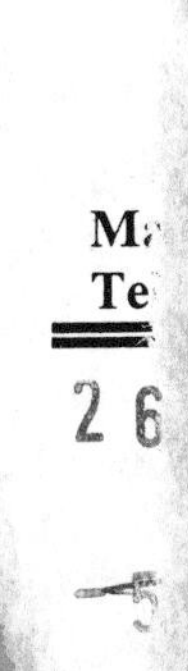

D0229871

ICONS

WITHDRAWN FROM
THE LIBRARY
UNIVERSITY OF

KA 0341692 5

Ed. Julius Wiedemann

TASCHEN

HONG KONG KÖLN LONDON LOS ANGELES MADRID PARIS TOKYO

CONTENTS

Flash, Evolution and the Web

Rob Ford (Favourite Website Awards)

THE EARLY YEARS OF FLASH. There can be no doubt that Macromedia's Flash has changed the shape and future of the web. Before designers and developers found Flash they were toiling with HTML, Java and animated gifs. In those days, if you wanted to have a cool website, you could wow the masses with a Java applet or maybe even a virtual creature, like a tarantula to adorn your portfolio. Flash truly opened the door for creatives to fulfil their ideas and web design dreams. A new era of the web was upon us and everyone was jumping on the wave. Sites like Flashkit, Flash Wave, Flash Planet, Were Here and Ultrashock created large communities almost overnight and by offering free downloadable flash files (flas), everyone was able to learn tricks and techniques they could only dream of by dissecting and playing with other people's code. The days of cutting edge web design being a hypertext link that turned purple when clicked were long gone. It was time for the Internet to go colour... enter Flash.

FLASH FINDING ITS FEET. If we go back to April 1999 we can see one of the first truly pioneering Flash sites, Full Throttle **<www.davidgarystudios.com/v1>** from David Gary Studios. Made entirely with Flash 3 this site covered all angles. You need to remember that a 33.6k modem was the standard at that time and if you had a 56.6k you were pushing the boundaries of surfing speed.

Today, the Full Throttle site loads in a couple of seconds but back then it took minutes, a problem a lot of Flash sites had. To overcome this, the site had a game of Pong for users to play as they waited for the site to load, which was seen as a very clever idea at the time.

Full Throttle boasted slick chrome graphics, all created within Flash and all vector, exactly what Flash was designed to do. Not forgetting the superb animations, which included a life-like exhaust flame with matching sound FX and music to complete the full package.

Site intros were all the rage in Flash's infancy, whilst creating rage amongst a number of users as well. A thirty day trial version of Flash and everyone thought they were one step away from Hollywood. Whilst a number of sites did create some clever site intros, like lookandfeel new media **<www.lookandfeel.com>** did in 2000, where they built their whole web presence around their intro which featured two cute stickmen characters, the huge majority of intros were nothing but fluff and left users looking for a "skip intro" button.

"Skip intro" buttons became a necessity for sites that had an intro, even though some of them didn't appear until after the intro had loaded! Eventually, people power won and intros became a big no-no and slowly started disappearing from sites or being replaced by fast loading splash/entrance pages.

It wouldn't be until 2004 and group94's site for the Magnum photographer, Carl de Keyzer **<www.carldekeyzer.com>**, when we would welcome the production and addition of a creative new intro to accompany his highly acclaimed work.

As we moved into 2001, everyone could agree that Flash was a great tool for animations and multimedia additions to websites but apart from these gimmicky effects being produced everywhere, what was it actually good for... functional for?

From the shores of Flashkit, the Sydney Opera House Virtual Tour **<www.sydneyoperahouse.com/sections/tours/virtual_tour/vrtour2.asp>** delivered the first real taste of what Flash could achieve, if used correctly.

Using 360 degree panoramic photographs and point-and-click navigation, users quite literally had an access all areas pass and could leave the site feeling they had "visited" the Opera House for real.

Again in 2001, Flash showed its power as an animation and storytelling powerhouse as Broken Saints **<http://bs.brokensaints.com/splash-page.htm>** launched their twenty four chapter animated series, which eventually went on to be released as a twelve hour DVD in 2005.

A plethora of experimental sites like Jamie Macdonald's nooflat **<www.nooflat.nu>** would leave their mark for years to come. nooflat's legacy being the resizing script that we still see used today, predominantly on photography websites.

2002, THE YEAR OF INNOVATION. In 2002 a new wave of sites began to address the anti-aliased small, blurry, text problem Flash had by using pixel fonts, specially designed for Flash and pioneered by the likes of Craig Kroeger of miniml **<www.miniml.com>**. The Fido Film **<www.fantasy-interactive.com/fido>** site from Fantasy Interactive was a perfect example of this new trend of polished and clean websites, a trend that would last for a number of years.

Flash also demonstrated its power as an application development tool, with sites like Looplabs **<www.looplabs.com>** who used back-end database integration to run this extremely popular music mixing tool that would go on to frequent a number of sites where users could mix tracks, upload vocals and much more.

Flash has always given the opportunity for creatives to fulfil their ideas. How many sites do we see today that use a page-turn effect? Lots of online magazines use this effect and whilst it now seems like such an obvious idea, you have to wonder if clever individuals, the likes of Perfect Fools and their first web presence **<www.perfectfools.com/book>** that started this new navigation method, hadn't produced such an obvious idea, would we be seeing it now?

We had seen a lot of very innovative and progressive ideas pushed through Flash but when Who's We **<www.whoswestudios.com/flashsite.html>** unleashed their attitude in May 2002 we knew something new would take off. With their bitmap and png sequencies a whole new door opened up just in time to capitalise on the ever expanding size of cable and broadband pipes.

2002 proved to be an amazing year for taking Flash forward. Brands such as Fred Perry **<www.fredperry.com>** took the leap and pretty much gambled on running their whole ecommerce operation through a Flash website. Fred Perry's seamless ecommerce application, still online today, proved how robust and secure Flash could be in the online environment.

With new releases of Flash, new features became available and video integration was one of those new features that had arrived for good. One of the first to use video and to add a new personality to websites was the site of Alex Trépanier. His site, Meet Alexis **<www.pixelpharmacy.com>** won instant international acclaim and made people realise that adding personality to websites was a crucial element.

Flash in itself provided designers and developers with a huge tool to realise their projects but a number of other, third party tools, were fast appearing, Swift 3D from Electric Rain being one of them.

After such a powerful year in 2002 I began to wonder

if creativity had peaked for a while but that thought was short lived as tokyoplastic **<www.tokyoplastic.com/tokyoplastic1.html>** launched a new and exciting web presence showcasing their animation skills and unique style, by harnessing the capabilities of Swift 3D and Flash. Once again, Flash had enabled unknown individuals to establish themselves, almost overnight, as industry respected creatives and would see them go on to produce work for companies including MTV.

A VERSATILE TOOL. Not only has Flash lent itself to web design and development but also to game production. The truly unique and original point and click adventure, Samorost **<www.amanitadesign.com/samorost>** from 2003 and the crazy survival shooter, Heli Attack 3 **<www.miniclip.com/heliattack3.htm>**, proved exactly how versatile the software is.

An area that has always concerned a number of people is the usability of websites using Flash. First of all, to clarify the term usability, in that a site must be usable by the target audience. Some people's attitude is that if their mum cannot use a site then it isn't usable. I have never subscribed to this theory. Try putting your mum in a Ferrari F430 with an open-gate manual gearbox and watch her stall it five times in a row and then tell Ferrari that it's not very functional. The same principal applies to websites... it's all about target audience.

Not many sites have a very far reaching and eclectic target audience but one that has is the Time Warner Road Runner portal **<www.rr.com/flash>**. In 2004 Fantasy Interactive set a new standard and answered a number of questions by releasing a site that had everything covered. Back button in the browser worked; seamless video integration; live news, sports feeds, finance feeds; weather reports and even later the first Flash integration of Google, all under the same roof and everything tied in together with immense back-end programming and vision. The Road Runner site quickly established itself as the perfect web portal.

THE FUTURE OF FLASH. Without a doubt, Flash has proved that it is a universal tool that 9 out of 10 designers/developers could not work without. It has provided the perfect environment to push the web forward into the 21st century and has allowed seamless integration of a number of other tools, including 3D, video, sound and a host of other multimedia.

We have seen how it can be used to be cool, how it can produce the WOW! factor, how it can be used as an application both on and offline. It is an extremely versatile tool that _can_ produce very functional and usable websites.

I look at literally hundreds of websites each day whilst pre-screening for the FWA **<www.theFWA.com>** and am often asked what will become the next big thing on the web. Well, in my opinion we shall be seeing a lot more application style websites, the likes of the new FWA website, where the site runs and feels like software on your desktop. Plus, expect to see more virtual web experiences, loaded with interactive 3D and video.

Broadband pipes are getting bigger and ideas are becoming more progressive... the timing is perfect for the web to grow out of its infancy stage and on to the next level.

Power to the player.

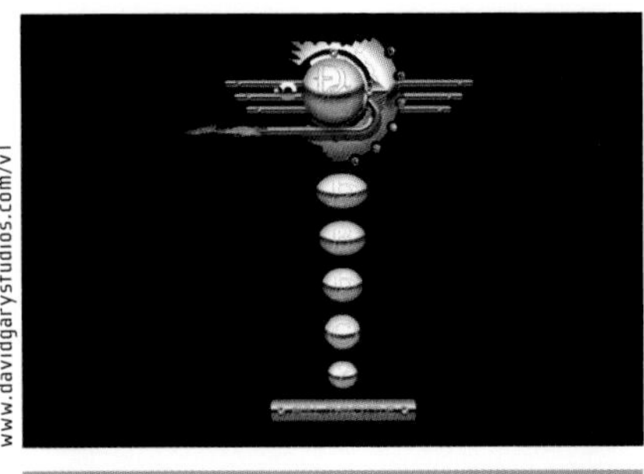

www.davidgarystudios.com/v1

www.carldekeyzer.com

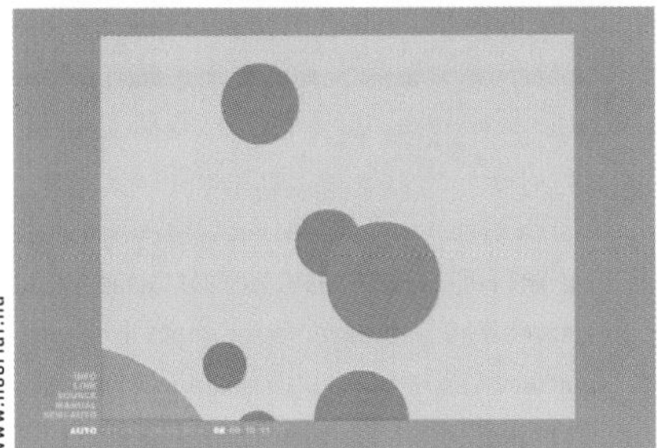

www.nooflat.nu

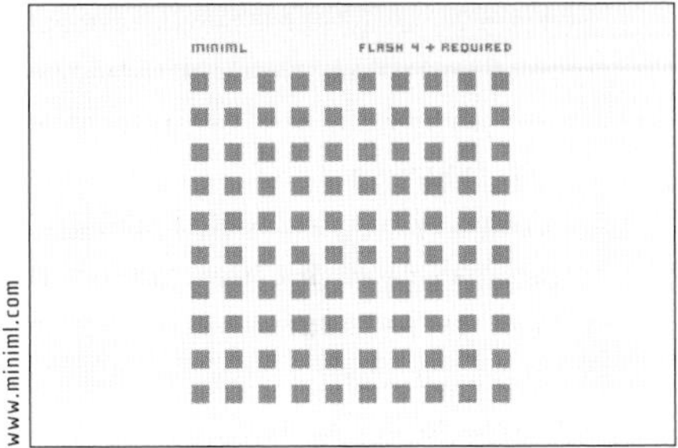

www.miniml.com

Rob Ford is FWA's **<www.theFWA.com>** Founder and General Manager. FWA (Favourite Website Awards) is the Flash designer's and developer's number 1 daily source of inspiration which serves millions of visitors each year from a broad global audience.
Born and bred in England with a background in finance, sales and project management, working for companies like Halifax PLC and American Express. He oversees the day to day running of the FWA project.
His work has been featured by Macromedia, Yahoo, The Guardian and numerous online and offline publications. He has judged for a number of industry award shows including: Webaward; the Flash Film Festival; SXSW Interactive; FlashintheCan; President of the Jury for the Latin American FFM Awards; and is a monthly judge for Web Standards Awards. He contributes regularly to other well-known web design community sites and magazines and is seen as one of the industry leaders in the field of new media.

Flash, évolution et Internet

Rob Ford (Favourite Website Awards)

LES DÉBUTS DE FLASH. Il ne fait aucun doute que le Flash de Macromedia a révolutionné la forme et l'avenir d'Internet. Avant de découvrir Flash, les designers et les développeurs peinaient avec l'HTML, Java et les gifs animés. À cette époque, si l'on voulait un site branché, on pouvait impressionner les foules avec un lac en applet, ou peut-être même une créature virtuelle, comme une tarentule pour décorer un portfolio. Flash a vraiment permis aux créatifs de réaliser leurs idées et leurs rêves de création de sites web. Une nouvelle ère de l'Internet arrivait, et tout le monde surfait sur la vague. Des sites comme Flashkit, Flash Wave, Flash Planet, Were Here et Ultrashock ont créé de vastes communautés presque d'un jour à l'autre, et ont proposé des fichiers Flash (flas) téléchargeables gratuitement. On pouvait soudain apprendre les trucs et les techniques dont on rêvait en disséquant et en jouant avec les codes d'autres personnes. L'époque où le dernier cri en matière de design Internet était un lien hypertexte qui devenait violet quand ont cliquait dessus était bien loin. L'heure était arrivée de se mettre en couleur... Bienvenue dans l'ère Flash.

FLASH S'INSTALLE. Si l'on remonte à avril 1999, on peut voir l'un des premiers sites pionniers en Flash, Full Throttle **<www.davidgarystudios.com/v1>** des studios David Gary. Entièrement réalisé avec Flash 3, ce site couvrait tous les aspects. Il ne faut pas oublier qu'à cette époque les modems 33,6 K étaient la norme, et que si vous aviez un 56,6 K vous repoussiez les limites de la vitesse de navigation.

Aujourd'hui, le site Full Throttle se charge en quelques secondes, mais à l'époque cela prenait plusieurs minutes, comme pour beaucoup de sites Flash. Pour résoudre ce problème, le site proposait aux utilisateurs de jouer à un jeu de ping-pong pendant qu'ils attendaient le chargement du site, ce qui était considéré comme une idée très astucieuse à l'époque.

Full Throttle présentait fièrement des graphismes rutilants et chromés, tous créés en Flash et tous vectoriels, exactement ce pourquoi Flash avait été conçu. Sans oublier les superbes animations, qui comprenaient une flamme de pot d'échappement plus vraie que nature avec les effets sonores correspondants, et de la musique pour compléter l'ensemble.

Au début, les introductions étaient le nec plus ultra, mais faisaient aussi s'arracher les cheveux à pas mal d'utilisateurs. Il suffisait d'une version d'essai de 30 jours de Flash pour se croire aux portes d'Hollywood. Un certain nombre de sites ont créé des introductions ingénieuses, comme lookandfeel new media **<www.lookandfeel.com>** en 2000. Ils ont construit toute leur présence web autour de leur intro qui présentait deux petits bonshommes sympas. Mais l'immense majorité des intros n'était que de l'esbroufe et donnait aux utilisateurs l'envie impérieuse de chercher le bouton « passer l'intro ».

Les boutons « passer l'intro » devinrent nécessaires pour les sites qui avaient une introduction, même si certains n'apparaissaient qu'après son chargement ! Finalement, le peuple a eu le dessus et les introductions, ça ne se faisait plus. Elles ont commencé à disparaître des sites ou à être remplacées par des pages d'accueil à chargement rapide.

Il aura fallu attendre 2004 pour accueillir avec plaisir la production d'une nouvelle introduction créative, accompagnant le travail admirable du photographe de

Magnum, Carl de Keyzer **<www.carldekeyzer.com>**, sur son site créé par group94.

En 2001, tout le monde s'accordait à penser que Flash était un outil formidable pour les animations et les compléments multimédias des sites web, mais à part ces gadgets reproduits partout, à quoi servait-il donc ?

Grâce à Flashkit, la visite virtuelle de l'Opéra de Sydney **<www.sydneyoperahouse.com/sections/tours/virtual_tour/vrtour2.asp>** a donné pour la première fois une idée de ce dont Flash était capable, pourvu qu'on l'utilise correctement. Il suffisait de pointer et cliquer pour naviguer dans des photographies panoramiques à 360 degrés. Les utilisateurs étaient littéralement munis d'un passe universel et quittaient le site en ayant l'impression d'avoir vraiment « visité » l'opéra.

Encore en 2001, Flash a démontré son potentiel narratif et d'animation lorsque Broken Saints **<http://bs.brokensaints.com/splash-page.htm>** ont lancé leur série animée de 24 chapitres, qui est finalement sorti sur un DVD de 12 heures en 2005.

Une pléthore de sites expérimentaux, comme le nooflat **<www.nooflat.nu>** de Jamie Macdonald, allaient laisser leur empreinte pour plusieurs années. L'héritage de nooflat est un script de redimensionnement qui est toujours utilisé aujourd'hui, surtout sur les sites de photographie.

2002, L'ANNÉE DE L'INNOVATION. En 2002, une nouvelle vague de sites ont commencé à résoudre le problème des petits textes anticrénelés et flous de Flash en utilisant des polices pixelisées, spécialement conçues pour Flash, et dont Craig Kroeger de miniml **<www.miniml.com>** et quelques autres ont été les pionniers. Le site Fido Film **<www.fantasy-interactive.com/fido>** de Fantasy Interactive était un exemple parfait de cette nouvelle tendance de sites élégants et raffinés, une tendance qui allait durer plusieurs années.

Flash a aussi montré son potentiel en tant qu'outil de développement d'application, avec des sites comme Looplabs **<www.looplabs.com>**, qui a utilisé l'intégration de base de données en arrière-plan pour faire tourner cet outil de mixage de musique extrêmement populaire qui allait par la suite être présent sur de nombreux sites où les utilisateurs pourraient mixer des pistes, télécharger des chants vers le serveur et bien plus encore.

Flash a toujours permis aux créatifs de réaliser leurs idées. Combien de sites voit-on aujourd'hui utiliser l'effet d'une page qu'on tourne ? Beaucoup de magazines en ligne utilisent cet effet, et maintenant cela semble une idée évidente, mais le verrait-on aujourd'hui si des petits malins comme Perfect Fools et leur premier site de présence web **<www.perfectfools.com/book>** n'avaient pas lancé cette nouvelle méthode de navigation soi-disant si évidente ?

On avait vu beaucoup d'idées progressives et innovantes se frayer un chemin grâce à Flash, mais lorsque Who's We **<www.whoswestudios.com/flashsite.html>** ont lancé leur attitude en mai 2002, on a su que quelque chose de nouveau allait commencer. Avec leurs séquences en bitmap et en png, une toute nouvelle porte s'est ouverte juste à temps pour tirer parti du débit toujours croissant des câbles et de la large bande.

2002 s'est révélé être une année étonnante pour les avancées de Flash. Des marques comme Fred Perry **<www.fredperry.com>** ont sauté le pas et ont fait le pari de gérer toutes leurs opérations d'e-commerce à travers un site en Flash. L'application d'e-commerce entièrement intégrée de Fred Perry est toujours en service aujourd'hui, et a prouvé la robustesse et la stabilité de Flash dans l'environnement en ligne.

Les nouvelles versions de Flash ont proposé de nouvelles fonctions, et parmi elles, l'intégration de la vidéo. L'un des premiers à utiliser la vidéo et à donner une nouvelle personnalité aux sites web a été Alex Trépanier. Son site, Je vous présente Alexis <**www.pixelpharmacy.com**>, a tout de suite été un succès international et a fait réaliser l'importance de la personnalité des sites web.

Flash a donné aux concepteurs et aux développeurs un formidable outil pour réaliser leurs projets, mais de nombreux autres outils tiers sont vite apparus, par exemple Swift 3D de Electric Rain.

Après une telle année 2002, je commençais à me demander si la créativité allait plafonner pendant un certain temps, mais cette pensée a vite été balayée lorsque tokyoplastic <**www.tokyoplastic.com/tokyoplastic1.html**> ont lancé une présence web nouvelle et captivante, qui présentait leur talent en animation et leur style unique en exploitant les capacités de Swift 3D et de Flash. Encore une fois, Flash avait permis à des inconnus de s'établir eux-mêmes, pratiquement du jour au lendemain, en tant que créatifs respectés dans le secteur qui allaient ensuite travailler pour des entreprises commerciales, dont MTV.

UN OUTIL POLYVALENT. Flash s'est prêté non seulement au design et au développement de sites web, mais aussi à la production de jeux. Samorost, une aventure à pointer et cliquer vraiment unique, <**www.amanitadesign.com/samorost**> de 2003 et l'incroyable jeu de survie Heli Attack 3 <**www.miniclip.com/heliattack3.htm**> ont prouvé à quel point le programme était polyvalent.

La facilité d'utilisation des sites Flash est un domaine qui a toujours préoccupé beaucoup de gens. Tout d'abord, pour clarifier le terme, un site doit être facile à utiliser pour l'audience qu'il cible. Certaines personnes pensent que si leur mère ne peut pas utiliser un site, alors il n'est pas utilisable. Je n'ai jamais souscrit à cette théorie. Mettez votre mère au volant d'une Ferrari F430 avec une boîte de vitesse manuelle, et lorsqu'elle aura calé cinq fois de suite, allez dire à Ferrari que leur voiture n'est pas très fonctionnelle. Le même principe à s'applique aux sites web... Ça dépend de l'audience que l'on veut atteindre.

Peu de sites ont une cible très vaste et éclectique, mais l'un d'eux est le portail Warner Road Runner <**www.rr.com/flash**>. En 2004, Fantasy Interactive a établi un nouveau standard et a répondu à beaucoup de questions en lançant un site qui couvrait tous les aspects. Le bouton de retour du navigateur fonctionnait, la vidéo était parfaitement intégrée, il y avait des informations en temps réel, les résultats sportifs, les données financières, les prévisions météorologiques et même, plus tard, la première intégration en Flash de Google, le tout sur le même site, avec une programmation et une vision en arrière-plan colossales. Le site Road Runner a vite été considéré comme le portail Internet parfait.

L'AVENIR DE FLASH. Flash s'est sans aucun doute révélé être l'outil universel dont 90 % des concepteurs/développeurs ne pouvaient pas se passer. Il a fourni l'environnement idéal pour faire entrer Internet dans le XXIe siècle et a permis l'intégration parfaite de nombreux autres outils, dont la 3D, la vidéo, le son et bien d'autres supports multimédias.

www.pixelpharmacy.com

www.whoswestudios.com/flashsite.html

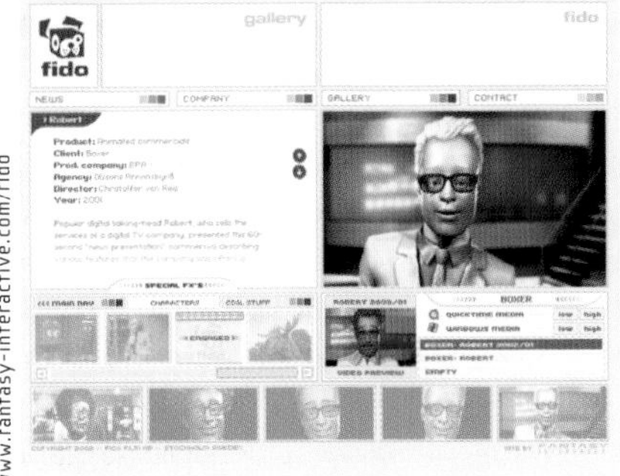

www.fantasy-interactive.com/fido

http://bs.brokensaints.com/splash-page.htm

Nous avons vu qu'il peut être utilisé pour être cool ou pour impressionner, et qu'il peut être utilisé comme application en ligne et hors connexion. C'est un outil extrêmement polyvalent qui peut donner des sites très fonctionnels et faciles à utiliser.

Je vois littéralement des centaines de sites chaque jour lorsque je présélectionne pour le FWA **<www.theFWA.com>**, et on me demande souvent quelle sera la prochaine mode sur le web. Eh bien, à mon avis, nous allons voir beaucoup plus de sites de style application, qui comme le site de la FWA ressembleront à un logiciel installé sur votre ordinateur. Attendez-vous aussi à davantage de virtuel, avec beaucoup de 3D et de vidéos interactives.

Le débit est de plus en plus rapide et les idées deviennent de plus en plus progressistes, c'est le moment idéal pour qu'Internet sorte de l'enfance et passe au niveau suivant.

Les joueurs au pouvoir.

Rob Ford est le fondateur et le directeur général de FWA **<www.theFWA.com>**. FWA (Favourite Website Awards) est la source d'inspiration quotidienne numéro un pour les concepteurs et développeurs de Flash, et reçoit des millions de visiteurs chaque année, d'horizons très divers.
Il est né et a grandi en Angleterre, et il a travaillé dans la finance, les ventes et la gestion de projet chez des entreprises comme Halifax PLC et American Express. Il supervise le fonctionnement quotidien du projet FWA.
Macromedia, Yahoo, The Guardian et de nombreuses publications en ligne et hors connexion ont parlé de son travail. Il a été juge pour de nombreux prix du secteur, dont : Webaward, le Flash Film Festival, SXSW Interactive et FlashintheCan. Il est président du jury pour les Latin American FFM Awards, et chaque mois il est juge pour les Web Standards Awards. Il collabore régulièrement à d'autres sites et magazines bien connus de la communauté du web design, et il est considéré comme l'un des leaders du secteur dans le domaine des nouveaux médias.

Flash, Evolution und das Web

Rob Ford (Favourite Website Awards)

DIE FRÜHEN JAHRE DES FLASH. Durch Macromedias Flash wurde das Web und seine Zukunft nachhaltig verändert. Darüber gibt es keine Zweifel. Bevor die Designer und Entwickler Flash erfunden hatten, arbeiteten sie mühevoll mit HTML, Java und animierten Bildern. Um damals mit einer Website zu beeindrucken, reichte es ein „Lake Applet" einzusetzen oder sein Portfolio vielleicht mit einer Tarantel, oder einer anderen virtuellen Kreatur zu schmücken. Als Flash aufkam, öffnete sich kreativen Menschen wahrhaftig die Tür zur Verwirklichung ihrer Ideen und Erfüllung ihrer Design-Träume. Eine neue Ära im Zeitalter des Webs fing an und jeder ließ sich von der Welle tragen. Fast über Nacht versammelten Websites wie Flashkit, Flash Wave, Flash Planet, Were Here und Ultrashock Internet-Communities um sich herum, und dank Flash-Dateien zum kostenlosen Herunterladen (flas), war jedem die Möglichkeit gegeben, Tricks und Techniken zu erlernen, von denen er nur hätte träumen können, zu Zeiten als es noch nötig war, die Codes von anderen Programmierern zu knacken und mit ihnen herumzuexperimentieren. Die Zeit des innovativen Webdesigns, das sich auf ein Hypertext-Link beschränkte, der nach dem Anklicken die Farbe veränderte, war nun endgültig vorbei. Für das Internet war es an der Zeit, wirklich lebhaft zu werden, und zwar durch Flash.

FLASH ERLERNT DAS LAUFEN. Wenn wir auf den April 1999 zurückblicken, stoßen wir auf eine der ersten echten Pionier-Flash-Websites namens Full Throttle **<www.davidgarystudios.com/v1>** von David Gary Studios. Die Website wurde vollständig mit Flash 3 erstellt und deckte alle Bereiche ab. Dabei sollte man bedenken, dass ein 33.6k-Modem damals Standard war und dass man sich mit 56.6k jenseits der Übertragungs-Höchstgeschwindigkeit befand. Heute wird die Full Throttle-Site innerhalb von wenigen Sekunden geladen, damals dauerte es Minuten. Das Problem der Ladegeschwindigkeit hatten jedoch viele andere Web-Designer auch. Um diese Schwierigkeit zu meistern, wurde auf der Website ein Ping-Pong-Spiel programmiert, damit der Besucher die Wartezeit spielend überbrücken konnte. Das galt damals als eine sehr gute Idee.

Die Betreiber von Full Throttle waren stolz auf die mit Flash- und Vektor-Programmen erstellte raffinierte Chromgrafik. Die Programmierung solcher Grafiken war auch die Absicht, die hinter dem Entwurf von Flash steckte. Dazu kamen die beeindruckenden Animationen, unter anderem die naturgetreue Flamme mit passendem FX-Ton und Musik, die das gesamte Packet abrundeten.

Als Flash noch ziemlich neu war, wurden Website-Intros mit großer Vorliebe programmiert, obwohl sie bei manchen Benutzern auf heftige Ablehnung stießen. Es reichte schon aus, dass jemand eine 30-Tage-Testversion von Flash in die Finger bekam und schon hielt er sich für einen großen Designer. Es gab schon einige Websites, die über besonders clevere Intros verfügten, wie z.B. „lookandfeel new media" **<www.lookandfeel.com>** von 2000. Die gesamte Website wurde um das Intro herum gebaut, das zwei niedliche Strichmännchenfiguren zeigte. Die große Mehrheit der Intros war jedoch einfach nur schlecht, so dass die Besucher gleich nach dem „skip intro"-Button suchten.

„Skip intro"-Buttons wurden unerlässlich für Websites mit Intro, selbst wenn die Buttons erst dann zu sehen waren, wenn die gesamte Intro bereits geladen war! Letztendlich hat die Vernunft gesiegt und Intros wurden allmählich von den Websites verdrängt oder

durch schnell ladende Empfangsseiten ersetzt wurden.

Erst 2004, als group94 die Website für den Magnum Fotografen Carl de Keyzer **<www.carldekeyzer.com>** entwarf, sollte sich die Erstellung und Einsatz einer kreativen Intro für ein Unternehmen durchsetzen und hohe Anerkennung genießen.

Anfang 2001 waren sich alle einig, dass Flash ein tolles Werkzeug zur Erstellung von Animationen und multimedialen Spezialeffekten war. Doch wofür waren sie eigentlich wirklich gut? Was genau war ihre Funktion? Bis jetzt hatten sie doch nicht mehr als nur massenhaft marktschreierische Effekte produziert. Auf diese Fragen wusste niemand eine Antwort.

Die Website für die Sydney Opera House Virtual Tour **<www.sydneyoperahouse.com/sections/tours/virtual_tour/vrtour2.asp>** von Flashkit war das erste Beispiel dafür, was man bei richtiger Handhabung mit Flash erreichen konnte. Naturgetreue 360° Panorama-Fotos mit „point-and-click"-Navigation. Der Besucher bekommt wortwörtlich einen Zugang zu allen Bereichen und wenn er die Website verlässt, hat er das Gefühl, das Opera House tatsächlich „besucht" zu haben.

Im Jahre 2001 bewehrte sich Flash als das A und O für Animationen und das Geschichtenerzählen. Dazu trugen Broken Saints **<http://bs.brokensaints.com/splash-page.htm>** bei, als sie ihre 24-Kapitel lange Serie mit Animationen veröffentlichten, die letztendlich 2005 auf DVD mit zwanzig Stunden Spielzeit herausgegeben wurde.

Eine Fülle von experimentellen Websites, wie „nooflat" von Jamie Macdonald **<www.nooflat.nu>** haben für Jahre hinweg einen bleibenden Eindruck hinterlassen. Das Vermächtnis von „nooflat" ist die Funktion der Veränderbarkeit durch verschiedene Schrifteffekte, die heute immer noch genutzt wird, und zwar überwiegend auf Foto-Websites.

2002, DAS JAHR DER INNOVATION. 2002 gab es eine neue Welle von Websites, die sich mit dem Problem von Anti-Aliasing von kleinen, undeutlichen Schriften bei Flash befasste, indem sie Pixel-Schriftarten einsetzte. Einer der Pioniere auf diesem Gebiet war Craig Kroeger von miniml **<www.miniml.com>**. Die Website für Fido Film **<www.fantasy-interactive.com/fido>** von Fantasy Interactive stellte ein perfektes Beispiel für den neuen Trend dar, mit seinen glatten und sauberen Seiten. Dieser Trend sollte noch mehrere Jahre lang andauern.

Flash bewährte sich auch als ein Werkzeug für Anwendungsentwicklung. Websites wie Looplabs **<www.looplabs.com>** nutzten die Back-End-Datenbank-Integration für den Einsatz des äußerst populären Musik-Mix-Tools, das auf zahlreichen Websites genutzt wurde und den Benutzern die Möglichkeit gab, Musik zu Mixen, Songs zu laden und vieles mehr.

Dank Flash war kreativen Menschen schon immer die Möglichkeit gegeben, ihre Ideen zu verwirklichen. Wie oft finden wir heute Websites, die den Effekt von Seitenblättern nutzen? Viele Online-Zeitschriften nutzen ihn. Obwohl uns diese Funktion heute so selbstverständlich erscheint wie nur was, sollte man sich fragen, ob es sie heute wirklich gäbe, wenn nicht clevere Menschen auf die Idee gekommen wären und sie auf ihren Websites umgesetzt hätten. In diesem Zusammenhang sind die Perfect Fools und ihr erster Internetauftritt **<www.perfectfools.com/book>** zu erwähnen.

Wir haben es mitverfolgt, wie zahlreiche innovative und fortschrittliche Ideen dank Flash umgesetzt wurden.

Als jedoch Who's We **<www.whoswestudios.com/flashsite.html>** ihre Website in Mai 2002 veröffentlichten, war uns allen klar, dass sich etwas Revolutionäres anbahnte. Mit ihren bitmap- und png-Sequenzen eröffneten sie ganz neue Perspektiven. Und das gerade zur rechten Zeit, um von den immer leistungsstärkeren Kabeln und Breitband-Leitungen zu profitieren.

2002 wurde zu einem besonders dynamischen Jahr für Flash. Marken wie Fred Perry **<www.fredperry.com>** haben den Sprung gewagt und sind ein recht großes Risiko eingegangen, indem sie ihren gesamten elektronischen Handel über eine Flash-Website abwickelten. Fred Perrys problemlose E-Commerce-Anwendung, die heute immer noch online ist, zeigte wie robust und sicher Flash in einer Online-Umgebung sein kann.

Mit neuen Versionen von Flash, die auf den Markt kamen, wurden neue Funktionen zugänglich. Die Einbindung von Video war unter den gut etablierten. Einer der ersten, der Video einsetzte, um seiner Website eine neue Persönlichkeit zu verleihen war Alex Trépanier. Seine Website „Meet Alexis" **<www.pixelpharmacy.com>** gewann dauerhaften internationalen Zuspruch und zeigte, wie wichtig der persönliche Charakter einer Website war.

Schon Flash alleine war ein recht umfangreiches Werkzeug, mit Hilfe dessen Designer und Entwickler ihre Projekte realisieren konnten. Sehr schnell kam jedoch eine Vielzahl von anderen Werkzeugen auf den Markt. Eines von ihnen war Swift 3D von Electric Rain.

Nach dem so erfolgreichen Jahr 2002 fing ich an zu überlegen, ob das schon der Gipfel der Kreativität war. Diese Frage blieb jedoch nicht lange unbeantwortet, denn „tokyoplastic" **<www.tokyoplastic.com/tokyoplastic1.html>** kam mit einer neuen und aufregenden Webpräsenz auf den Markt. Sie schöpften die Möglichkeiten von Swift 3D und Flash aus und stellten somit ihre Animationskunst und einzigartigen Stil unter Beweis. Und wieder konnten unbekannte Menschen dank Flash von einem Tag auf den anderen groß herauszukommen und sich etablieren. Die Industrie schätzt nämlich kreative Menschen und möchte sie gerne für die Unternehmen arbeiten lassen, MTV inklusive.

EIN VIELSEITIGES WERKZEUG. Flash zeigte sich nicht nur für Webdesign und –entwicklung von Nutzen sondern auch für die Spiele-Produktion. Das wirklich einzigartige und originelle „point and click"-Abenteuer „Samorost" **<www.amanitadesign.com/samorost>** von 2003 und das verrückte Überlebensschießeisen Heli Attack 3 **<www.miniclip.com/heliattack3.htm>**, zeigten deutlich die Vielseitigkeit der Software.

Das Thema Brauchbarkeit der Websites, die mit Flash erstellt wurden, war schon immer kontrovers. Und wenn ich von Brauchbarkeit spreche, dann sollte ich zuerst den Terminus Brauchbarkeit erklären. Damit ist gemeint die Brauchbarkeit der Website für eine bestimmte Zielgruppe. Es gibt Menschen, die behaupten, dass eine Website nicht brauchbar ist, wenn sie von ihrer Mutter nicht benutzt werden kann. Ich war nie Verfechter dieser Theorie. Versuchen sie doch, Ihre Mutter in einen Ferrari F430 mit dem manuellen Formel1-Getriebe zu stecken und schauen Sie, ob sie den Motor fünfmal hintereinander anlassen kann, ohne ihn abzuwürgen. Wenn das nicht gelingt, dann gehen Sie zu Ferrari und erklären Sie, dass das Auto nicht sehr brauchbar ist. Das gleiche Prinzip gilt für die Websites... Es kommt ganz auf die Zielgruppe an.

Nicht viele Websites haben eine weit reichende und breit gefächerte Zielgruppe. Bei der Website Time

Warner Road Runner-Portal <**www.rr.com/flash**> ist das der Fall. 2004 stellte Fantasy Interactive einen Standard auf und beantwortete durch die Einführung einer umfangreichen Website automatisch viele Fragen. Der Back-Button im Browser funktionierte; eine Problemlose Video-Einbindung war auch gegeben; Es gab Nachrichten live, Sport, Finanzen, Wetter-Vorhersage und später sogar auch die erste Flash-Einbindung für Google. All das unter einem Dach und alles zusammengetragen mit immensem Back-End-Programmierungsaufwand und Vision. Die Website von Road Runner etablierte sich schnell als das perfekte Web-Portal.

DIE ZUKUNFT VON FLASH. Zweifellos hat Flash bewiesen, dass es ein universelles Werkzeug ist, auf das 9 von 10 Designer/Entwickler bei ihrer Arbeit nicht verzichten können. Flash kreierte für das Web die perfekte Basis für den Durchstart in das 21. Jahrhundert und erlaubte problemlose Integration von vielen anderen Werkzeugen, inklusive 3D, Video, Ton und einer Menge anderer Multimedien.

Wir haben jetzt gesehen, wie man sich damit profilieren kann, wie man damit den AHA-Effekt auslösen kann, wie man es als Anwendung für den On- und Offline-Betrieb nutzen kann. Es ist ein äußerst vielseitiges Werkzeug, womit sehr funktionelle und brauchbare Websites erstellt werden _können .

Ich schaue mir buchstäblich Hunderte von Websites jeden Tag an, um eine Vorauswahl für die FWA <**www.theFWA.com**> zu treffen und sehr häufig werde ich gefragt, was jetzt der große Newcomer im Web sein wird. Meiner Meinung nach werden wir jetzt verstärkt anwendungsbetonte Websites erleben, wie etwa die neue Website von FWA, die so läuft und sich so anfühlt wie die Software auf dem Desktop. Hinzu werden mehr virtuelle Erlebnisse kommen, die mit interaktiven 3D und Video geladen werden.

Breitbandleitungen werden immer leistungsfähiger und Ideen werden fortschrittlicher... Die Zeit ist reif für das Web, aus seinen Kinderschuhen herauszuwachsen und ein höheres Entwicklungsstadium zu erreichen.

Macht dem Spieler!

Rob Ford ist Gründer und General Manager von FWA <**www.theFWA.com**>. FWA [Favourite Website Awards] ist die Nummer Eins unter den Inspirationsquellen, die den mit Flash arbeitenden Designern und Entwicklern täglich zur Verfügung stehen. Das kommt jedes Jahr Millionen von Besuchern aus einem breiten Publikum rund um den Globus zugute.
Rob Ford ist in England geboren und aufgewachsen, ausgebildet im Bereich Finanzen, Vertrieb und Projektmanagement und arbeitete für Unternehmen wie Halifax PLC and American Express. Er beaufsichtigt das Tagesgeschehen im FWA-Projekt.
Für seine Arbeit genießt er die Anerkennung von Macromedia, Yahoo, The Guardian und zahlreichen online und offline Herausgebern. Er war in der Jury vieler industrieller Preisverleihungen, unter anderem: Webaward; the Flash Film Festival; SXSW Interactive; FlashintheCan; Vorsitzender der Jury der lateinamerikanischen FFM Awards-Preisverleihung; und er ist jeden Monat Richter in Web Standards Awards. Er trägt regelmäßig zu anderen bekannten Designer-Websites und Magazinen bei und wird als ein Vorreiter der Industrie im Bereich Neue Medien betrachtet.

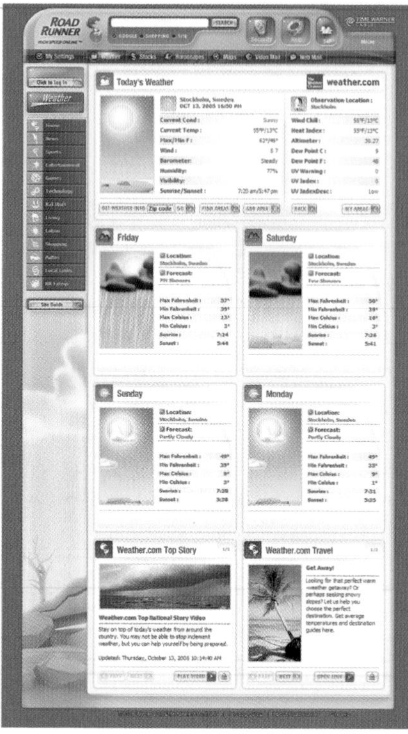

www.rr.com/flash

www.tokyoplastic.com

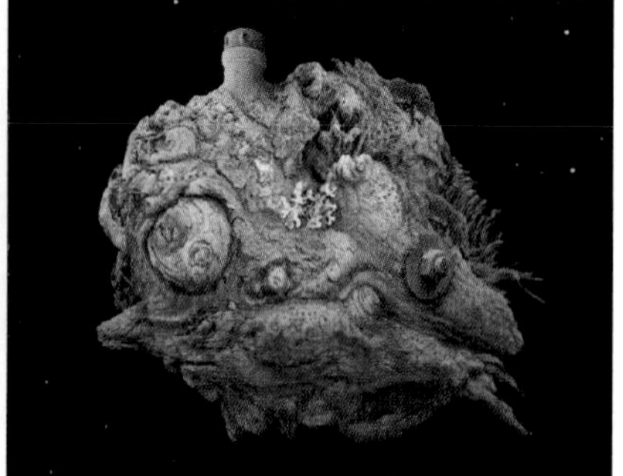

www.amanitadesign.com/samorost

www.looplabs.com

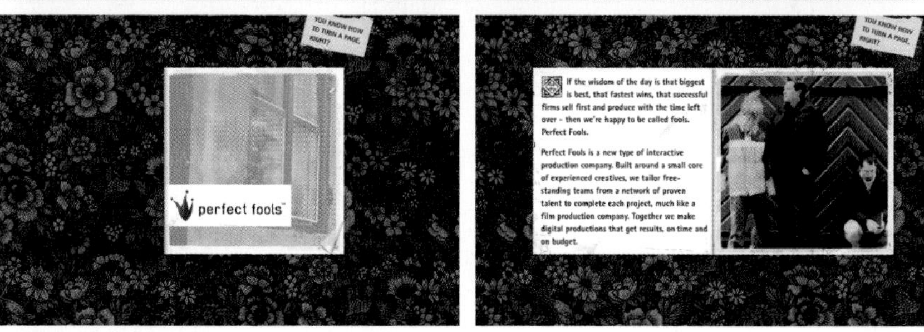

www.perfectfools.com

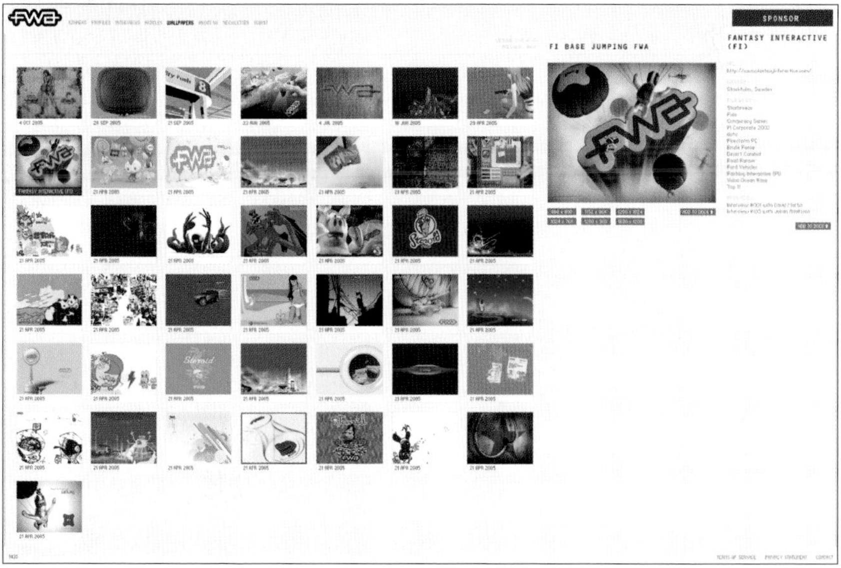

FWA
WALLPAPERS
SPONSOR
FANTASY INTERACTIVE (FI)
FI BASE JUMPING FWA

www.theFWA.com

CASE:01

BACARDI®Live.com

Kurt Noble (KNI)

BACARDI® does very little print advertising and, instead, focuses almost the entire balance of its marketing budget on Live, sweepstakes-driven events, Commercial Broadcast spots, and, of course, sexy photographic collateral. As the name of this site strongly suggests, BACARDI®Live.com needed to be an extremely sexy and fun online representation of all these various marketing initiatives. The project also needed to be very carefully planned so that whatever we designed, engineered and launched, was also then very capable of meeting on-going seasonal updates, many of which would have their own unique look and feel. For instance, the site would launch with a Vegas theme, but then in the late fall need to take on a Halloween theme. The site also had to have a massive amount of content that all looked and worked well together, and each element had to be dynamic for the ever-changing promotional schedule. This promotional agenda also include quite a number of contest signups and email opt-ins, each of which had to be configured to post data to a managed database of customers. On top of all that, the site had to be configured to also post user behavior to a custom tracking system. So, figuring out how to make all that work AND still end up with a site that looked and acted sexy was definitely the major challenge of this project.

As with any successful project, it's always important to note how helpful it was that we that we had a great client, who came to us because they liked our work and wanted to bring our design-making decisions into the project and then also give us a great deal of freedom and room to really spread our wings.

We also had a fairly well established brand, in that BACARDI® had already developed a nicely established service mark, the Bat icon, and also a ballpark color spectrum.

So, we set out with these aforementioned parameters and set out to see if we could set up a grid. To make sure the grid made visual sense, we asked the client to give us an absolute hierarchy of their visual priorities, or, in other words, a list of the homepage elements in order of promotional importance. Once we had this list, we then knew, at least, how to visually prioritize the grid, which allowed us to begin the design process, in earnest, and comp up the homepage grid. Because our preproduction homework with the client was fairly extensive and thorough, we were actually able to nail the homepage grid proportions on our first pass at it. Many of the individual modules within the grid would go through many more iterations, to get them feeling just right on an individual basis, but the proportions of our first grid didn't actually need to ever change after our first comp.

Again, having a great, easy-going client who trusted us a lot, really, really helped. Because we convinced the client not to get too hung up on in each individual module in the grid, which had been comped up a bit roughly, and to think of the design as a "shell", which could later be massaged into perfection on a module-by-module basis, after we had a chance to actually engineer the shell and get it all action-scripted, figure out how it would all preload, what rollovers would look like, and, how the background elements would work with and support the grid of content. We also had to really flesh out animation issues and make sure that whatever rollover states and loading animations we came up with

Kurt Noble

Daniel

Eric

Michael

would be easy to replicate out across an entire site and be changed to support and compliment seasonal changes. For example, the first sets of rollovers would have playing card themes, but the upcoming Halloween rollovers would clearly not have those same themes. So, we obviously had to then set up the animation for those rollovers so that it was math-based, rather than time-line based; this would be an essential ingredient to keeping our maintenance over-head with the client streamlined and at its most optimal during updates. Similarly, we had this "liquefied" idea for pre-loaders and spent a great deal of time figuring out how to do this concept without taxing computer processors and bogging down the flow of the animations. This was another feat of action-scripting for us and we figured out a really low file-size, smooth, and processor-friendly way to do that as well.

Once we had the grid finalized and the Flash system all shelled and planned out, we could then proceed forward to the sub sections of the site, gridding them out in a consistent and fairly similar way, but adding secondary and in some cases tertiary navigation. Again, we were blessed from a work-flow standpoint, by having the client support our idea to continue building out the shell of all pages in the site. So, rather than getting bogged down in individual page-by-page reviews of all the modules in each page's grid, we were able to proceed forward with all the grids in the shell, knowing that in the later stages of our work, we'd circle back to each individual module in the grid, and work out exact copy and asset approval on a module by module basis. This actually worked out better for the client, as well, because they didn't have copy that was 100% approved yet, anyways. So, in many regards this was not only the most beneficial way to proceed with design, but also the only logical way to proceed with the build. In many ways, the success of the project really hinged on this ability to continue to push forward, knowing we had a ton of trust from the client.

The Girls section of the site that presented particularly fun challenge, and, as you can see, the grid was really pushed much further down on the list of visual priorities, because, the girls, themselves, needed prominence. Originally, we'd earmarked them for just the gallery section of the site, but mid-way into pre-production, we were tasked by the client to build something much more grand and special, a really impressive and more interactive gallery, exclusively for the girls. So, we came up with this great idea to have this really large-scale gallery system for them, giving visitors a fun way to scroll through the photos, "supersize" the images, and even send "autographed" photos to one another through a component in the Flash. Here, again, as with the rest of the site, had to make sure that, even this massive, over-sized photo-viewing interface was still every bit as scalable and dynamic as the rest of the site. Because, a new batch of girls would be coming to the site once a year, and the number of photos would change, the girls names would change, and all that new content would need to be easily wired into the voting system and the viral components in this section. The result is probably one of our proudest accomplishments within the site.

After we finished up all of the grids and pages within the shell, we then circled back, finally, with the client, and spent the last 6 weeks of the project piecing together all the revisions, copy edits, and visual tweaks to all the various modules across the entire grid of page content. The end result is what you see today, although, as discussed, it will undergo dramatic visual and content infusions 3 times a year!

Kurt Noble - Profile:
In addition to managing the overall corporate duties of KNI, Kurt develops KNI's client-relationships, cultivates creative concepts with those clients and also works with the KNI crew to make sure KNI produces visual, motion and engineering deliverables that exceed client expectations.
<www.kurtnoble.com>

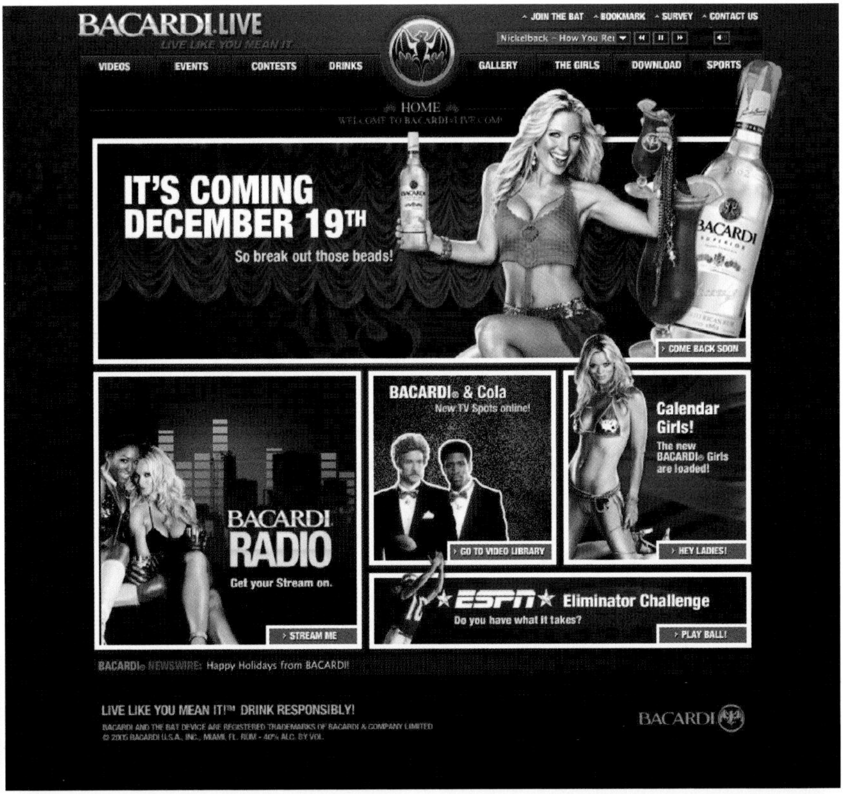

BACARDI LIVE
LIVE LIKE YOU MEAN IT
JOIN THE BAT
BOOKMARK
SURVEY
CONTACT US
Nickelback - How You Rei
VIDEOS
EVENTS
CONTESTS
DRINKS
GALLERY
THE GIRLS
DOWNLOAD
SPORTS
HOME
WELCOME TO BACARDILIVE.COM

IT'S COMING DECEMBER 19TH
So break out those beads!
COME BACK SOON

BACARDI RADIO
Get your Stream on.
STREAM ME

BACARDI® & Cola
New TV Spots online!
GO TO VIDEO LIBRARY

Calendar Girls!
The new BACARDI® Girls are loaded!
HEY LADIES!

ESPN Eliminator Challenge
Do you have what it takes?
PLAY BALL!

BACARDI® NEWSWIRE: Happy Holidays from BACARDI!

LIVE LIKE YOU MEAN IT!™ DRINK RESPONSIBLY!
BACARDI AND THE BAT DEVICE ARE REGISTERED TRADEMARKS OF BACARDI & COMPANY LIMITED
© 2005 BACARDI U.S.A., INC., MIAMI, FL. RUM - 40% ALC. BY VOL.
BACARDI

www.bacardilive.com

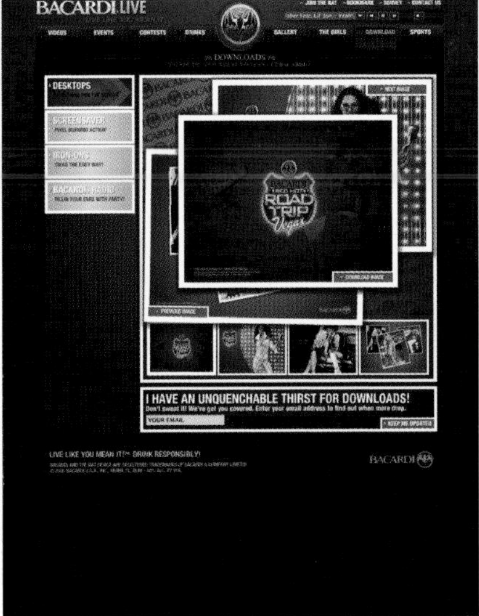

CASE: 01

BACARDI®Live.com

Kurt Noble (KNI)

BACARDI® fait très peu de publicité imprimée et concentre plutôt tout le reste de son budget marketing sur Live, les concours et les loteries, les spots de publicité diffusés à la radio ou à la télévision, et bien sûr des visuels sexy. Comme le nom du site le suggère fortement, BACARDI®Live.com devait être une représentation en ligne extrêmement séduisante et ludique de toutes ces différentes initiatives marketing. Le projet devait également être planifié très soigneusement afin que tout ce que nous aurions conçu, réalisé et publié puisse ensuite s'adapter sans problème aux mises à jour saisonnières, dont la plupart auraient un esprit et une image bien particuliers. Par exemple, le site allait être lancé avec un thème Las Vegas, et à la fin de l'automne il basculerait sur un thème Halloween. Le site devait aussi héberger une énorme quantité de contenus cohérents et avec une image harmonieuse, et chaque élément devait être dynamique pour s'adapter à un calendrier promotionnel en perpétuelle évolution. Cet agenda promotionnel comprend également un nombre considérable d'inscriptions à des concours et à des listes de distribution qui devaient être configurées pour envoyer les données vers une base de données de clients. En plus de tout cela, le site devait également être configuré pour envoyer des données sur le comportement des utilisateurs à un système de suivi sur mesure. Alors, trouver la manière de faire tout cela ET que le site soit sexy a vraiment été le plus grand défi de ce projet.

Comme pour tout projet réussi, il est toujours important de remarquer à quel point le client nous a aidés. Il nous a contactés parce qu'il aimait notre travail et qu'il voulait intégrer nos décisions sur le design au projet, et il nous a vraiment donné une grande liberté d'action.

Nous avions aussi une marque assez bien établie, dans le sens où BACARDI® avait déjà développé une marque de service solide, l'emblème de la chauve-souris, ainsi qu'un spectre de couleurs approximatif.

Nous sommes partis de ces paramètres et nous avons essayé de mettre une grille en place. Pour être sûrs que la grille soit visuellement cohérente, nous avons demandé au client de nous donner une hiérarchie absolue de leurs priorités visuelles ou, en d'autres termes, une liste des éléments de la page d'accueil par ordre d'importance promotionnelle. Une fois cette liste en main, nous savions, au moins, comment établir les priorités visuelles de la grille, ce qui nous a permis d'attaquer sérieusement la conception graphique, et de composer la grille de la page d'accueil. Comme le travail de préparation que nous avions fait avec le client en préproduction avait été assez complet et détaillé, nous avons pu définir les proportions de la grille de la page d'accueil du premier coup. Certains modules à l'intérieur de la grille allaient devoir être revus plusieurs fois pour les fignoler individuellement, mais nous n'avons jamais vraiment eu besoin de modifier les proportions de notre première grille après notre première composition.

Encore une fois, le fait d'avoir un très bon client, facile à vivre et qui nous a fait confiance, nous a vraiment, vraiment aidés. Nous l'avions convaincu de ne pas prêter trop d'attention à chaque module individuel de la grille, qui avait été composée un peu grossièrement, et de considérer le design comme une « coquille ». Il pourrait ensuite être fignolé jusqu'à la perfection module par module, mais il fallait d'abord construire la coquille et la programmer en ActionScript, trouver comment tout ça allait se précharger, de quoi auraient l'air les rollovers,

Kurt Noble

Daniel

Eric

Michael

et comment les éléments de l'arrière-plan allaient fonctionner avec la grille de contenus et la mettre en valeur. Nous avons aussi dû étudier à fond les questions d'animation et nous assurer qu'absolument tous les états de rollover et toutes les animations de téléchargement que nous proposions seraient ensuite faciles à reproduire sur tout le site et à modifier en fonction des changements saisonniers. Par exemple, les premiers rollovers auraient pour thème des cartes à jouer, mais les rollovers d'Halloween n'allaient évidemment pas avoir le même thème. Alors nous avons bien sûr dû baser l'animation de ces rollovers sur les maths plutôt que sur la chronologie. C'était un ingrédient essentiel pour alléger nos frais de maintenance et être performants lors des mises à jour. Et puis, nous avions cette idée « liquide » pour les préchargements et nous avons passé beaucoup de temps à chercher comment la réaliser sans taxer les processeurs des ordinateurs ni ralentir le flux des animations. Pour nous, cela a été une autre prouesse de programmation en ActionScript, et nous avons aussi trouvé une solution très fluide, pas trop lourde pour le processeur et avec une taille de fichier réduite.

Une fois que nous avions finalisé la grille et que le système Flash avait été entièrement structuré et planifié, nous pouvions continuer avec les sous-sections du site, et construire leurs grilles de manière similaire et cohérente, mais en ajoutant un deuxième et parfois même un troisième niveau de navigation. Là encore, du point de vue de la séquence de travail, ça a été une vraie bénédiction que le client soutienne notre idée de continuer à construire la « coquille » de toutes les pages du site. Au lieu de s'enliser dans des révisions individuelles page par page de tous les modules dans chaque grille de page, nous avons pu avancer avec toutes les grilles dans la coquille, en sachant que plus tard nous allions revenir sur chaque module individuel, et que nous allions obtenir une approbation de la copie définitive module par module. En fait, cela convenait mieux au client aussi, parce que de toute manière il n'avait pas encore une copie approuvée à 100 %. Alors, à de nombreux points de vue, c'était non seulement le meilleur moyen d'avancer dans le design, mais aussi le seul moyen logique d'avancer dans la construction. Le succès du projet a vraiment tenu à cette possibilité de continuer à avancer, en sachant que le client nous faisait confiance.

La partie consacrée aux « girls » nous a posé un défi particulièrement amusant, et comme vous pouvez le voir, la grille est vraiment passée au second plan dans la liste des priorités visuelles, parce que les filles devaient être mises en valeur. Au départ, nous les avions simplement destinées à la galerie du site, mais au cours de la préproduction le client nous a chargés de construire quelque chose de bien plus ambitieux, une galerie vraiment impressionnante et plus interactive, exclusivement pour les filles. Nous avons eu cette grande idée : un système de galerie à grande échelle rien que pour elles, qui permet au visiteur de feuilleter les photos de façon ludique, d'agrandir les images, et même d'envoyer des photos « autographiées » à travers un composant du Flash. Ici encore, nous devions nous assurer que cette énorme interface de photos surdimensionnées soit quand même tout aussi modulable et dynamique que le reste du site. Parce qu'un nouveau groupe de filles allait arriver sur le site une fois par an, et le nombre de photos allait changer, le nom des filles allait changer, et tout ce nouveau contenu devrait pouvoir être relié facilement au système de vote et aux composants de marketing viral de cette section. C'est sans doute l'une des réalisations dont nous sommes les plus fiers pour ce site.

Après avoir terminé toutes les grilles et les pages à l'intérieur de la coquille, nous sommes finalement revenus sur l'ensemble du projet avec le client, et nous avons passé les six dernières semaines à vérifier toutes les révisions, les modifications de copie et tous les ajustements visuels de tous les différents modules dans l'ensemble de la grille de contenus. Le résultat final est ce que vous voyez aujourd'hui, mais comme nous l'avons dit, il y aura des changements visuels et de nouveaux contenus spectaculaires trois fois par an !

Kurt Noble - Portrait:
En plus de la gestion des obligations de KNI, Kurt s'occupe du développement des relations de KNI avec ses clients et cultive avec eux des concepts créatifs. Il travaille aussi avec l'équipe de KNI pour s'assurer que le travail visuel, d'animation et de conception dépasse les attentes des clients.
<www.kurtnoble.com>

BACARDI.LIVE
LIVE LIKE YOU MEAN IT

JOIN THE BAT · BOOKMARK · SURVEY · CONTACT US

VIDEOS EVENTS CONTESTS DRINKS GALLERY THE GIRLS DOWNLOAD SPORTS

BACARDI® GIRLS

2005–2006 BACARDI® Girls

PREV IMAGE

PHOTO TOOLBOX

NEXT IMAGE

WHAT'S MY NAME?!

HELLO
my name is

Get your own personally autographed picture from your favorite BACARDI® girl! (must be 21 years of age or older)

Select your girl:
Summer
YOUR NAME
YOUR EMAIL

SEND ME THE SIG!

WHO'S THE DIME?
Cast your vote for your favorite BACARDI® girl.
Summer
CAST YOUR VOTE

WE GOT VIDEO!
Click here for your viewing pleasure!
ROLL THE CLIP

LIVE LIKE YOU MEAN IT!™ DRINK RESPONSIBLY!

BACARDI

www.bacardilive.com

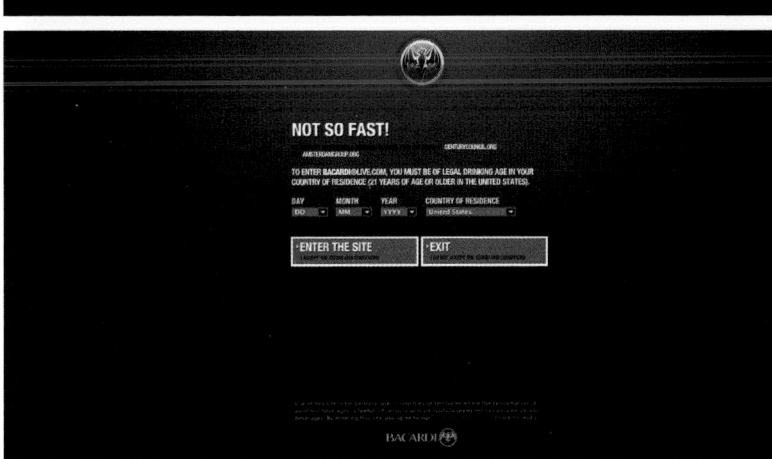

CASE·01

BACARDI®Live.com

Kurt Noble (KNI)

BACARDI® macht sehr wenig Druckwerbung und stützt stattdessen seine Marketingstrategie auf Live-Spielen, Werbespot-Übertragungen und natürlich auf sexy Fotos. Wie bereits der Name der Website zu erkennen gibt, legt BACARDI®Live.com bei der Umsetzung seiner vielfältigen Marketing-Strategien Wert auf eine ausgesprochen sexy und spaßbetonte Online-Präsenz. Das Projekt wurde äußerst sorgfältig geplant, so dass alles, was von uns entworfen, konstruiert und ins Internet gestellt wurde, mit geringem Aufwand auf die verschiedenen Jahreszeiten angepasst werden kann. Die explizite Darstellung der einzelnen Jahreszeiten soll dem Betrachter ein besonderes Gefühl vermitteln. Die Website könnte z. B. mit dem Vegas-Thema erstmalig ins Netz gestellt werden und im Herbst durch das Halloween-Thema aktualisiert werden. Sie sollte vor allem zahlreiche, gut miteinander harmonierende Elemente aufweisen. Jedes Element sollte so dynamisch sein, dass es problemlos an die ständig wechselnden Anforderungen der Werbung angepasst werden kann. Sie sollte außerdem viele Anmeldungen zu Spielen sowie Email-Optionen beinhalten, um Kundendaten an eine Datenbank weiterzuleiten. Schließlich sollte die sie so konfiguriert sein, dass jeder einzelne Schritt der Besucher im System ausgewertet und festgehalten werden kann. Unter Berücksichtigung dieser Faktoren ist die Erstellung einer Website für uns eine echte Herausforderung. Ganz besonders dann, wenn sie auch noch sexy wirken sollte.

Wir erkannten, wie wichtig es für den Erfolg eines Projektes ist, einen guten Kunden zu haben, dem unsere Art mit Design-Fragen umzugehen generell zusagt und der uns jegliche Freiheiten lässt, unsere Kreativität für ihn frei entfalten zu können.

Wir hatten hier mit einer guten Marke zu tun. Das Markenzeichen war schon bestens etabliert; Das bekannte Logo mit der Fledermaus und das Farbspektrum hatte BACARDI® bereits zuvor entwickelt.

Also machten wir uns an die Arbeit und versuchten, unter Berücksichtigung aller oben genannten Parameter eine Struktur aufzubauen. Um sicher zu gehen, ob unsere Struktur visuell Sinn macht, baten wir den Kunden, uns seine visuellen Prioritäten darzulegen, oder anders ausgedrückt, eine Liste der Homepage-Elemente nach Wichtigkeit für die Werbung gestaffelt zu unterbreiten. Anhand dieser Liste war nun wenigstens ungefähr zu erkennen, wie die visuellen Prioritäten innerhalb der Struktur eingeordnet werden sollten. Somit konnten wir mit dem Design-Prozess beginnen und die endgültige Homepage-Struktur aufzustellen. Da wir mit unserem Kunden gute Vorarbeit geleistet hatten, waren wir imstande, den Aufbau der Homepage schon beim ersten Versuch endgültig festzulegen. Viele der einzelnen Module in der Struktur mussten wiederholt überarbeitet werden, um das beabsichtigte Gefühl überzeugend zu vermitteln, aber der anfängliche Aufbau der Website blieb in seinen wesentlichen Strukturen erhalten.

Ich möchte es noch einmal betonen: Es hat uns wirklich, wirklich sehr geholfen, dass wir einen guten und unkomplizierten Kunden hatten, der uns großes Vertrauen entgegenbrachte. Wir überzeugten ihn, sich nicht zu sehr auf jedes einzelne Modul in der grob geplanten Struktur festzulegen und das Design als „Entwurf" zu betrachten, der noch auf Modul-Basis bis zur Perfektion auszuarbeiten war. Nachdem wir die Zustimmung für den Entwurf erhalten hatten, galt es, diesen funktionsfähig zu machen und zu sehen, wie alles geladen wird, wie die

Kurt Noble

Daniel

Eric

Michael

Rollover-Aktionen aussehen und wie die Hintergrundelemente mit der Struktur übereinstimmen sowie diese unterstützen. Wir mussten auch die animationsrelevanten Funktionen ausarbeiten und uns vergewissern, dass unabhängig von der Art der einzusetzenden Rollovers und Animationen, es nachher problemlos sein wird, diese nachzubilden und Änderungen websiteweit durchzuführen, so dass die Anforderungen der jeweiligen Jahreszeit berücksichtigt werden können. Die ersten Rollovers sollten zum Beispiel mit dem Thema Spielkarten arbeiten, die nachfolgenden sollten jedoch dem Thema Halloween gewidmet sein. Also mussten wir eine Animation für diese Rollovers einsetzen, die auf Berechnungen basiert und nicht auf Zeitenfolgen. Das war unbedingt erforderlich für die Aktualisierung der Website, um den sich ständig wechselnden Anforderungen des Kunden gerecht zu werden. Als wir dann die „zündende" Idee für den Pre-loader hatten, überlegten wir, wie das Konzept umgesetzt werden könnte, ohne dass die Computer-Prozessoren überfordert und die Qualität der Animationen beeinträchtigt würde. Das war eine große Herausforderung für uns als Programmierer, aber schließlich ist es ist uns gelungen, eine reibungslose und prozessorfreundliche Lösung zu finden, die mit einer geringen Datengröße funktioniert.

Nach Festlegung der Makro-Struktur für die Website und des Flash-Systems konnten wir mit der Ausarbeitung der Mikro-Struktur der Website fortfahren, und zwar indem wir diese in die Makro-Struktur eingefügt haben. Diese Mikro-Struktur war ähnlich aufgebaut, wie die Makro-Struktur, hatte jedoch eine zweite, und in manchen Fällen eine dritte Navigationsebene. Auch in diesem Entwicklungsstadium ging der Kunde auf unseren Vorschlag ein, zunächst einen Entwurf für die einzelnen Seiten der Website auszuarbeiten. Wieder ließ uns der Kunde freie Hand beim Entwurf der einzelnen Module für die Mikro-Struktur. Erst in einer späteren Arbeitsphase wurden die Details der Module mit dem Kunden noch einmal überarbeitet. Diese Vorgehensweise kam auch dem Kunden entgegen, der zu Beginn selbst noch keine endgültige Vorstellung von allen Details der Website hatte und somit seine Zustimmung erst zu einem späteren Zeitpunkt geben konnte. Das ist die einfachste Lösung, mit der Entwicklung des Designs umzugehen und auch die einzig logische Möglichkeit, an dem Aufbau zu arbeiten. Der Schlüssel zum Erfolg war hier das uneingeschränkte Vertrauen des Kunden.

Die Girls-Section der Website war eine besondere Herausforderung und hat viel Spaß gemacht. Wie Sie sehen, war diese Struktur im unteren Bereich der visuellen Prioritäten angeordnet. Ursprünglich waren die Mädchen nur für die Galerie auf der Website vorgesehen. Im Zuge der Vorproduktion jedoch hat uns der Kunde damit beauftragt, die Galerie auffallend und interaktiv zu gestalten, exklusiv für die Mädchen. Also sind wir auf die glorreiche Idee gekommen, ein wirklich groß angelegtes Galerie-System für die Mädchen einzubauen. Der Besucher soll Spaß daran haben, durch die Fotos zu scrollen, die Bilder im Großformat anzusehen und sogar Fotos mit „Autogrammen" mit Hilfe des Flash-Programms an andere Benutzer zu versenden. Auch hier, wie auf der gesamten Website, mussten wir sicherstellen, dass auch die Schnittstelle zum Einsehen übergroßer Fotos genauso größenvariabel und dynamisch war, wie der Rest der Website. Jedes Jahr sollten neue Mädchen auf der Website erscheinen, dabei sollten die Anzahl der Fotos und die Namen der Mädchen variieren. Diese neuen Faktoren sollten auf einfachste Weise in das Auswahlsystem und die Viren-Komponenten eingebunden werden. Das Resultat steht für Erfolg und darauf sind wir stolz.

Nachdem wir alle Strukturen des Entwurfs erstellt hatten, haben wir sechs Wochen der Projektlaufzeit damit zugebracht, mit dem Kunden alle Details der verschiedenen Module innerhalb der gesamten Struktur der Website zu überarbeiten, ggf. zu revidieren und visuelle Schwachpunkte zu beseitigen. Das Endresultat ist das, was Sie heute sehen, auch wenn jetzt schon klar ist, dass diese Website drei Mal im Jahr komplett überholt wird und zwar inhaltlich und visuell!

Kurt Noble – Profil:
Neben der Abwicklung der allgemeinen unternehmerischen Aufgaben der Fa. KNI, baut Noble die Kundenkontakte der Firma auf, pflegt die Konzepte mit diesen Kunden und arbeitet auch mit dem Personal von KNI zusammen, um sicherzustellen, dass KNI visuelle und technisch ausgereifte Ergebnisse liefert, die die Erwartungen der Kunden übertreffen.
<www.kurtnoble.com>

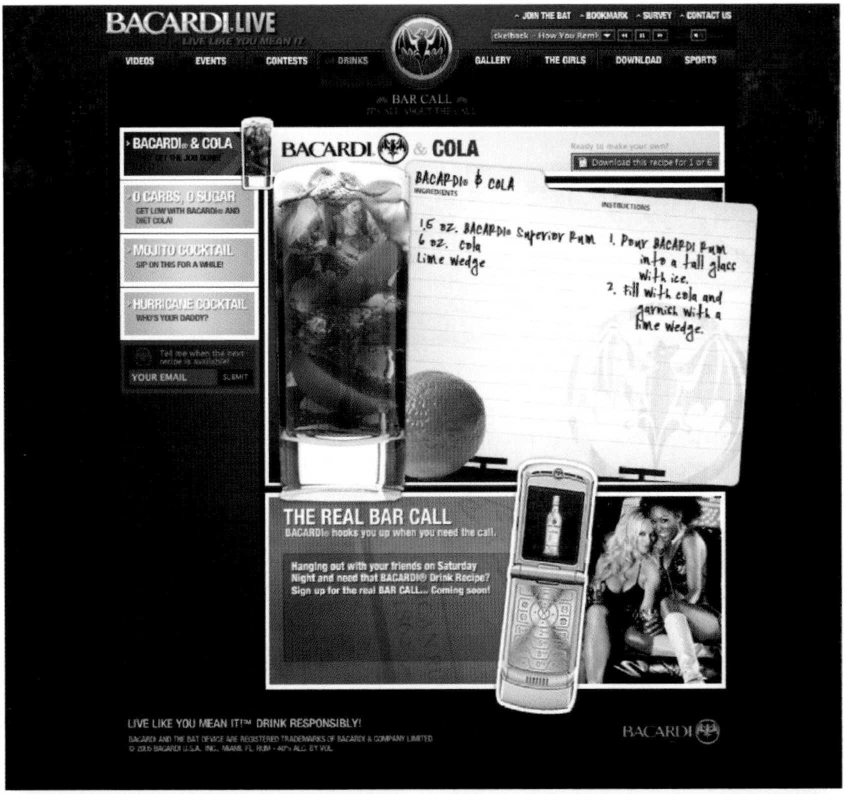

www.bacardilive.com

CASE·02

Interview:
Pascal Leroy (group94)

1) You work hard on navigation systems. How do you start planning a new site? Is it from a navigation point of view?

Not really. A client contacts us because he has certain needs and requirements: he wants to broadcast information, he wants to provide certain online functionality; he wants to do business... It is our job to devise the best possible vehicle for his needs. At first every g94-project starts with a clean sheet. We never use site templates; we always start from scratch with as few constraints as possible. We study, we think, we examine, we discuss things with the client, we evaluate his target audience, we check his existing publications, etc. We try to figure out a site concept that matches all aspects of the project and all the client's other requirements. Next step is to figure out the design architecture and that sometimes leads to an unusual navigation. But that is a consequence; it is never the goal itself. And an uncommon navigational system is only justified if it makes sense, if the user understands it immediately and if it works fluently and perfectly. The navigation is the engine that will make the site work or fail and thus it is worth paying a lot of attention to it.

2) What are the biggest challenges when doing a project from scratch?

Most important is to take enough time to think the project over at startup. Building a site should happen meticulously and according to a well thought plan. The first phase in the production process is to lay out each scene and to make sure that the system is logical and makes sense. Draw wireframes, make sure that the site will be built according to the user requirements, avoid pitfalls and make sure that all technical issues are sorted out.

Secondly it's important to communicate well with the client and make sure that he understands the project in all its aspects: that he agrees with the concept, that he approves the design, and that he understands what the site will do and – important - what it will not do: the worst nightmare would definitely be to spend a few weeks on programming a site and then end up with a client who's unhappy with the result...

3) What are basic parameters/priorities for a good working website for you?

From a content point of view I think a site should give what it promises. It should be obvious, well structured. From a navigational point of view it should be easy to understand, intuitive. From a technical point of view every aspect, every detail should be well thought out, fast and efficient.

That should result in a believable project, stripped of all unnecessary bells and whistles. In my opinion, being essential and to the point is being trustworthy.

4) How complicated can be a navigation system and what is the usual timeframe for the programming?

From a technical point of view there are hardly any limitations. Up till now we managed to build about every system exactly as we had conceived it without too many technical compromises. It is true that some navigation systems we've built were really complex. Weirdly enough the most evident and easy to use navigation sometimes were the toughest ones to program. The in-text navigation we created for **<www.mortierbrigade.com>** for

instance is extremely obvious and fluent from a user point of view. Nonetheless it took us more than a week just to program the effect of pushing the non-selected text aside.

One of the toughest ones was definitely the portfolio site we built for **<www.dart-design.de>**, which navigates via an intuitive 3d environment (one can even use the arrow keys...) where projects are represented by smoothly floating round objects. The site is fully database driven and the information structure is relational: information that is related to the selected project will be added to the scene, non-related projects will vanish. The menu acts as a filtering system. It took more than two months to build the whole system.

5) What is the biggest advantage of using flash in your view?

The technique we use always depends on the message or the subject.

Compare it to printed matter: some communication, say a campaign for a new mobile phone, will be done via advertisements in magazines while a fashion designer will promote his latest collection in an exclusive full color catalogue. Although both are printed matter they are different and they serve a different purpose.

Same for the web: Flash and html are very different techniques, they serve different purposes and they result in a very different surfing experience.

The navigational element of a html site is limited to providing a user with an efficient and straightforward way of allocating specific information. Due to technical limitations, surfing an html site is uni-dimensional. In contrast surfing a Flash site, if it's well done, can be more like taking a journey, that ultimately creates an experience that portrays an idea or image. A Flash website can be multi-layered.

We do both Flash and html projects. As a matter of fact one of our largest recent projects was a strictly xhtml project as we have redesigned the global presence for **<www.agfa.com>**. For example: I cannot imagine making an emotive photographer's portfolio site like **<www.sksantos.com>** by means of html techniques. On the other hand it would be stupid to build a site for a multinational like Agfa with Flash techniques only. We recently also mixed techniques: **<www.hotham.com.au>** for instance is structured as an html site which allows typical browser functionality and which makes the site fully scannable by Google, but we utilized Flash technology where appropriate: navigation, multimedia, interactive maps etc. Best of both worlds...

6) What is to be avoided when you do a flash-based site?

Personally I hate loading sequences, which is why one will rarely encounter a 'please wait while loading' in a g94-project.

7) How do you keep a client happy with his website?

The client wants us to provide him with a good solution for his requirements. He is prepared to pay for this but obviously his investment should pay off afterwards. His project should not only meet with his current requirements but also be built in such a flexible way that it may be easily adapted to future needs as well. Our job doesn't finish upon delivery and we keep in contact with most of our clients long after their project is online. And I must admit that it always feels great to suddenly receive an email from a client photographer saying that he's got, yet again, a new assignment via his website. Having most satisfied clients while producing quality work is our main commitment.

8) Do you think there is a specific visual language related to websites or to flash-designed sites?

Definitely. Basically the web is a very new communication channel besides other – older – media and although it has its very own specific rules and regulations and possibilities, I think that a designer should always keep in mind the basic rules of communication when designing for the web. Again: it's essential that people understand how a site is structured and how it works.

Having said that, I'm not convinced that interface design evolution has stopped somewhere at the end of the previous millennium and that Jacob Nielsen is the Internet Moses who wrote down the ultimate laws.

The discipline we're active in is definitely in motion and the surfing audience is becoming more and more mature. That allows us to question each dogma over and over again and that's what keeps our job so exciting.

Pascal Leroy is founder of and creative director at group94. Located in Gent, Belgium. **<www.group94.com>**

www.dart-design.de

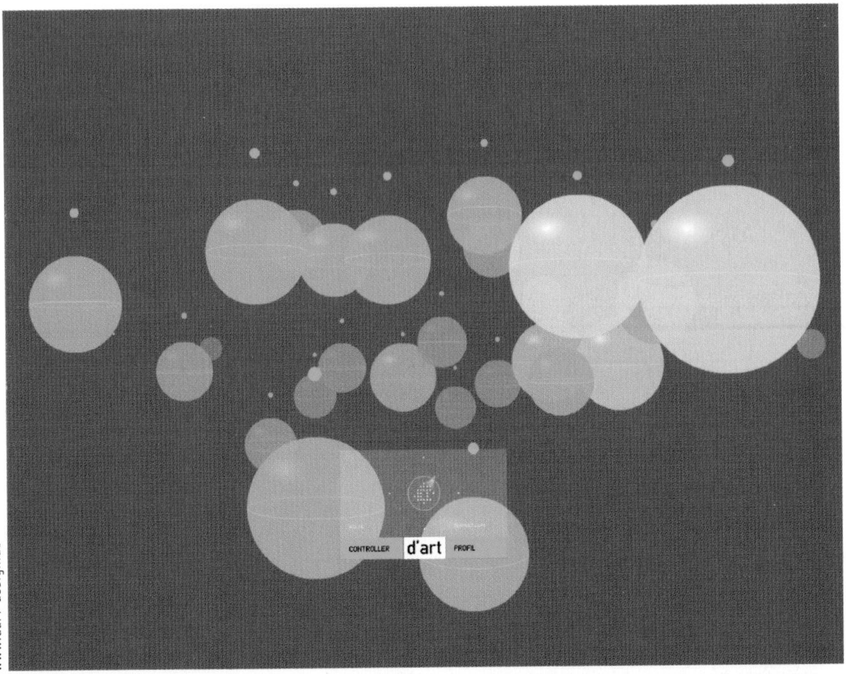

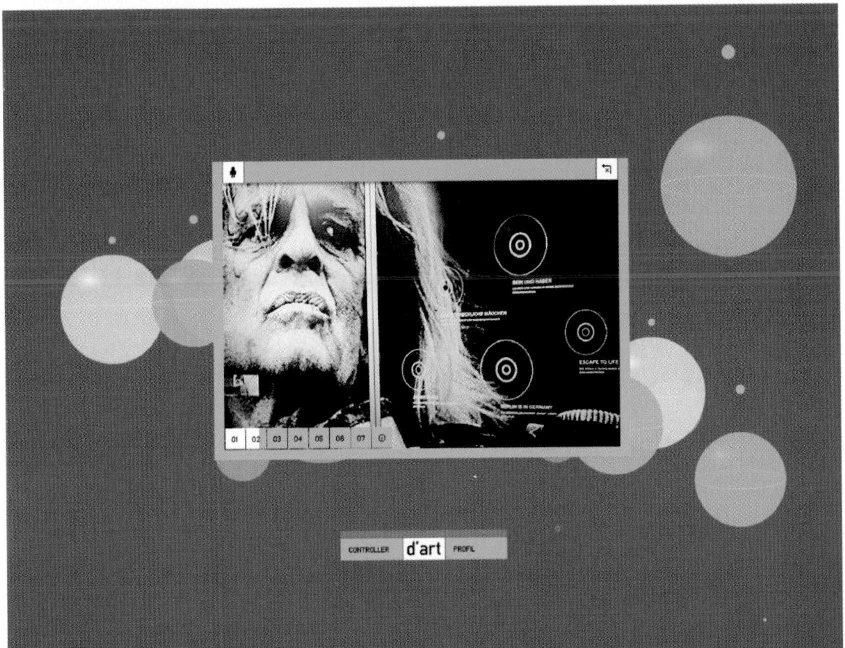

CONTROLLER d'art PROFIL

01 02 03 04 05 06 07

CONTROLLER d'art PROFIL

L'entretien :

Pascal Leroy (group94)

1) Vous travaillez dur sur les systèmes de navigation. Par quoi commencez-vous lorsque vous planifiez un nouveau site ? Par la navigation ?

Pas vraiment. Lorsqu'un client nous contacte, c'est parce qu'il a certains besoins et certaines exigences : il veut diffuser des informations, il veut proposer une certaine fonctionnalité en ligne, il veut faire du commerce... Notre travail, c'est d'imaginer le meilleur véhicule possible pour ses besoins. Au départ, chaque projet de g94 commence par une feuille blanche. Nous n'utilisons jamais de modèles de sites. Nous commençons toujours de zéro, avec aussi peu de contraintes que possible. Nous étudions, nous réfléchissons, nous examinons, nous discutons avec le client, nous évaluons son audience cible, nous consultons ses publications, etc. Nous essayons de trouver un concept de site qui correspond à tous les aspects du projet et à toutes les autres exigences du client. L'étape suivante est de trouver l'architecture, et cela mène parfois à une navigation inhabituelle. Mais c'est une conséquence, ce n'est jamais le but en lui-même. Et un système de navigation inhabituel ne se justifie que s'il a un sens, si l'utilisateur le comprend immédiatement et s'il fonctionne parfaitement et de manière fluide. La navigation est le moteur qui fera du site un succès ou un échec, et cela vaut la peine d'y accorder beaucoup d'attention.

2) Et qu'est-ce qui est le plus dur lorsqu'on commence un projet de zéro ?

Le plus important, c'est de prendre assez de temps pour bien réfléchir au projet dès le départ. La construction d'un site doit être méticuleuse, et suivre un plan bien défini. La première phase du processus de production est de planifier chaque scène et de s'assurer de la logique et du sens du système. Dessiner les cadres en fil de fer, s'assurer que la construction du site respectera les exigences du client, éviter les pièges et s'assurer de la résolution de tous les problèmes techniques.

Ensuite, il est important de bien communiquer avec le client et de s'assurer qu'il comprend le projet dans tous ses aspects : qu'il est d'accord avec le concept, qu'il approuve le design, et qu'il comprend ce que le site pourra faire et - important - ce qu'il ne pourra pas faire : le pire cauchemar ce serait vraiment de passer plusieurs semaines à programmer un site et que le client ne soit pas content du résultat...

3) Quels sont les paramètres/priorités essentiels pour un site Internet qui fonctionne bien, selon vous ?

Du point de vue du contenu, je pense qu'un site devrait tenir ses promesses. Il devrait être clair, bien structuré. Du point de vue de la navigation, il devrait être facile à comprendre et intuitif. Du point de vue technique, chaque aspect, chaque détail doit être bien pensé, rapide et efficace.

Cela devrait donner un projet crédible, dépouillé de tout le superflu. D'après moi, aller directement à l'essentiel c'est être digne de confiance.

4) Jusqu'où un système de navigation peut-il aller dans la complexité, et combien de temps prend la programmation en général ?

Du point de vue technique, il n'y a pratiquement aucune limite. Jusqu'à maintenant nous avons réussi à

construire pratiquement chaque système exactement comme nous l'avions conçu sans trop faire de compromis techniques. C'est vrai que certains des systèmes de navigation que nous avons construits étaient vraiment complexes. C'est assez bizarre, mais les systèmes de navigation les plus évidents et les plus faciles à utiliser ont parfois été les plus durs à programmer. Par exemple, la navigation textuelle que nous avons créée pour **<www.mortierbrigade.com>** est très évidente et fluide pour l'utilisateur. Ça nous a pourtant pris plus d'une semaine rien que pour programmer l'effet de pousser le texte non sélectionné sur le côté.

L'un des plus difficiles a vraiment été le site de présentation que nous avons fait pour **<www.dart-design.de>**. On y navigue dans un environnement 3D intuitif (on peut même utiliser les flèches du clavier...) où les projets sont représentés par des sphères qui flottent doucement. Le site est entièrement construit sur une base de données et la structure de l'information est relationnelle : l'information associée au projet sélectionné est ajoutée à la scène, les projets non associés disparaissent. Le menu agit comme un système de filtrage. Il a fallu plus de deux mois pour construire tout le système.

5) Selon vous, quel est le plus grand avantage de Flash ?

La technique que nous utilisons dépend toujours du message ou du sujet.

On peut faire une comparaison avec les supports imprimés : un certain type de communication, disons une campagne pour un nouveau téléphone portable, se fera grâce à des publicités dans les magazines, alors qu'un créateur de mode fera la promotion de sa dernière collection dans un catalogue très chic en pleine couleur. Bien que les deux soient des supports imprimés, ils sont différents, et ils servent un but différent.

C'est la même chose pour Internet : Flash et l'HTML sont des techniques très différentes, elles servent des buts différents et elles donnent des navigations très différentes.

L'élément navigationnel d'un site HTML se limite à donner à l'utilisateur une façon simple et efficace de localiser des informations spécifiques. À cause des limites techniques, naviguer sur un site en HTML est unidimensionnel. En revanche, naviguer sur un site Flash, si c'est bien fait, peut se rapprocher davantage d'un voyage qui en fin de compte fait le portrait d'une idée ou d'une image. Un site web en Flash peut comporter plusieurs couches.

Nous faisons des projets en Flash et en HTML. D'ailleurs, l'un de nos principaux projets récents était un projet strictement en XHTML, car nous avons revu la conception de la présence globale pour **<www.agfa.com>**. Par exemple : je n'arrive pas à imaginer un portfolio de photographe qui véhicule aussi bien l'émotion que **<www.sksantos.com>** avec des techniques HTML. D'un autre côté, il serait stupide de construire un site pour une multinationale comme Agfa avec seulement des techniques Flash. Nous avons aussi mélangé les techniques récemment : **<www.hotham.com.au>**, par exemple, est structuré comme un site HTML avec la fonctionnalité de navigateur typique. Cela permet que le site soit entièrement scanné par Google, mais nous avons utilisé la technologie Flash là où c'était approprié. Navigation, multimédia, cartes interactives, etc. Le meilleur des deux mondes...

6) Que doit-on éviter lorsque l'on fait un site en Flash ?

Personnellement, je déteste les séquences de chargement, c'est pourquoi vous rencontrerez rarement un message « veuillez patienter pendant le chargement » dans un projet de g94.

7) Que faites-vous pour qu'un client soit content de son site web ?

Le client veut que nous lui trouvions une solution efficace. Il est prêt à payer pour cela, mais évidemment son investissement doit être rentable ensuite. Son projet ne doit pas seulement correspondre à ses exigences actuelles, il doit aussi être construit de manière à pouvoir être adapté à ses besoins futurs. Notre travail ne s'arrête pas à la livraison et nous restons en contact avec la plupart de nos clients bien après que leur projet soit mis en ligne. Et je dois admettre que c'est toujours très agréable de recevoir soudain un e-mail d'un client photographe disant qu'il a encore reçu une nouvelle mission à travers son site web. Notre engagement principal est de satisfaire les clients tout en produisant un travail de qualité.

8) Pensez-vous qu'il existe un langage visuel spécifique associé aux sites web ou aux sites en Flash ?

Tout à fait. En fait, Internet est un moyen de communication très nouveau à côté des autres médias (plus vieux), et bien qu'il ait ses propres règles et possibilités, je pense qu'un designer devrait toujours garder à l'esprit les règles de base de la communication lorsqu'il travaille pour Internet. Encore une fois : il est essentiel que les gens comprennent la structure et le fonctionnement d'un site.

Maintenant, je ne crois pas que l'évolution de la conception d'interface se soit arrêtée à la fin du dernier millénaire, ni que Jacob Nielsen soit le Moïse de l'Internet et ait gravé les tables de la loi.

Notre discipline est vraiment en mouvement et l'audience mûrit de plus en plus. Cela nous permet de remettre chaque dogme en question encore et encore, et c'est ce qui rend notre travail si excitant.

Pascal Leroy est le fondateur et le directeur de la création de group94. Situé à Gent, Belgique. **<www.group94.com>**

www.sksantos.com

01 RENEGADED | 02 PURE R | 03 POTERNITY | // THE SHORT | Sean Kennedy Santos. fotographie

AUDIENCE INCLUDE | 24/7 4U | LCR

04

MENU

Das Interview:
Pascal Leroy (group94)

1) Sie arbeiten intensiv an der Programmierung von Navigationssystemen von Websites. Wie gehen Sie bei der Planung einer neuen Website vor? Fangen Sie mit der Navigation an?

Nicht ganz. Ein Kunde nimmt Kontakt mit uns auf, weil er bestimmte Bedürfnisse hat und Anforderungen erfüllt bekommen will. Er möchte Informationen im Internet zur Verfügung stellen. Er möchte eine bestimmte Funktion online stellen. Er möchte Geschäfte machen... Unsere Aufgabe besteht darin, das möglichst beste Werkzeug für seine Bedürfnisse zu entwickeln. Jedes Projekt von g94 beginnt mit einem leeren Blatt Papier. Wir benutzen keine Schablonen. Wir fangen immer bei Null an, mit so wenigen Einschränkungen wie möglich. Wir forschen nach, wir überlegen, wir überprüfen, wir diskutieren mit dem Kunden, wir schätzen seine Zielgruppe ein, wir schauen uns seine bereits vorhandenen Publikationen an etc. Wir versuchen, ein Konzept für eine Website zu erarbeiten, die alle Aspekte des Projektes und alle anderen Anforderungen des Kunden berücksichtigt. Im nächsten Schritt erarbeiten wir ein allgemeines Design. Die Umsetzung des Designs wiederum erfordert manchmal eine ganz ungewöhnliche Navigation. Also ist die Navigation die Konsequenz und nicht das Ziel an sich. Ein ausgefallenes Navigationssystem ist jedoch nur dann gerechtfertigt, wenn es sinnvoll ist, wenn der Benutzer es sofort verstehen kann und wenn es reibungslos funktioniert. Die Navigation ist das Triebwerk, von dem die Funktionsfähigkeit oder der Misserfolg der gesamten Internetpräsenz abhängt, deshalb muss sie ganz besonders sorgfältig geplant werden.

2) Welchen großen Herausforderungen muss sich ein Webdesigner stellen, der ein Projekt von Grund auf startet?

Das Wichtigste ist, sich genügend Zeit zu nehmen, um das Projekt bereits am Anfang gut zu durchdenken. Die Herstellung einer Website sollte auf akribische Weise und gemäß einem sehr gut durchdachten Plan vonstatten gehen. Die erste Phase des Herstellungsprozesses besteht darin, alle Bereiche festzulegen und sicherzustellen, dass das gesamte System logisch aufgebaut ist und einen Sinn ergibt. Man sollte Modelle zeichnen, überprüfen, ob die Website den Anforderungen des Kunden entspricht, mögliche Fallen umgehen und überprüfen, ob alle technischen Anforderungen umsetzbar sind. Dann ist es wichtig, mit dem Kunden in gutem Kontakt zu stehen und sich zu vergewissern, dass er das Projekt mit allen Facetten versteht. Der Kunde sollte mit dem Konzept einverstanden sein, das Design akzeptieren, verstehen, welche Funktion die Website erfüllen wird und – das ist ganz wichtig – welche Funktion sie nicht erfüllen wird. Es wäre doch ein Alptraum, wenn der Kunde nach wochenlangem Programmieren mit dem Resultat nicht zufrieden wäre...

3) Was sind Ihrer Meinung nach die wichtigsten Merkmale einer gut funktionierenden Website?

Ich glaube, wenn man die Inhalte betrachtet, so sollte eine Website erfüllen, was sie verspricht. Sie sollte klar und gut strukturiert sein. Was die Navigation anbetrifft, so sollte sie intuitiv und leicht verständlich sein. Aus technischer Sicht sollte jeder Aspekt, jedes Detail gut durchdacht, schnell und effizient sein. Es sollte insgesamt betrachtet ein glaubwürdiges Projekt sein,

ohne unnötigen Schnickschnack. Ich bin der Ansicht, dass man Vertrauen erweckt, wenn man sich auf das Nötige beschränkt und geradlinig ist.

4) Wie kompliziert kann ein Navigationssystem sein und wie sieht im Allgemeinen der Zeitrahmen für die Programmierung aus?

Technisch gesehen gibt es kaum Einschränkungen. Bis jetzt ist es uns gelungen, fast jedes System genau nach unserem Plan zu bauen, und zwar ohne viele technische Kompromisse eingehen zu müssen. Zugegeben, manche der von uns gebauten Navigationssysteme waren wirklich komplex. Komischerweise waren oft die übersichtlichsten und benutzerfreundlichsten Navigationssysteme am schwierigsten zu programmieren. Die Text-Navigation, die wir z.B. für **<www.mortierbrigade.com>** programmiert haben ist absolut übersichtlich und benutzerfreundlich und dennoch haben wir über eine Woche gebraucht, nur um den Effekt des Wegschiebens des nicht ausgewählten Textes zu programmieren. Eine der schwierigsten Websites war eindeutig die Portfolio-Site für **<www.dart-design.de>**. Die Navigation funktioniert in einer intuitiven 3D-Umgebung (man kann für die Navigation sogar die Pfeil-Tasten auf der Tastatur benutzen...), die Projekte verbergen sich hinter langsam schwebenden, runden Objekten. Die Website ist Datenbank-gestützt und die Informationsstruktur ist relational, d.h. dass die zum ausgewählten Projekt gehörende Information eingeblendet wird, während alle anderen Projekte verborgen bleiben. Das Menu funktioniert wie ein Filtersystem. Der Aufbau des gesamten Systems dauerte über zwei Monate.

5) Was ist Ihrer Meinung nach der größte Vorteil von Flash?

Wir wählen die richtige Technik aus, je nach Botschaft oder Thema der Website.

Lassen Sie mich das am Beispiel Printmedien erklären. Manche Werbekampagnen, sagen wir mal, für ein neues Mobiltelefon, erscheinen in Zeitschriften, während z. B. ein Modedesigner für seine neue Kollektion in einem exklusiven, farbigen Katalog werben wird. Obwohl die Werbung in beiden Fällen gedruckt wird, ist doch jede von ihnen anders und dient einem anderen Zweck. Das gilt auch für das Internet: Flash und HTML sind ganz unterschiedliche Techniken, sie dienen unterschiedlichen Zwecken und resultieren in unterschiedlichen Surferlebnissen. Ein Navigationselement bei einer HTML-Website bietet dem Benutzer lediglich eine effiziente und einfache Möglichkeit an genaue Informationen heranzukommen. Aufgrund technischer Einschränkungen ist das Surfen auf einer HTML-Website uni-dimensional. Im Gegensatz dazu kann das Surfen auf einer Flash-Website, wenn sie gut programmiert ist, mit einer Reise verglichen werden, die letztendlich zu einem bildhaften und ideenreichen Erlebnis wird. Eine Flash-Website kann mehrschichtig sein. Wir bearbeiten sowohl Flash- als auch HTML-Projekte. Tatsächlich ist eines unserer größten Projekte der letzten Zeit ein XHTML-Projekt. Es handelt sich dabei um ein Neudesign für den globalen Webauftritt von **<www.agfa.com>**. Um ein Beispiel zu nennen: Ich kann mir nicht vorstellen, dass eine gefühlsbetonte Portfolio-Website für einen Fotografen, wie **<www.sksantos.com>**, mit Hilfe der HTML-Technik erstellt werden könnte. Auf der anderen Seite wäre es nicht angebracht, eine Website für ein internationales Unternehmen wie Agfa ausschließlich mit Hilfe von Flash-Techniken zu erstellen. Wir haben in letzter Zeit auch beide Techniken miteinander kombiniert. **<www.hotham.com.au>** ist z.B. HTML-strukturiert. Das bringt den Vorteil der typischen Funktionalität des Browsers mit sich, wodurch auch ein gutes Google-Ranking erreicht wird. Wir haben jedoch überall dort, wo es sinnvoll erschien, die Flash-Technik eingesetzt: in der Navigation, für Multimedia, interaktive Karten etc. Wir haben das Beste aus beiden Techniken herausgeholt und umgesetzt.

6) Was sollte man beim Erzeugen einer Flash-Website vermeiden?

Ich persönlich kann das Laden von Sequenzen nicht leiden. Das ist auch der Grund, warum Sie bei g94-Projekten nur ganz selten lesen werden „please wait while loading".

7) Wie erreichen Sie, dass die Zufriedenheit des Kunden mit seiner Website anhält?

Der Kunde wünscht, dass wir ihm eine gute Lösung für seine Anforderungen bieten. Er ist bereit, dafür Geld zu bezahlen, aber natürlich sollte sich seine Investition nachher auch lohnen. Das Projekt sollte nicht nur die gegenwärtigen Anforderungen des Kunden erfüllen, sondern so flexibel konzipiert sein, dass es auch künftig an neue Anforderungen angepasst werden kann. Unsere Aufgabe ist mit dem Tag der Lieferung nicht beendet, zu den meisten Kunden halten wir Kontakt, auch wenn das Projekt längst online ist. Ich muss zugeben, dass es immer wieder ein tolles Gefühl ist, wenn man von seinem Kunden, einem Fotografen, eine Email bekommt, in der steht, dass er zum wiederholten Male dank seiner guten Website einen neuen Auftrag erhalten hat. Unser Ziel ist es, unsere Kunden durch hohe Qualität unserer Arbeit zufrieden zu stellen.

8) Glauben Sie, dass es in Bezug auf Websites und Flash-Websites eine besondere visuelle Sprache gibt?

Natürlich. Grundsätzlich stellt das Internet, neben anderen – älteren – Medien, ein ganz neues Kommunikationsmittel dar. Obwohl das Web seine eigenen sehr spezifischen Regeln und Möglichkeiten hat, glaube ich, dass der Designer immer die Grundregeln der Kommunikation im Auge behalten sollte, wenn er an einer Website arbeitet. Nochmal: Es ist außerordentlich wichtig, dass die Menschen verstehen, wie eine Website strukturiert ist und wie sie funktioniert.

Auch wenn ich das gesagt habe, bin ich nicht davon überzeugt, dass die Evolution im Webdesign irgendwann gegen Ende des letzten Jahrtausends angehalten hat und dass Jacob Nielsen der Internet-Moses ist, der die 10 Gebote niedergeschrieben hat.

Der Bereich, in dem wir arbeiten, entwickelt sich ständig weiter und die Internetsurfer werden immer reifer. Das erlaubt uns, jedes Dogma immer wieder in Frage zu stellen, und genau dass macht unsere Arbeit so aufregend.

Pascal Leroy ist der Gründer und zugleich der Creative Director bei group94 mit Sitz in Gent, Belgien. **<www.group94.com>**

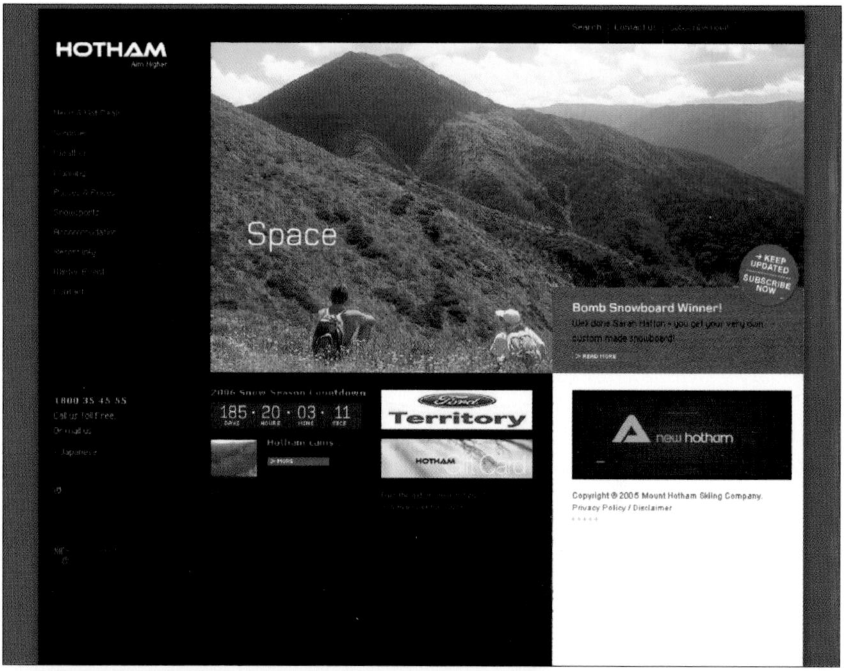

www.hotham.com.au

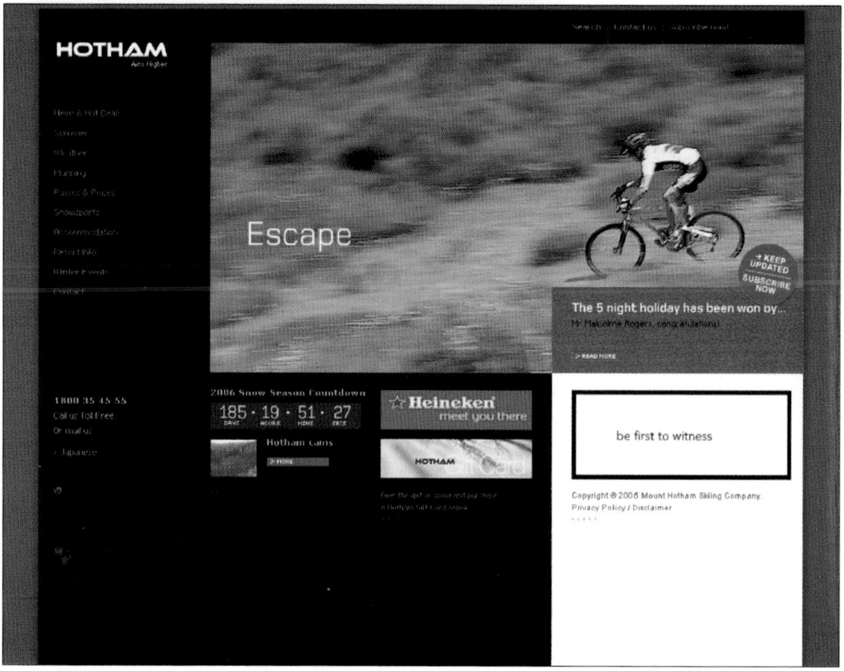

212BOX

USA

www.212box.com

2005

Concept

A 3D cube acts as the interface. Lines flow between project icons to illustrate their connections across disciplines. /// C'est un cube en 3D qui sert d'interface. Des lignes fluides relient les icônes des projets pour montrer les connexions entre disciplines. /// **Auf dieser Website dient ein 3D-Würfel als Benutzeroberfläche. Die Projekt-Icons sind durch Linien verbunden, die die Bezüge zwischen den einzelnen Fachgebieten bildhaft darstellen.**

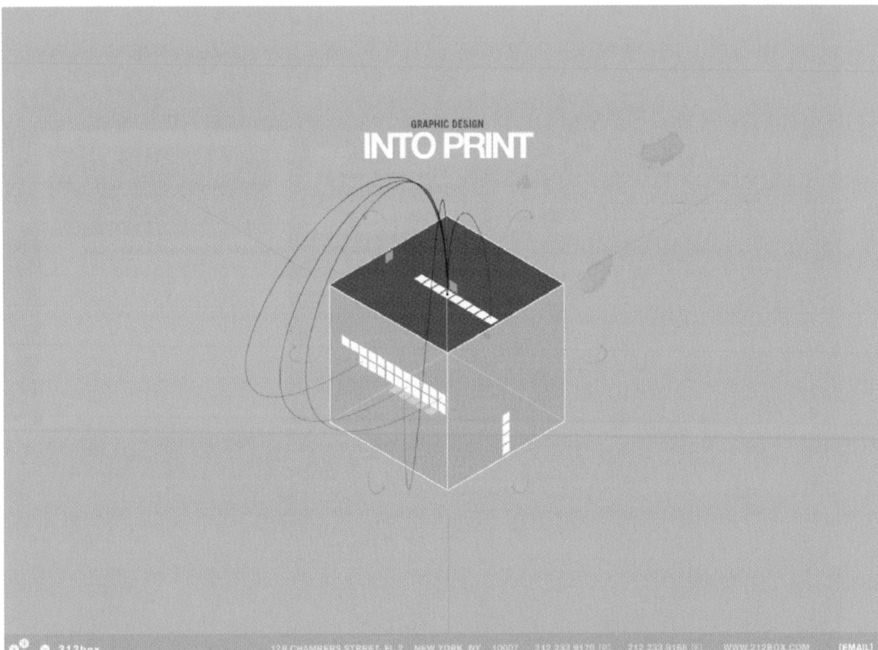

Info

Design and Programming: CRIMSON Design Group <www.crimsonmade.com>. /// **Tools:** Macromedia Flash, XML, PHP, MySQL, Maya. /// **Contents:** photography and renderings. /// **Cost:** 150 hours.

DAMIÁN DI PATRIZIO

ARGENTINA

www.22-10-78.com

2004

Concept

You have to maintain simplicity. That is why I developed a strong idea (a voyage across my head), but with a graphic surrounding and a very simple navigation: home is the web. /// Il faut privilégier la simplicité. C'est pourquoi j'ai développé une idée forte (un voyage dans ma tête), mais avec un environnement graphique et une navigation très simple : le web, c'est comme à la maison. /// Alles muss einfach bleiben. Aus diesem Grund entwickelte ich ein besonderes Konzept (eine Reise durch meinen Kopf), in einer grafischen Umgebung und mit einer sehr einfachen Navigation. Web ist das Zuhause.

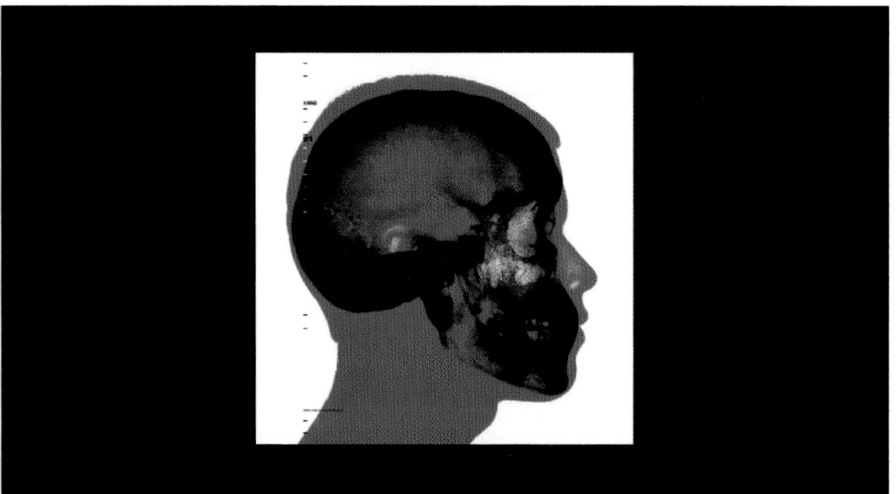

Info

Design and Programming: Damián Di Patrizio. /// **Tools**: Macromedia Flash, Adobe Photoshop, Adobe Illustrator. /// **Contents**: graphic design, art direction, web, photo. /// **Awards**: American Design Awards; Design TAXI; DOPE Awards; e-Creative; Plasticpilots; Pura Raza; Up Award Link; NewWebPick; Res72; Netdiver. /// **Cost**: 45 hours.

300K

SPAIN

www.300k.com

2003

Concept

Simply Magic! /// Tout simplement magique ! /// Einfach zauberhaft!

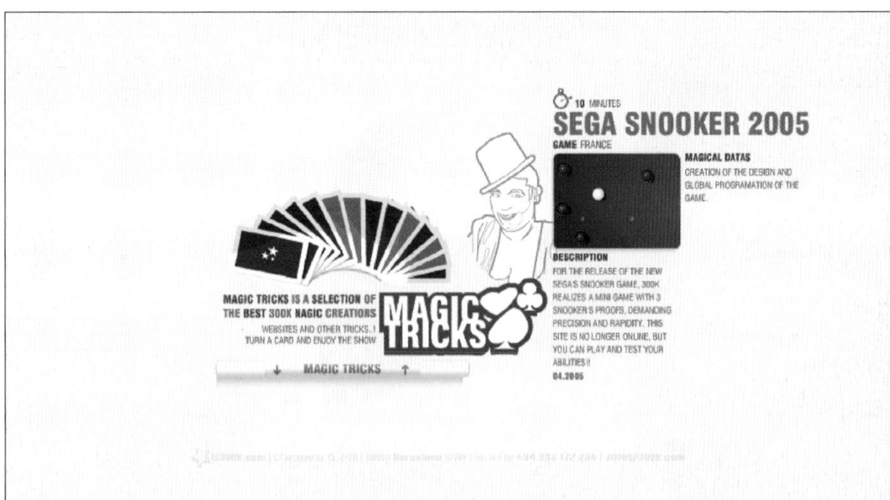

Info

Design and Programming: Guillaume Fenwick "Guitz" (300k.com). /// **Tools**: Macromedia Flash, Adobe Photoshop, Adobe Illustrator. ///
Contents: animations, games, and magics. /// **Awards**: e-Creative (Site of the Month), Flahxpress, FWA (Site of the Day), Praktica (Site of the Day). ///
Cost: 1 month.

3DSIGN

ITALY

www.3dsign.it

2005

Concept

I have tried to create an effective navigation system to leaf through an articulate showcase without neglect of the character and the style of the client. /// J'ai essayé de créer un système de navigation efficace pour parcourir toute une présentation sans négliger le caractère et le style du client. /// Ich habe versucht, ein effektives Navigationssystem zum Durchsehen der in einem klaren Schaukasten dargestellten Projekte zu programmieren, ohne den Charakter und den Stil des Kunden zu vernachlässigen.

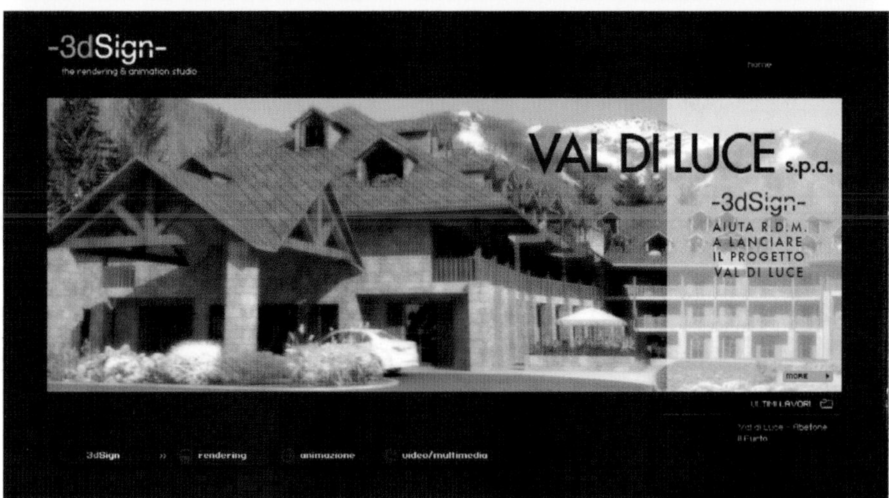

Info

Design: Federico Lupo (JABOH) <www.jaboh.it>. /// **Tools**: Macromedia Flash, ASP, XML. /// **Contents**: photo, animation, movie. /// **Awards**: fcukstar.com, TINY. /// **Cost**: 3 months.

STREETBALL

HONG KONG/CHINA/TAIWAN/KOREA

www.adidas.com.hk/streetball

2005

Concept

"City is your Playground". Player navigated the website by walk-through the city, buildings & player's action are keys of site. How to keep good performance of site is the focus on our technical team. /// « La ville est votre terrain ». Un joueur marchant dans la ville sert de système de navigation, les bâtiments et les actions du joueur sont les éléments clé du site. La priorité de notre équipe technique est la performance du site. /// „Die Stadt ist dein Spielfeld". Der Spieler navigiert durch die Website wie bei einem Spaziergang durch die Stadt. Die Gebäude und die Handlungen des Spielers sind Objekte der Website. Unser technisches Team beschäftigt sich schwerpunktmäßig mit der Leistungsfähigkeit der Website.

Info

Design: Rice 5 <www.rice5.com>. /// **Programming**: Daniel Yuen <www.120fps.com>. /// **Tools**: Macromedia Flash, Macromedia Fireworks, Adobe Photoshop, Adobe After Effects, XML, ASP, CMS (TEAMSITE). /// **Contents**: photo, music, video, animation, games, viral interactive ecard, gallery. /// **Cost**: 4 men team for 2 months.

AGENCYNET.COM

USA

www.agencynet.com

2005

Concept

We provide visitors with a first-hand look inside our day-to-day lives at AgencyNet. This personal approach allows for an innovative and unique interactive experience that touches the user's senses. /// Nous donnons aux visiteurs un regard direct sur nos vies quotidiennes à AgencyNet. Cette approche personnelle touche les sens de l'utilisateur de façon originale, nouvelle et interactive. /// Der Besucher bekommt einen direkten Einblick in das tägliche Leben bei AgencyNet. Dieser persönliche Ansatz schafft ein innovatives, einzigartiges und interaktives Erlebnis, die Sinne des Besuchers unmittelbar ansprechend.

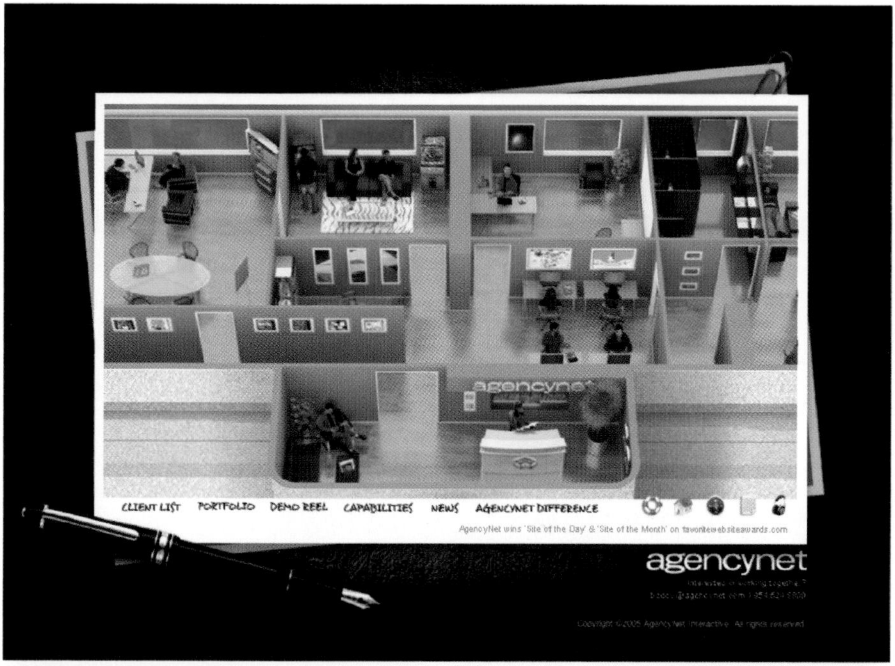

Info

Design and Programming: AgencyNet Interactive. /// **Tools:** Adobe Photoshop, Adobe Illustrator, Macromedia Flash, Lightwave, Macromedia Dreamweaver, Microsoft SQL Server 2000, ASP.NET, XML. /// **Contents:** 3D, animations, digitally-captured footage of office personnel, video, game, portfolio, newsletter and much more. /// **Awards:** FWA (Site of the Day/Site of the Month), Bombshock, Interactive Emmy Award, Well Vetted (Top Flash Site), Linkdup, Design TAXI (Site of the Week), Wow Factor, DOPE Awards, Fcukstar.com, TINY, Crossmind. /// **Cost:** Well over 1,000 development hours.

ALBERTO CERRITENO

MEXICO

www.albertocerriteno.com

2004

Concept

Personal Portfolio with fun own character style and creative navigation. /// Portfolio personnel avec un style ludique et plein de caractère, et un système de navigation créatif. /// **Bei dieser Website handelt es sich um ein persönliches Portfolio mit Humor, eigenem Charakter und kreativer Navigation.**

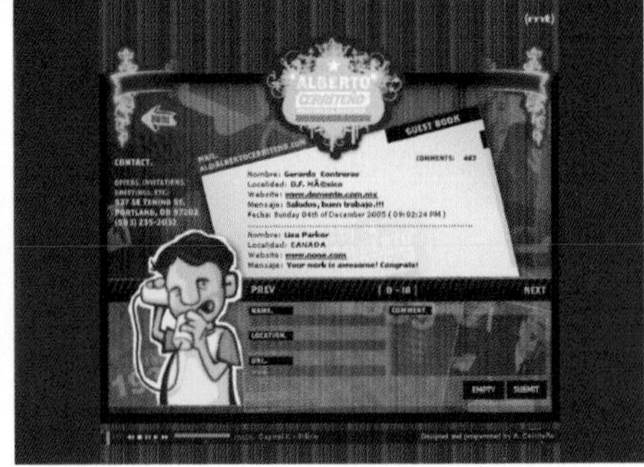

Info

Design and Programming: Alberto Cerriteno <www.albertocerriteno.com>. /// **Tools:** Macromedia Flash, Macromedia Dreamweaver, Adobe Photoshop, Adobe Illustrator, PHP, XML. /// **Contents:** animation, showcase portfolio, music. /// **Awards:** FWA (Site of the Day), TINY (Site of the Day), How Top Ten WebSites, Gold Portfolios.com (Personal WebSite), King for a Week, Best Design WebSite FFM Awards (Flashformexico.org), Pixelmakers (Site of the Month), Flashla/Flavoritos (Site of the Month). /// **Cost:** 50 hours.

AMPLIFIER

USA

www.amplifier.com

2004

Concept

Amplifier has a sense of humor, yet is a real company with employees. The site "comes alive" in the story section via the use of 'teleplays', which involve recorded voices and poorly lip synched characters. /// Amplifier a le sens de l'humour, mais c'est pourtant une véritable entreprise avec des employés. Le site « prend vie » dans la partie histoire grâce à des « saynètes » avec des voies enregistrées et des personnages mal doublés. /// **Amplifier hat Sinn für Humor, denn es ist ein echtes Unternehmen mit Mitarbeitern. Die Geschichten auf der Website „wirken lebendig" dank des Einsatzes von ‚Telespielen', für die Stimmen aufgenommen wurden, für die die Sprache der Figuren allerdings schwach synchronisiert wurde.**

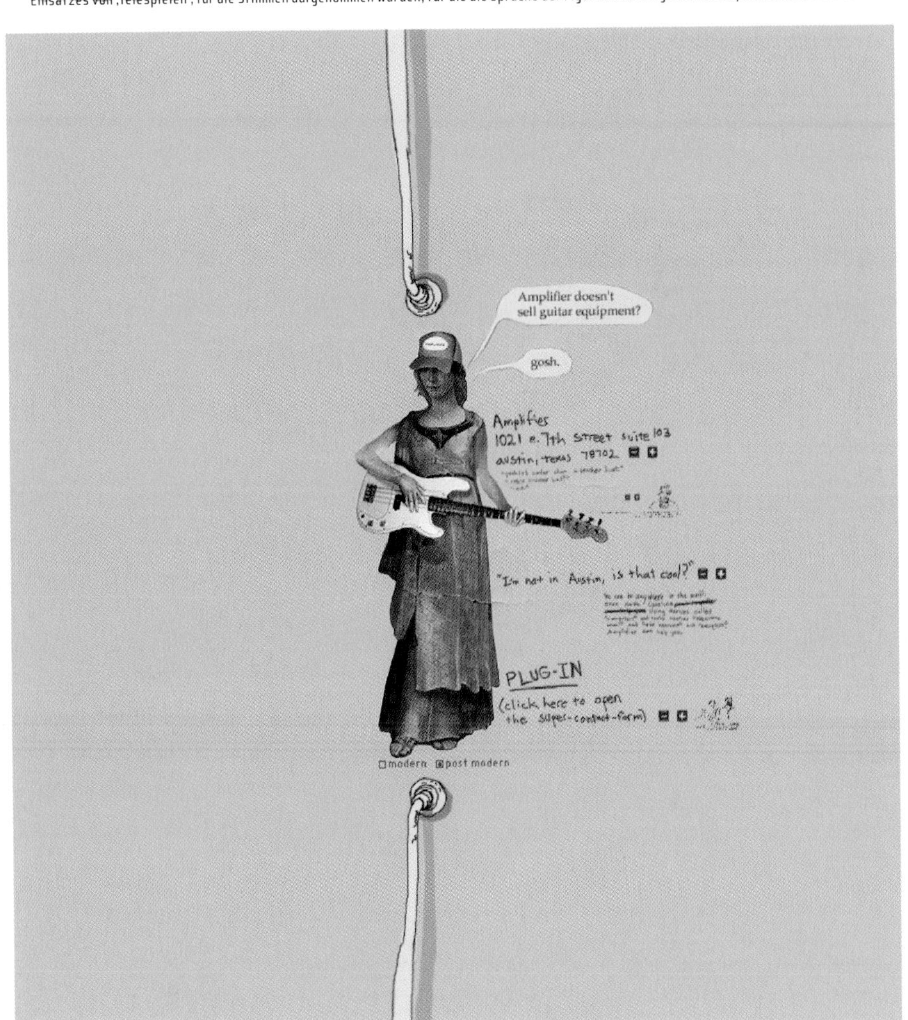

Info

Design: Sofake <www.sofake.com> and Amplifier. /// **Programming**: Sofake. /// **Tools**: Macromedia Flash, Adobe Photoshop. /// **Contents**: video, information, teleplays. /// **Awards**: FWA, Bombshock, SXSW. /// **Cost**: 3-4 months.

ANDREESCU & GAIVORONSKI

ROMANIA

www.andreescu-gaivoronski.com

2005

Concept

User interaction and customization. The drag and drop smart favourites toolbar, the help section and project filtering option make this site very user friendly and encourage repeated visits. /// Les utilisateurs peuvent interagir et personnaliser. Grâce à sa barre de favoris intelligente, l'aide et l'option de filtrage de projets, ce site est très agréable à utiliser et donne envie d'y revenir souvent. /// Die interaktive Website ist kundenorientiert. Sie verfügt über eine intelligente Werkzeugleiste mit Drag and Drop. Der Hilfe-Bereich und die Projekt-Filter-Option tragen zur hohen Benutzerfreundlichkeit bei und laden zu weiteren Besuchen ein.

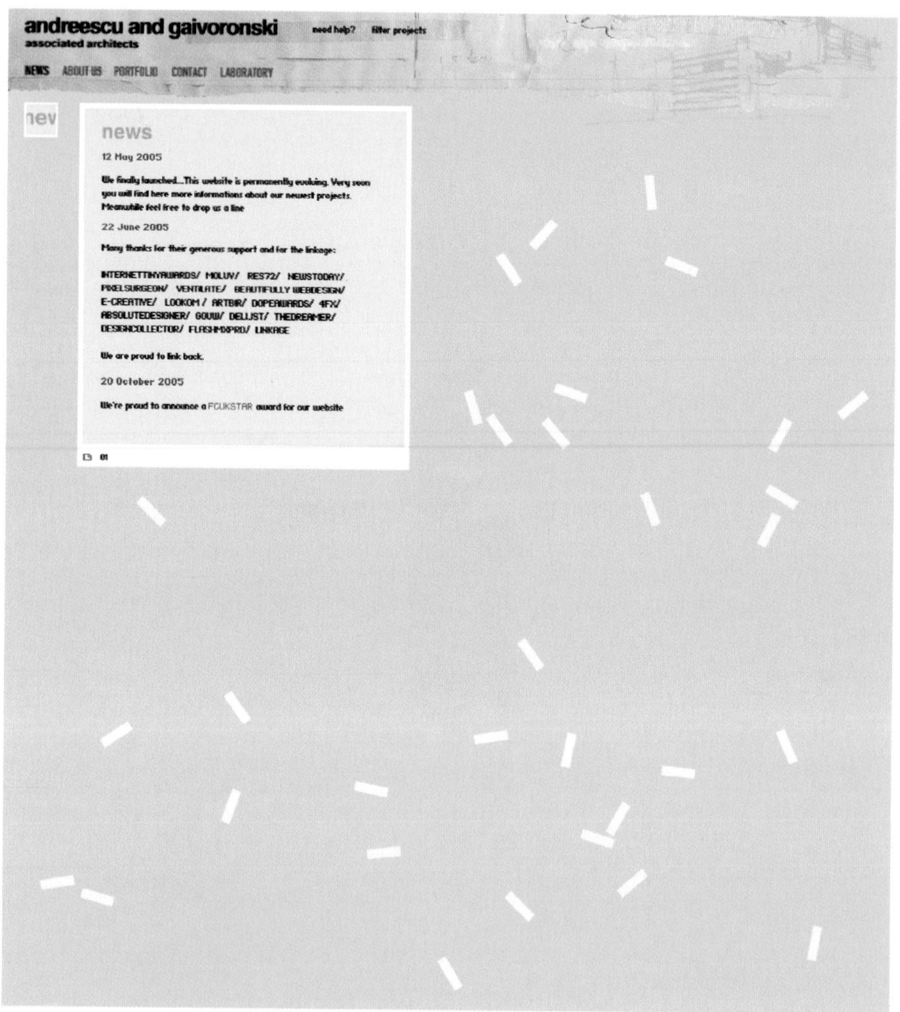

Info

Design: Vlad Ardeleanu <www.raise-media.com>. /// **Programming**: Zoltan Csibi <www.raise-media.com>. /// **Tools**: Macromedia Flash, php, Adobe Photoshop. /// **Contents**: photo. /// **Awards**: FWA, TINY, Moluv, Res72, Newstoday, e-Creative, DOPE, 4FX, Fcukstar, and more. /// **Cost**: 200 hours.

A PLAT VENTRE

FRANCE

2004

www.aplatventre.com

Concept

A simple and straight-to-the-point light thematic navigation to clearly and efficiently drive the users' attention towards the photographs showing the site's two creators laying on their stomach in various environments. /// Une navigation thématique, simple et sans détour attire clairement l'attention du visiteur sur les photographies des deux créateurs du site à plat ventre dans différents environnements. /// Die einfache und zielgerichtete sowie leichte und thematische Navigation ist so konzipiert, dass sie die Aufmerksamkeit der Besucher auf die Fotos der beiden Schöpfer der Site lenkt, die in verschiedenen Umgebungen auf dem Bauch liegen.

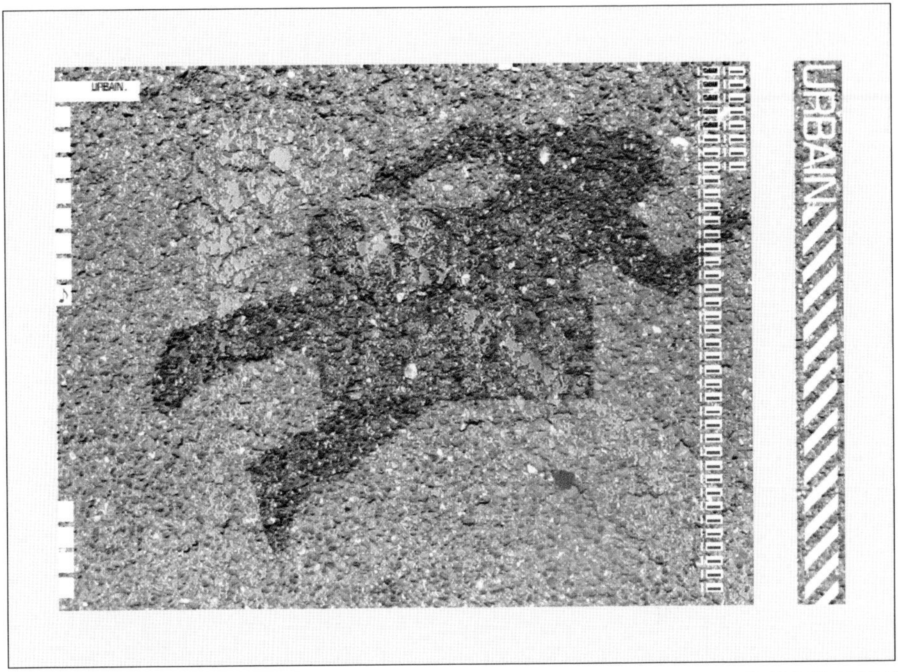

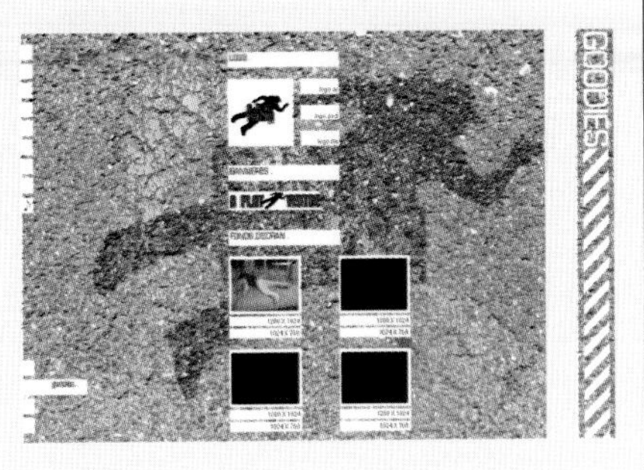

Info

Design: Stenkat <www.stenkat.com>. /// **Programming**: Franck Sinatra <www.flasheur.com>. /// **Tools**: Macromedia Flash, Adobe Photoshop, Adobe Illustrator, CMS, php, Scite|Flash. /// **Contents**: photo. /// **Cost**: 12 hours.

BACARDI MOJITO COCKTAIL

USA

www.bacardimojito.com

2005

Concept

Lot's of .NET back-end functionality. Clever presentation of the cocktail recipe. Video tour of product origin. /// Un grand nombre de fonctionnalités .NET en arrière-plan. Présentation astucieuse de la recette du cocktail. Visite vidéo sur les origines du produit. /// **Die Website weist jede Menge von .NET Back-End-Funktionen auf. Ein Cocktail-Rezept wird clever präsentiert und es gibt eine Video-Tour zum Thema Produkt-Herkunft.**

Info

DESIGN: driftlab <www.driftlab.com> in affiliation with Godfather Studios. /// **PROGRAMMING**: driftlab. /// **TOOLS**: .NET, Macromedia Flash, Adobe Photoshop, Adobe After Effects. /// **CONTENTS**: promotional imagery and animation to promote the Mojito cocktail. /// **AWARDS**: FWA, Bombshock. /// **COST**: 180 hours.

BAJTI PLAYGRRRRRR

POLAND

www.bajti.com

2004

Concept

Unique climate, grotesque figures created on the model of my personality. Sense of humour and also amazing music. The whole resembles old school graphic. /// Une atmosphère unique, des personnages grotesques modelés sur ma personnalité. De l'humour et une musique magnifique. Le tout ressemble au graphisme de la vieille école. /// Es herrscht eine einzigartige Atmosphäre, groteske Figuren wurden in Anlehnung an meine eigene Persönlichkeit kreiert. Alles mit Sinn für Humor und auch fantastischer Musik. Das Ganze erinnert an eine alte Schulgrafik.

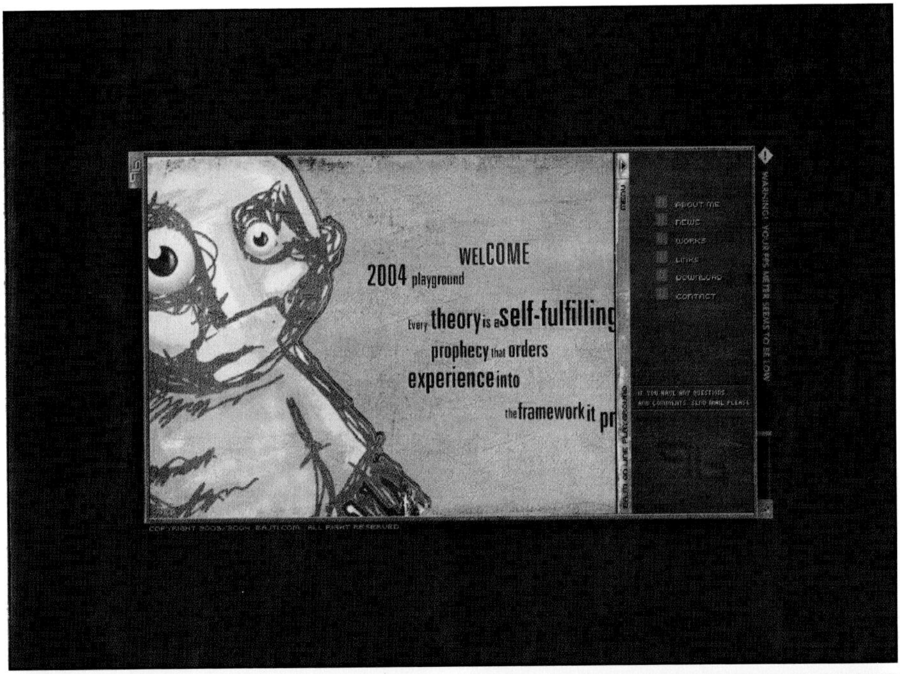

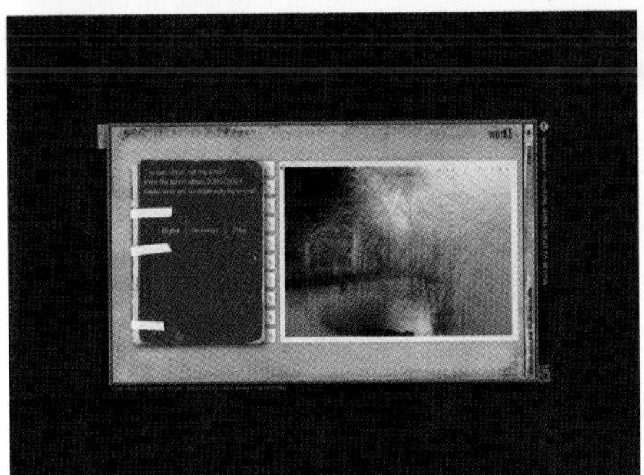

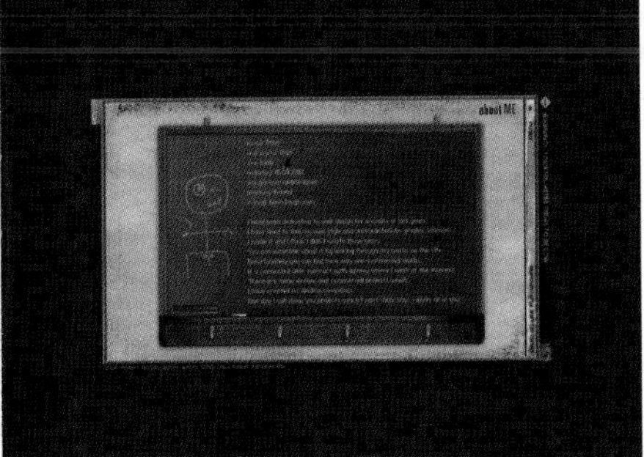

Info

Design: Piotr Bajtała (Bajti). /// **Tools**: Macromedia Flash, Adobe Photoshop. /// **Contents**: draw, digital. Music by <www.stobierski.pl>. /// **Awards**: WellVetted, Visuellerorgasmus.de (site of the year), e-Creative (site of the day). /// **Cost**: 6 months.

BERNHARD WOLFF PHOTO

AUSTRIA

www.bernhardwolff.com

2004

Concept

Yellow as background color was first choice to represent Bernhard Wolff's photography. The interface displays the pictures generously in a catchy and foolproof manner. /// Le jaune de l'arrière-plan a été le premier choix pour représenter la photographie de Bernhard Wolff. L'interface présente les photos de façon généreuse, accrocheuse et infaillible. /// **Gelb war die erste Wahl für die Hintergrundfarbe der Präsentation der Fotografie von Bernhard Wolff. Die Bilder werden auf der Oberfläche in einer großzügigen, attraktiven und kinderleichten Weise gezeigt.**

Info

DESIGN AND PROGRAMMING: Michael Franken <www.mfranken.com>. /// **TOOLS:** Macromedia Flash, PHP. /// **CONTENTS:** photo. /// **AWARDS:** FITC Award 2005.

BIG STAR

POLAND

www.bigstar.pl

2005

Concept

The Big Star project of OPCOM.pl is a breakthrough in video usage in the Internet. The basic information available on the website has been equipped with over 20 video sequences. /// Le projet Big Star d'OPCOM.pl est une révolution dans l'utilisation d'Internet. L'information de base disponible sur le site a été complétée par plus de 20 séquences vidéo. /// Das Big Star-Projekt von OPCOM.pl bedeutet einen Durchbruch für den Einsatz von Video im Internet. Die grundlegende Information auf der Website wurde mit 20 Video-Sequenzen ausgestattet.

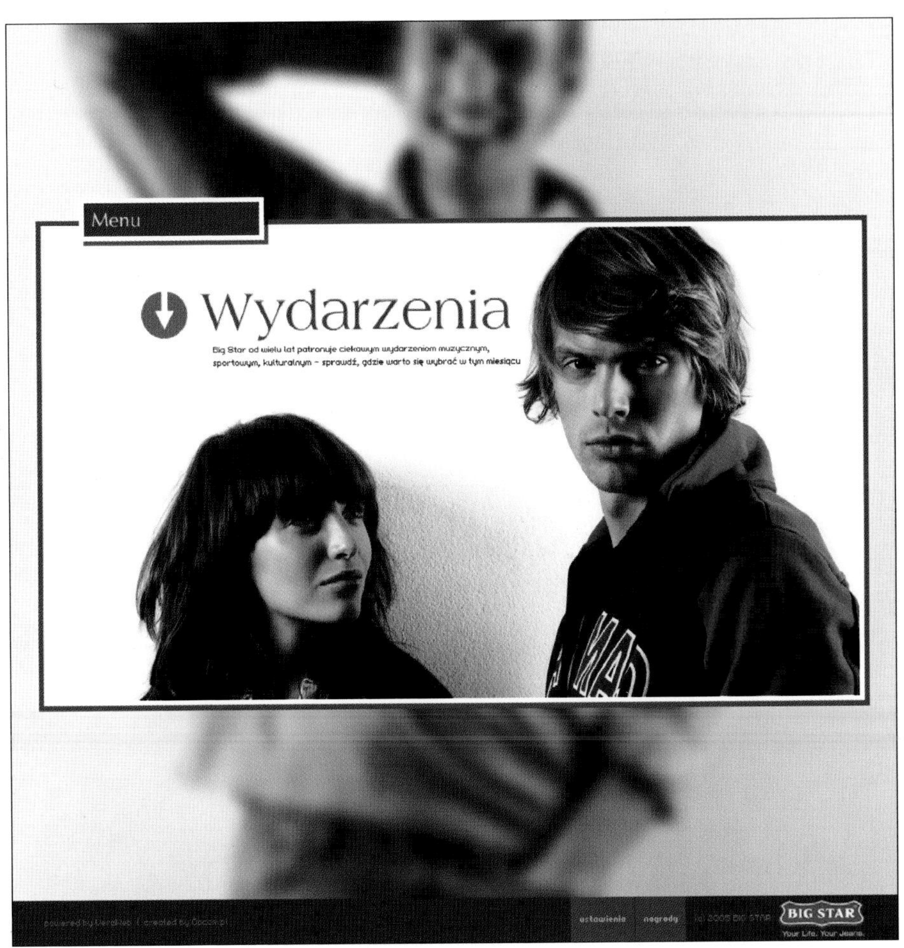

Info

DESIGN: OPCOM.pl <www.opcom.pl>. /// TOOLS: Macromedia Flash, VeraWEB CMS, php. /// CONTENTS: photo, music, video, animation. /// AWARDS: FWA (Site of the Day), Pixelmakers (Site of the Week), e-Creative. /// COST: 240 hours.

BIONIC SYSTEMS

GERMANY

www.bionic-systems.com

2002

Concept

Instead of simply re-designing our previous portfolio website we made up a little background story for a more mysterious and entertaining relaunch. /// Plutôt que de simplement revoir la conception de notre portfolio précédent, nous avons inventé une petite histoire pour que le nouveau site soit plus mystérieux et plus amusant. /// **Anstatt unser vorheriges Portfolio einfach neu zu entwerfen, haben wir uns eine kleine Geschichte einfallen lassen, um die Neueinführung geheimnisvoller und unterhaltsamer zu gestalten.**

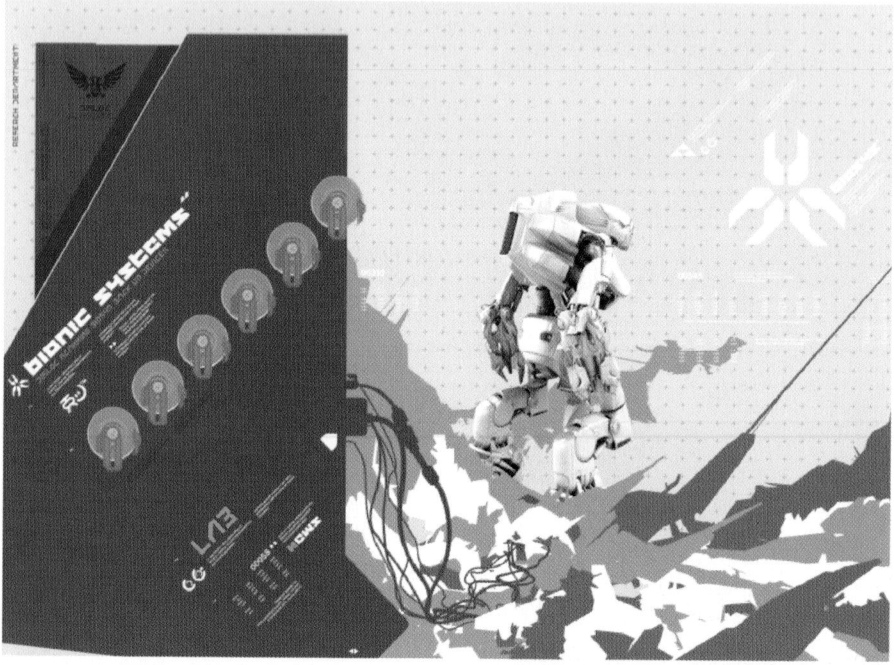

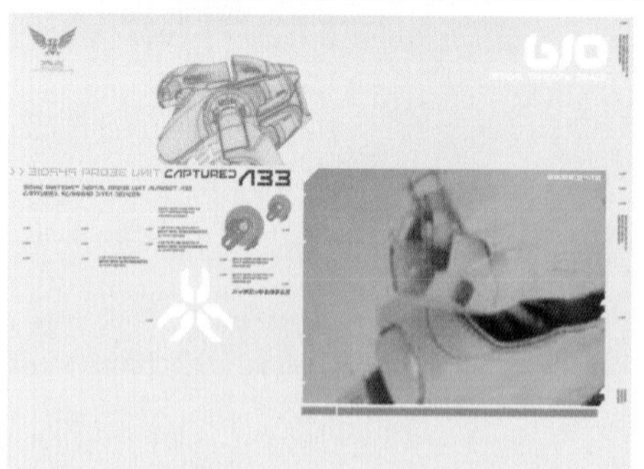

Info

DESIGN AND PROGRAMMING: Doris Fürst & Malte Haust (Bionic Systems). /// **TOOLS:** Macromedia Flash, Macromedia Freehand, Adobe Photoshop, html, php. /// **CONTENTS:** illustration, animation, typography, movie, 3D, sound.

BOB'S CUBE

USA

www.bobscube.com

2005

Concept

We wanted to have a user encounter something familiar and be compelled to explore, Expectations deny discovery. /// Nous voulions que l'utilisateur rencontre quelque chose de familier et soit poussé à explorer. Les attentes nient la découverte. /// **Wir wollten dem Benutzer eine vertraute Umgebung bieten und ihn zum Erforschen animieren. Erwartungen widersprechen Endeckungen.**

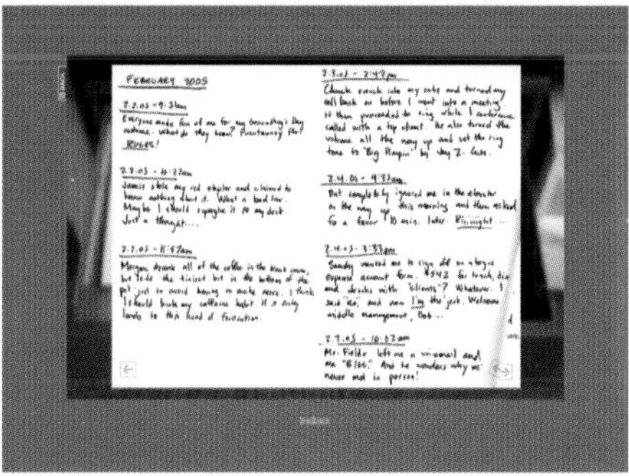

Info

Design and Programming: 15 letters inc. <www.15letters.com>. /// **Tools**: Adobe Illustrator, Adobe Photoshop, Macromedia Flash, ASP, SQL database, Autodesk 3ds Max, Adobe After Effects, Apple i-Movie, Digidesign Pro Tools, Sound Forge, and Reason. /// **Contents**: games, interactive experiences, photographs and films. /// **Cost**: lots and lots of hours.

BOOST MOBILE STREETBALL USA

www.boostmobilestreetball.com 2005

Concept

Build a site that becomes the content source for the And 1 Mix tape tour. Provide a content focused experience in an interactively engaging way. /// Nous voulions construire un site qui devienne la source de contenus pour le tour And 1 Mix tape. Le site est centré sur les contenus et invite à l'interaction. /// Erstelle eine Website als Quelle für die Inhalte zur „And 1 Mix Tape Tour". Erstelle interaktiv ein auf dem Inhalt basierendes, aufregendes Erlebnis.

Info

Design and Programming: Juxt Interactive <www.juxtinteractive.com>. /// **Tools**: Adobe Photoshop, Adobe Illustrator, Macromedia Freehand, Macromedia Flash. /// **Contents**: lots of content from the basketball tour, photos, video, blogs, pools, ringtones, etc. /// **Cost**: 3 months.

BRAD MILLER STUDIO

USA

www.bradmillerstudio.com

2005

Concept

Brad Miller Studio was designed to "break the grid"; the theme of "exploring Brad's tree of art" guided the design. Use of an XML layer allows for easy edits and re-organization of the site. /// Le Studio Brad Miller a été conçu pour « sortir de la grille »; le thème « explorer l'arbre d'art de Brad » a guidé le design. Un calque en XML permet de modifier et de réorganiser facilement le site. /// Die Website von Brad Miller-Studio wurde entworfen, um „das Raster zu durchbrechen"; das Leitthema für das Design war „die Erforschung von Brads Kunstbaum". Der Einsatz der XML-Schicht ermöglicht einfaches Editieren und Reorganisieren der Website.

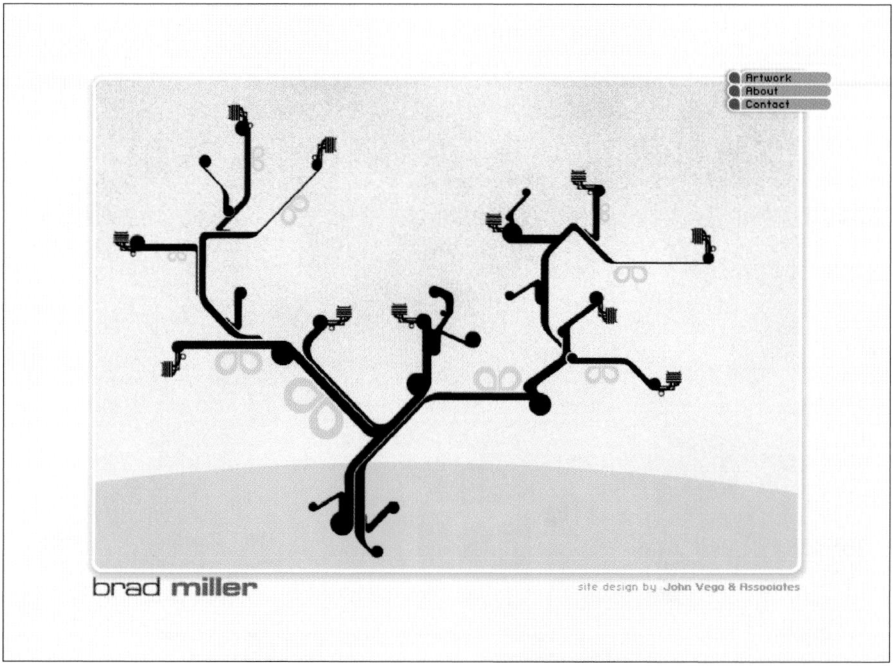

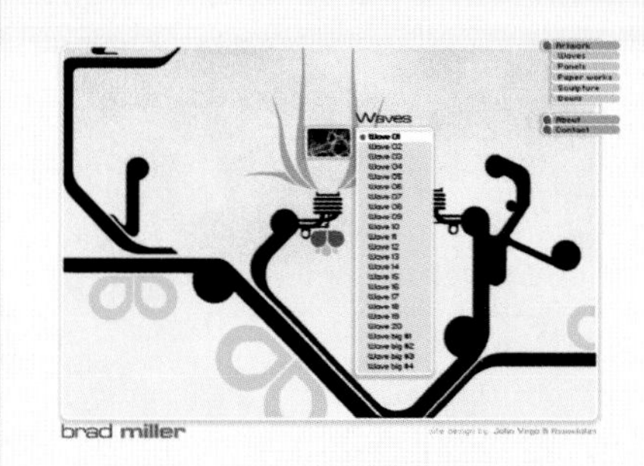

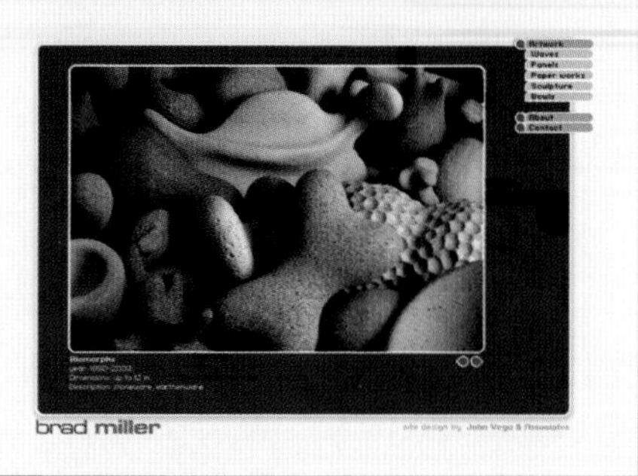

Info

Design: John Vega <www.johnvega.com>. /// **Programming:** Aaron Wilson <www.technic9.com>. /// **Tools:** Macromedia Flash, XML, HTML, Adobe Photoshop. /// **Contents:** text, flash animation, bitmap stills, digital audio. /// **Awards:** TINY, NewWebPick, DOPE Awards. /// **Cost:** 83 hours.

BREADNBUTTER

HONG KONG

www.breadnbutterstyle.com

2004

Concept

How to project the feel of youth and cheer is the brief requirement. 3D effect in flash is the most difficult challenge for technical team. We had developed a "3D engine" for the project to achieve the point. /// La seule condition est de projeter un sentiment de jeunesse et de gaieté. L'effet 3D en Flash a été le défi le plus difficile pour l'équipe technique. Nous avons développé un « moteur 3D » pour le projet afin d'y arriver. /// Das Gefühl der Jugend und der Lebensfreude sollten auf dieser Website vermittelt werden. 3D-Effekte in Flash stellen die schwierigste Herausforderung für ein technisches Team dar. Wir haben für das Projekt eine „3D-Engine" entworfen, um der Aufgabe gerecht zu werden.

Info

DESIGN: Rice 5 <www.rice5.com>. /// PROGRAMMING: Daniel Yuen <www.120fps.com>. /// TOOLS: Macromedia Flash, Macromedia Fireworks, Adobe Photoshop, XML. /// CONTENTS: photo, music, animation, viral interactive ecard. /// COST: 4 men team for 2 months.

ROBOTMANIA

MEXICO

www.caracolonline.com/robotmania

2005

Concept

Book-Photo gallery on line with a nice visual environment matched with the concept of the photo-galley and rich imagery treatment. /// Galerie Livre-Photo en ligne avec un environnement visuel agréable, en harmonie avec le concept de la galerie de photos, et un traitement de l'image très riche. /// **Eine online Buch-Foto-Galerie mit netter visueller Umgebung passte zum Konzept einer Foto-Galerie und einer umfangreichen Bilderverarbeitung.**

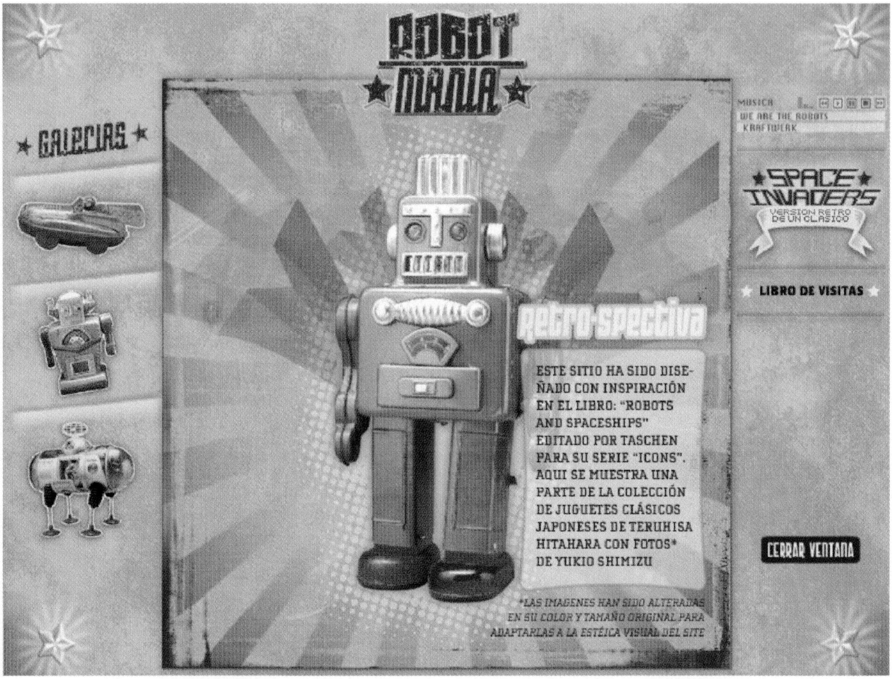

ROBOT MANIA
GALERIAS
MUSICA
WE ARE THE ROBOTS
KRAFTWERK
SPACE INVADERS
VERSION RETRO DE UN CLASICO
LIBRO DE VISITAS
Retro-spectiva
ESTE SITIO HA SIDO DISEÑADO CON INSPIRACIÓN EN EL LIBRO: "ROBOTS AND SPACESHIPS" EDITADO POR TASCHEN PARA SU SERIE "ICONS". AQUI SE MUESTRA UNA PARTE DE LA COLECCIÓN DE JUGUETES CLÁSICOS JAPONESES DE TERUHISA HITAHARA CON FOTOS* DE YUKIO SHIMIZU
*LAS IMAGENES HAN SIDO ALTERADAS EN SU COLOR Y TAMAÑO ORIGINAL PARA ADAPTARLAS A LA ESTÉICA VISUAL DEL SITE
CERRAR VENTANA

ROBOT MANIA
SOBRE-RUEDAS
Cerrar
-1950's-
Space Patrol Car, Ichiko, 217 x 85 x 82 mm
3
4

ROBOT MANIA
Cerrar
ASTRO-BOTS
CERRAR VENTANA
entrar

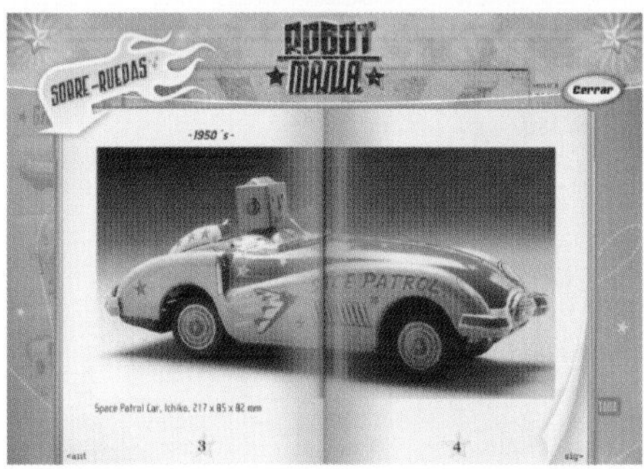

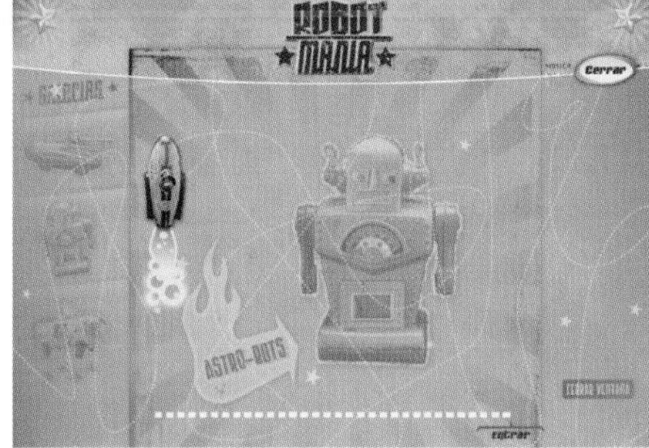

Info

DESIGN AND PROGRAMMING: Alberto Cerriteno <www.albertocerriteno.com>. /// **TOOLS**: Macromedia Flash, Macromedia Dreamweaver, Adobe Photoshop, Adobe Illustrator. /// **CONTENTS**: photo gallery, game, music. /// **AWARDS**: TINY (Site of the Day), How Top Ten WebSites, Gold Portfolios (Miscelaneous), Best Experience WebSite FFM Awards, Flashla/Flavoritos(Site of the Week), Silver Ojo de Iberoamerica 2004. /// **COST**: 35 hours.

CHRISTO CARAN PHOTO

GREECE

www.christocaran.com

2004

Concept

Is in the way of browsing and its minimal design. My goal was to design a site perfectly match with the content to bring out the work of the artist. The photos make the difference. /// La navigation et le design sont d'esprit minimaliste. Mon but était de créer un site en parfaite harmonie avec le contenu pour mettre en valeur le travail de l'artiste. Ce sont les photos qui font la différence. /// **Das Besondere an dieser Website ist die Navigation und das minimalistische Design. Mein Ziel war es, eine Website zu entwerfen, die inhaltlich perfekt dazu geeignet ist, die Arbeit der Künstler hervorzuheben. Die Fotos machen den Unterschied.**

Info

Design and Programming: Vassilis A. Alexiou - em[phaze] <www.emphaze.com>. /// **Tools**: Macromedia Flash, Adobe Photoshop, xml, php, cms, Sound Forge, Reason. /// **Contents**: photos. /// **Awards**: FWA. /// **Cost**: 2 months.

THE CORPSE BRIDE MOVIE

USA

www.corpsebridemovie.com

2005

Concept

Re-creation of Tim Burton's characters in 3D allowed for many custom animations. Every environment is unique in interactivity, gameplay and sound design. /// Une recréation des personnages de Tim Burton en 3D pour de nombreuses animations sur mesure. Chaque environnement est unique en termes d'interactivité, de jeu et de conception sonore. /// **Die Nachstellung der Figuren von Tim Burton in 3D ermöglichte viele einzigartige Animationen. Jede Umgebung ist interaktiv und einzigartig in Spiel- und Ton-Design.**

Info

Design and Programming: BLITZ <www.blitzagency.com>. /// **Tools:** Macromedia Flash, Adobe Photoshop, XML, PHP, Remoting, Digidesign Pro Tools, Autodesk 3ds Max. /// **Contents:** movie trailer, animation, games. /// **Awards:** iMedia.com, Ultra Bombshock. /// **Cost:** 3 months.

COUNT OLAF

USA

www.countolaf.com

2004

Concept

From a world of ugly children and really bad actors, Count Olaf contracted us to make him stand out. His personality was so potent, it into every detail of the site. Unfortunately. /// Depuis son monde d'enfants laids et d'acteurs vraiment très mauvais, le comte Olaf nous a engagés pour le mettre en valeur. Sa personnalité était si puissante qu'on peut la sentir dans chaque détail du site. Désastreux. /// Graf Olaf gab uns den Auftrag, ihn aus der Welt hässlicher Kinder und wirklich schlechter Schauspieler herausragen zu lassen. Seine Persönlichkeit war so mächtig, dass sie sich in jedem Detail der Website widerspiegelt. Leider.

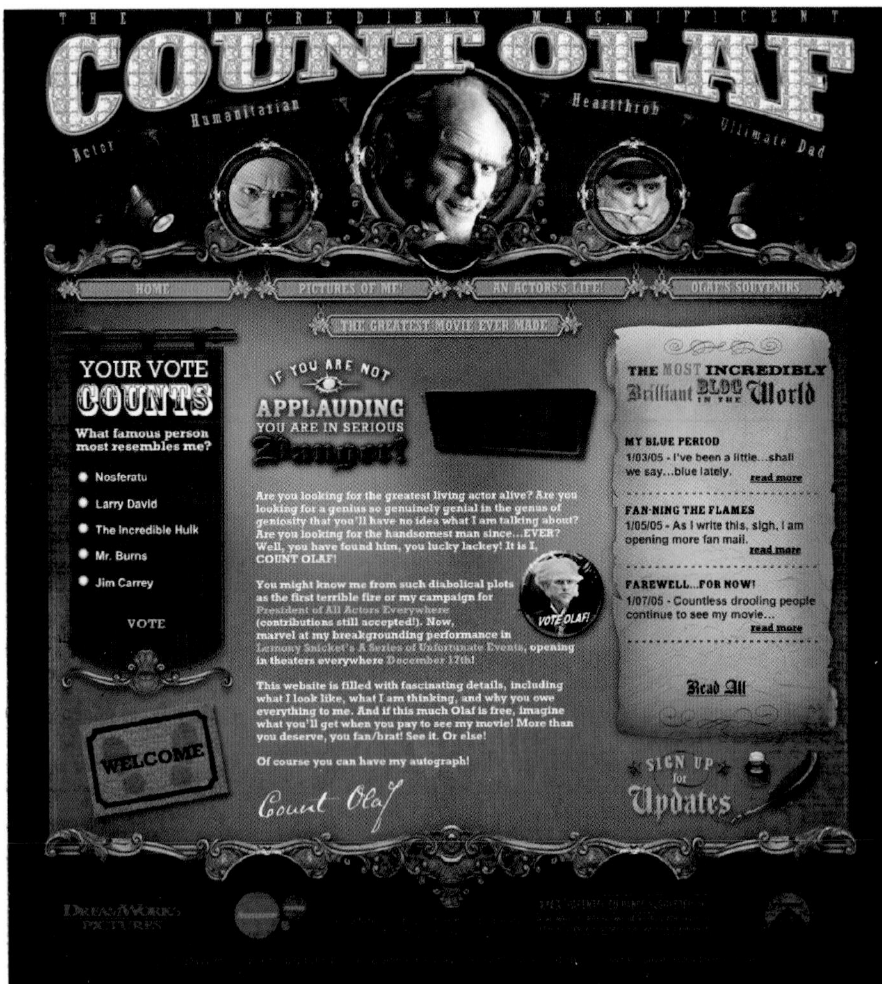

Info

Design: Creative Director: Doug Fitzsimmons (Tribal DDB) <www.fitzsimmons.net>; Art Director: Paul Novoa (Tribal DDB) <www.novoa.net>; Graphic Artist: Ali Moradi (Tribal DDB) <www.jadou.com>. /// **Programming**: Lawrence Aaron Buchanan <www.lab-media.com>. /// **Tools**: Html, CSS, Adobe Photoshop, Adobe Illustrator, Macromedia Flash. /// **Contents**: photos, film, animations, blog. /// **Cost**: 8 months.

CRASH!MEDIA

CANADA

www.crashmedia.com

2005

Concept

This site uses a specialized 3D timeline and custom keyword/search filtering system. /// Ce site utilise une ligne temporelle spécialisée en 3D et un système de filtre avec recherche et mot clé sur mesure. /// Diese Website nutzt eine spezialisierte 3D-Zeitleiste und ein kundenspezifisches Schlüsselwort/Such-Filtersystem.

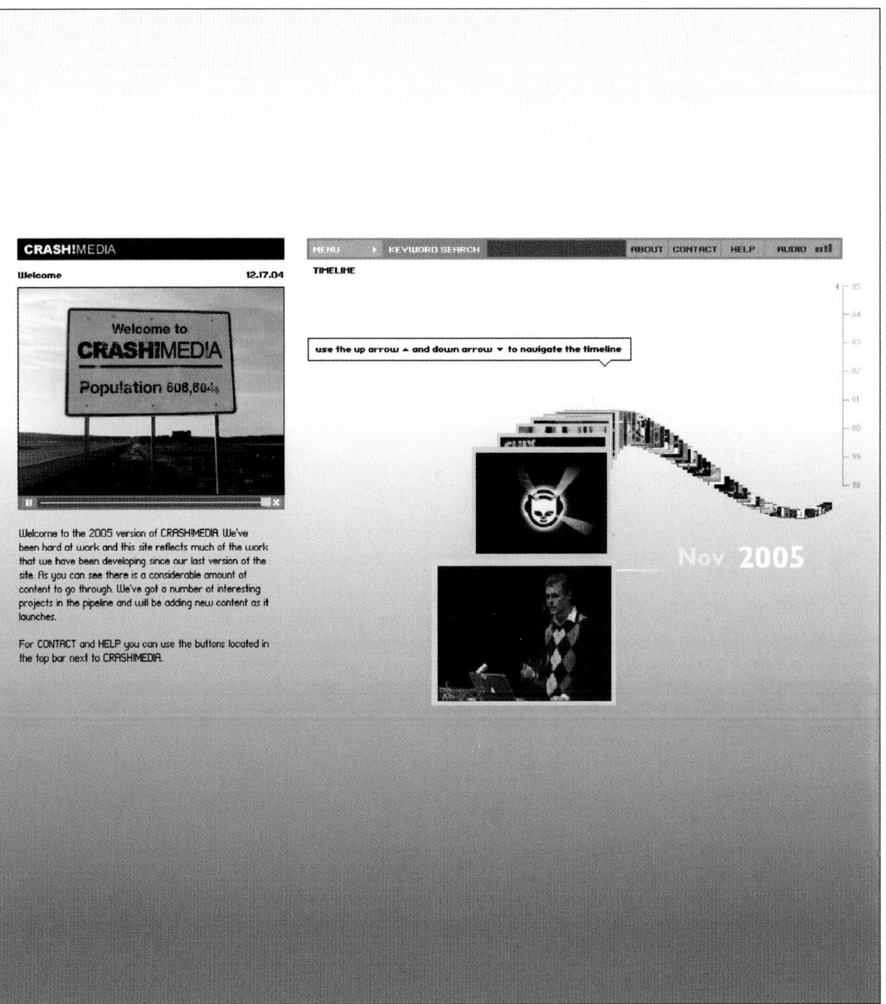

Info

DESIGN AND PROGRAMMING: CRASH!MEDIA Corp. <www.crashmedia.com>. /// TOOLS: Macromedia Flash, Adobe Photoshop. /// CONTENTS: image, video, audio. /// COST: 500 hours.

CRIMINAL CLOTHING

UK

www.criminalclothing.com

2005

Concept

The Drop-Off is a unique cinematic experience created to showcase Criminal Clothing's Autumn / Winter 05/06 collection. Its edgy design builds upon Criminal's brand and creates an engaging user experience. /// Le Drop-Off est une expérience filmique unique en son genre, créée pour présenter la collection de prêt-à-porter Criminal automne/hiver 05/06. Son design nerveux s'inspire de la marque Criminal et rend la visite captivante. /// Das Drop-Off ist ein einzigartiges Filmerlebnis, welches geschaffen wurde, um die Kollektion Criminal Clothing Herbst/Winter 05/06 zu präsentieren. Das ausgefallene Design stützt sich auf die Marke Criminal und erzeugt ein ansprechendes Benutzererlebnis.

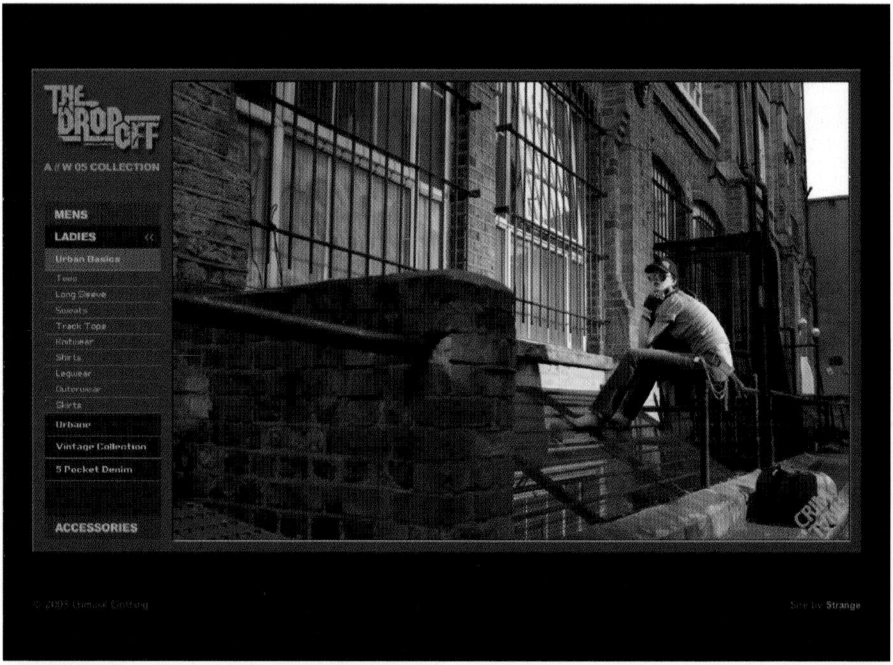

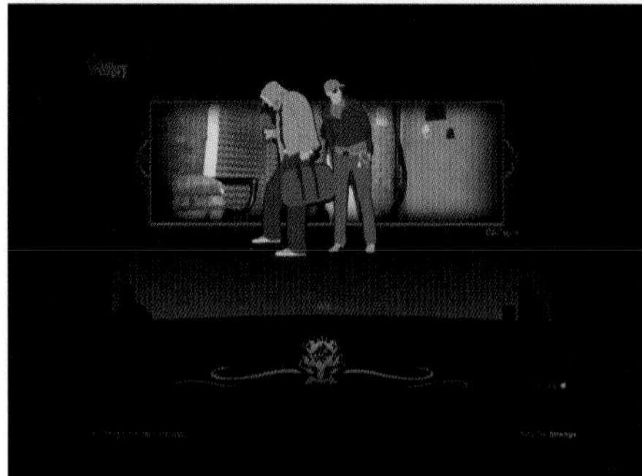

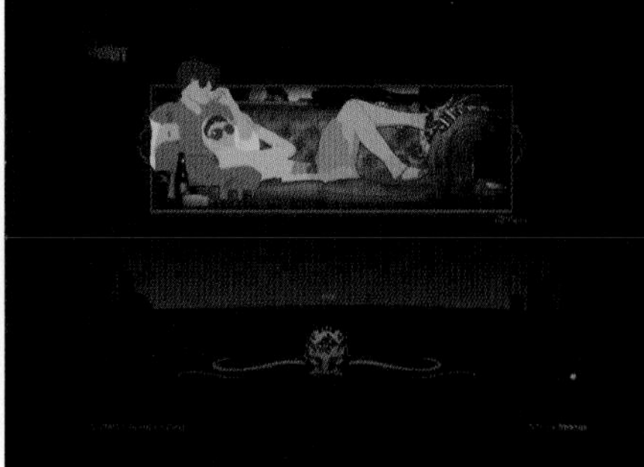

Info

Design: Strange Corporation <www.strangecorp.com>. /// **Tools**: php, Macromedia Flash, Adobe Photoshop, Adobe Illustrator. /// **Contents**: photography specially commissioned for Strange. Music 'The Drop Off' was written specifically for the site by Strange Corporation. /// **Awards**: Ades Design, Click of the Day, Design Firms, e-Creative, Pixel Gangster, Visuell Orgasmus. /// **Cost**: 1 month.

CROMM CRUAC

POLAND/UK

www.crommcruac.com

2005

Concept

The idea for the site is the reflection of my personal fascinations. Come and visit the ancient corridors and halls build by lost civilization. Find the four parts of the key to enter the treasure room. /// L'idée du site est une réflexion sur mes fascinations personnelles. Venez visiter les couloirs et les salles antiques construits par une civilisation perdue. Trouvez les quatre morceaux de la clé pour entrer dans la salle du trésor. /// Die Idee für die Website ist eine Reflexion meiner persönlichen Faszinationen. Komm und besuche die alten Flure und Hallen, die von einer verlorenen Zivilisation gebaut wurden! Finde die vier Teile des Schlüssels zur Schatzkammer!

Info

Design and Programming: Marcin Zemczak (Cromm Cruac). /// **Tools**: Adobe Photoshop, Macromedia Flash, Autodesk 3ds Max, Curious Labs Poser. /// **Contents**: portfolio, 3d gallery, web design gallery, music, animation, downloads. /// **Awards**: Web Design Library (Site of the Day/Site of the Month), FWA (Site of the Day), CoolStop (Site of the Day), WebEsteem.pl (Site of the Month). /// **Cost**: 1000 hours.

DENGG/KATZUNG/MIEZE SCHINDLER AUSTRIA

www.dengg.co.at;www.cafe-katzung.at;www.mieze-schindler.at 2004

Concept

One single design delivers the structure for 3 connected websites, each of them using its own corporate color. Large images in the background communicate both the ambience and culinary range. /// Une seule conception graphique donne la structure pour 3 sites web connectés, qui ont chacun leur propre identité couleur. De grandes images en arrière-plan transmettent l'atmosphère et le style de cuisine. /// Ein gemeinsames Design liefert die Struktur für drei miteinander verbundene Websites. Jede von ihnen hat ihre markeneigene Farbe. Große Bilder im Hintergrund vermitteln sowohl die Atmosphäre als auch das kulinarische Angebot.

Info

DESIGN: transporter* <www.transporter.at>. /// **PROGRAMMING:** Rainer Fabrizi (trnsporter*). /// **TOOLS:** Macromedia Flash, Macromedia Dreamweaver, Adobe Photoshop, Macromedia Freehand, Soundedit, PHP, mySQL, cargo*CMS, Javascript, Transmit. /// **CONTENTS:** photos done with a digicam, sound effects recorded on the powerbook. /// **COST:** 100 hours.

DIMAQUINA

BRAZIL

www.dimaquina.com

2005

Concept

The layout structure allows a random background use, random display of the projects button as well as a very easy update. /// La structure de présentation permet une utilisation en arrière-plan aléatoire, un affichage aléatoire des boutons des projets ainsi qu'une mise à jour très facile. /// Die Layout-Struktur ermöglicht die Nutzung des Hintergrunds und die Präsentation von Projekten nach dem Zufallsprinzip sowie eine sehr einfache Aktualisierung.

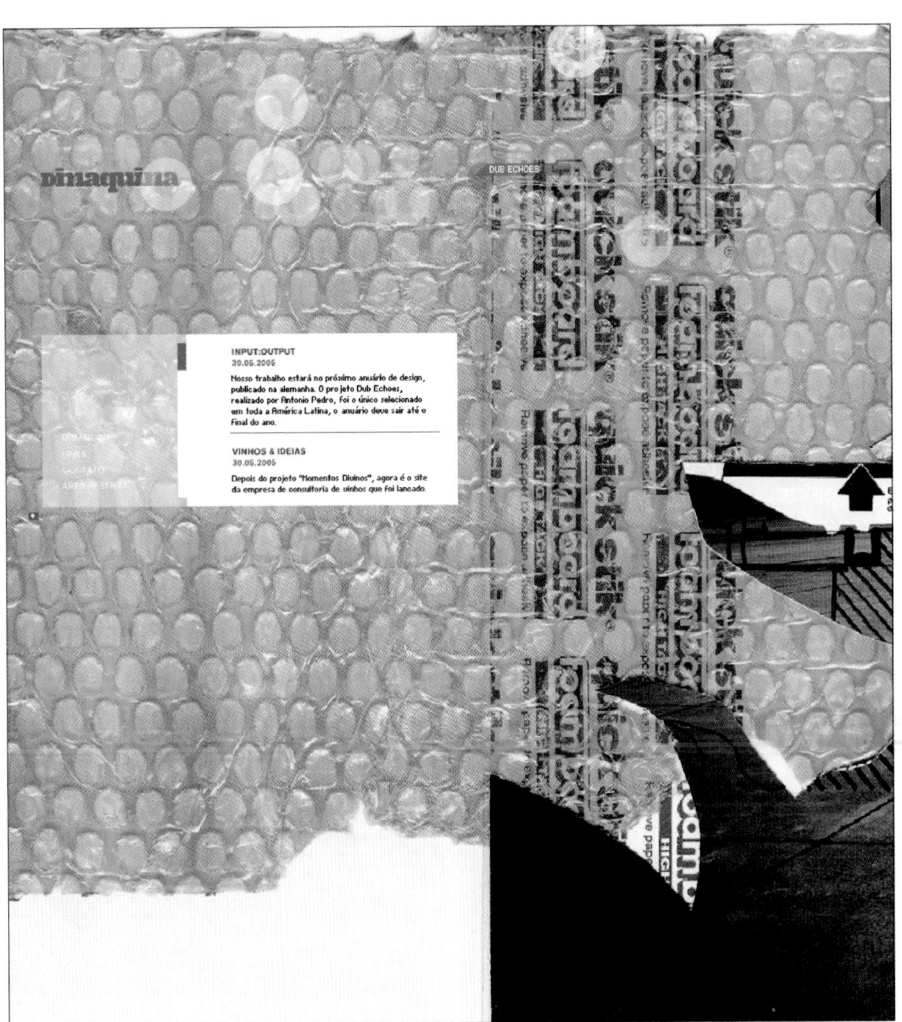

Info

Design and Programming: Antonio Pedro, Daniel Neves and Nako (dimaquina). /// **Tools**: Macromedia Flash, Adobe Photoshop, Adobe Illustrator. /// **Contents**: photos of the the design projects, as well as quicktime movies and links. /// **Awards**: Netdiver, Creative Behavior, Netinspiration, Destyler, Funkbuilders. /// **Cost**: 3 weeks.

KID CUPID

www.domanistudios.com/kidcupid

USA

2005

Concept

With engaging game play, quirky characters, a custom-built 3D environment, and a integrated viral marketing system, "Kid Cupid" was an immediate success. /// Avec des jeux captivants, des personnages excentriques, un environnement 3D sur mesure et un système de marketing viral intégré, « Kid Cupid » a été un succès immédiat. /// Durch den Einsatz von Spielen, schrulligen Charakteren, einer maßgeschneiderten 3D-Umgebung und einem integrierten Marketingsystem wurde „Kid Cupid" zum sofortigen Erfolg.

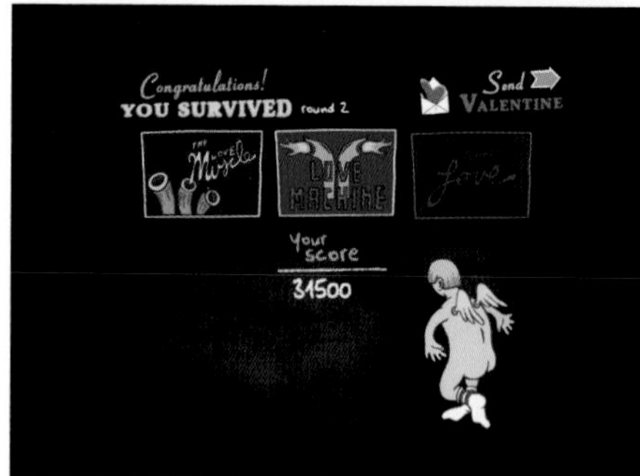

Info

Design and Programming: Domani Studios <www.domanistudios.com>. /// **Tools:** Macromedia Flash, Adobe Photoshop, Adobe Illustrator, PHP, MySQL, Unix. /// **Contents:** viral game. /// **Awards:** STEP Inside Design's Best of the Web. /// **Cost:** 3 months (design and development cycle).

DONTCLICK.IT

GERMANY

www.dontclick.it

2005

Concept

Dontclick.it lets you explore a digital world without clicking. Experience an interface that plays with your navigational habits and find out how it feels. /// Dontclick.it vous donne l'occasion d'explorer un monde numérique sans clic. Essayez cette interface qui joue avec vos habitudes de navigation et explorez vos sensations. /// Bei Dontclick.it erforschen Sie eine digitale Welt ohne zu klicken. Erleben Sie eine Oberfläche, die mit Ihren Navigationsgewohnheiten spielt und finden Sie heraus, wie sie sich anfühlt.

DONTCLICK.IT
INSTITUTE FOR INTERACTIVE RESEARCH

UNDERSTAND | LEARN | EXPLORE | COMMUNICATE

CAN YOU RESIST TO CLICK?

MAKE YOURSELF HEARD.
EXPERIENCE A BUTTON-FREE WORLD.
GET A GLIMPSE ON THE IDEA BEHIND THIS.

Info

Design and Programming: Alex Frank (LXFX) <www.lxfx.de>. /// **Tools**: PHP, MySQL, Adobe Photoshop, Macromedia Freehand, Macromedia Flash. /// **Contents**: photos, sound, animation, game, messageboard. /// **Awards**: FWA, DartAward, TINY, Design TAXI, etc. /// **Cost**: 3 months.

DOUBLE PLUS++

GERMANY

www.doubleplus.info

2005

Concept

Creation of a clean easy to use and manage portfolio to present my work and demonstrate my skills as a designer and programmer for potential clients. /// J'ai créé un portfolio sans fioritures, facile à utiliser et à gérer pour présenter mon travail et montrer mes talents de designer et de programmateur aux clients potentiels. /// **Ich hatte es mir zum Ziel gesetzt, ein Portfolio zu erstellen, das sauber, einfach zu nutzen und zu verwalten ist. Auf diese Weise wollte ich meinen potentiellen Kunden meine Arbeit und meine Fertigkeiten als Designer und Programmierer präsentieren.**

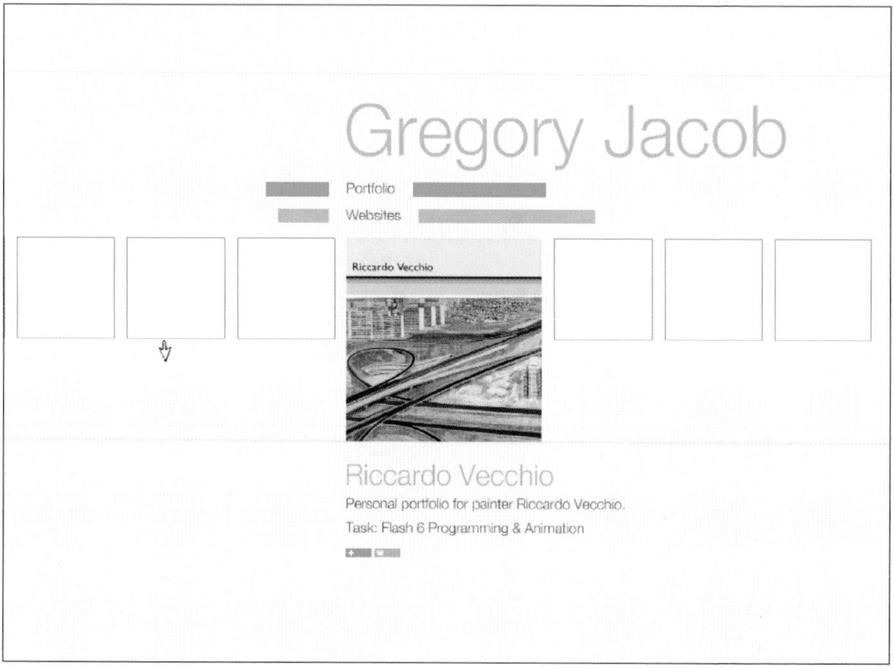

Gregory Jacob
Portfolio
Websites
Riccardo Vecchio
Riccardo Vecchio
Personal portfolio for painter Riccardo Vecchio.
Task: Flash 6 Programming & Animation

Gregory Jacob
Address
Telephone
Email

Gregory Jacob

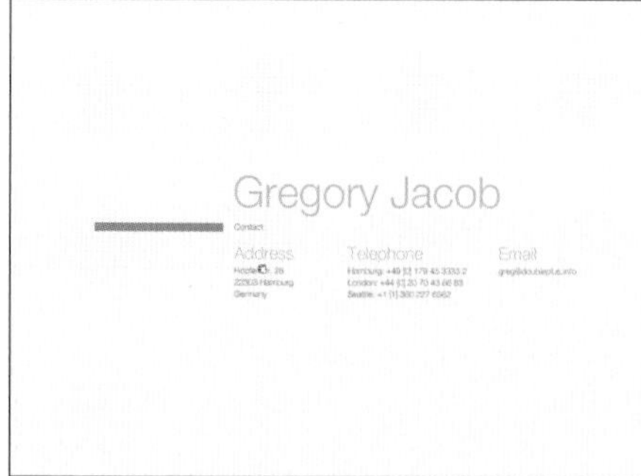

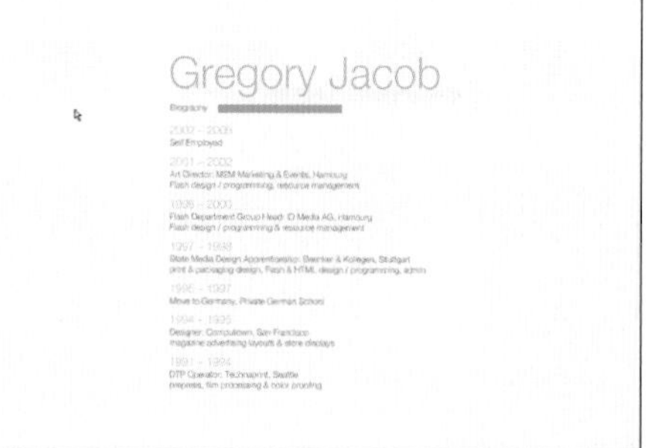

Info

DESIGN AND PROGRAMMING: Gregory Jacob (Double Plus++). /// **TOOLS:** Macromedia Flash, Adobe Photoshop, Macromedia Fireworks, Altova XML Spy. /// **CONTENTS:** personal portfolio. /// **AWARDS:** DOPE Awards, TINY, fcukstar.com, Moluv, King For A Week, Behind The Curtin, Res72. /// **COST:** 5 days.

DREAM STUDIO DESIGN

CANADA

www.dreamstudiodesign.com

2005

Concept

Aside from the little green army and a flipping robot, DSD showcase a full vector 3D experience that played a big role for its crisp n' sharp flavor and keeping a relatively small file size. /// À part la petite armée verte et un robot sautillant, DSD présente une panoplie complète en vecteur 3D qui a joué en grand rôle dans l'esprit tonique et affûté de ce site, et dans la taille des fichiers, relativement petite. /// Die Website von DSD bietet dem Besucher - abgesehen von kleinen, grünen Soldaten und einem Roboter - ein Vektor 3D-Erlebnis, welches für die geschickte Darstellung und die Beschränkung auf geringe Dateigrößen sehr wichtig ist.

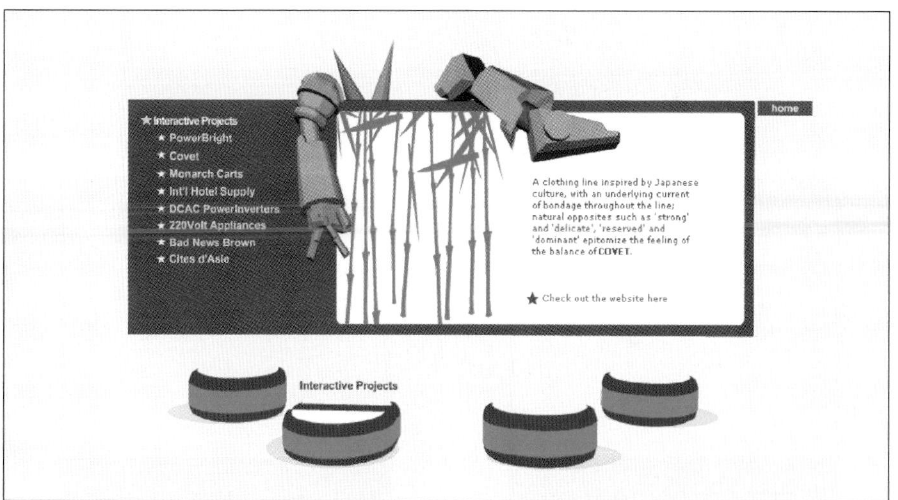

Info

Design: DREAM Studio Design. /// **Tools**: php, Swift 3D, Macromedia Flash, Macromedia Dreamweaver. /// **Contents**: 3d vector animations. /// **Awards**: FWA, TINY. /// **Cost**: 120 hours.

DRIFTLAB

USA

www.driftlab.com

2005

Concept

The Driftlab site throws trends to the wind by combining rich textures and smooth clean animations with a clever play on an old-western theme. It's easy to navigate and the work samples remain the focus. /// Le site de Driftlab lance les tendances en combinant des textures riches et des animations fluides, et joue avec astuce sur le thème des vieux westerns. La navigation est simple et les échantillons de travail sont au centre de l'attention. /// Die Website von Driftlab wirft alle Tends über Bord, indem sie texturreiche, glatte und saubere Animationen mit einem intelligenten Spiel mit altem Western-Thema kombiniert. Die Navigation ist einfach und die Arbeitsbeispiele bleiben im Vordergrund.

Info

Design and Programming: driftlab <www.driftlab.com>. /// **Tools**: Adobe Photoshop, Macromedia Flash, Actionscript, PHP, XML. /// **Contents**: smooth script driven animations. Work samples of web projects. /// **Awards**: FWA, Bombshock, fcukstar.com. /// **Cost**: 100 hours.

DZINENMOTION

CANADA

www.dzinenmotion.com

2000

Concept

dZinenmOtion changes on a monthly basis, each month reveals a new theme or chapter of a story. /// dZinenmOtion change chaque mois, et chaque mois révèle un nouveau thème ou un nouveau chapitre d'une histoire. /// dZinenmOtion ändert sich monatlich. Jeden Monat gibt es ein neues Thema oder ein Kapitel einer Geschichte.

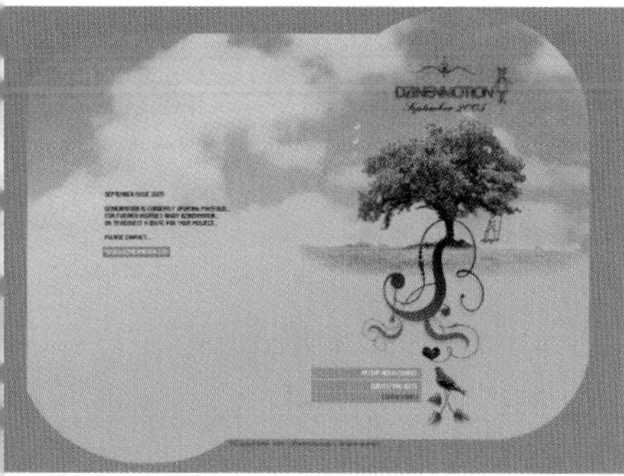

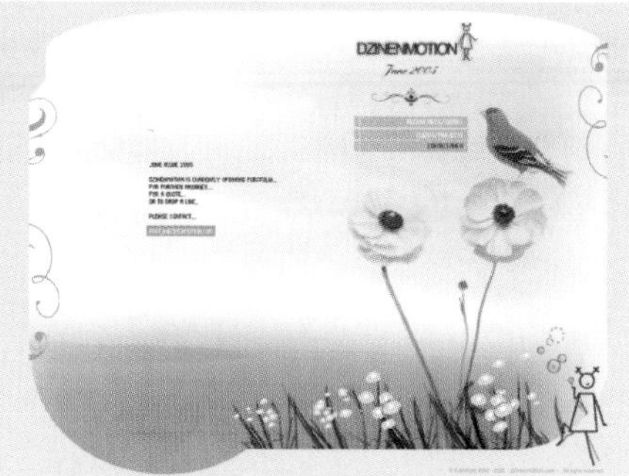

Info

Design: Rose Pietrovito (dZinenmOtion). /// **Tools**: Macromedia Flash, Adobe Photoshop. /// **Contents**: animation & portfolio. /// **Awards**: Cannes Cyber Lions (Shortlist), Lotus Award. /// **Cost**: Approximately 5-10 hours/month.

EMAGIC ENTERTAINMENT THE NETHERLANDS

www.emagicentertainment.com 2004

Concept

The difference lies in the visual concept. Only few sites use photos of real appliances as a visual interface. And it has a content management system using asp coding for updating the site. /// Le concept visuel fait toute la différence. Très peu de sites utilisent des photos de véritables appareils comme interface visuelle. Et le système de gestion des contenus utilise le codage asp pour les mises à jour du site. /// Das Besondere an dieser Website ist das visuelle Konzept. Nur wenige Sites benutzen Fotos von Geräten als visuelle Oberfläche. Für die Aktualisierung der Website wird ein Content Management System mit asp-Coding eingesetzt.

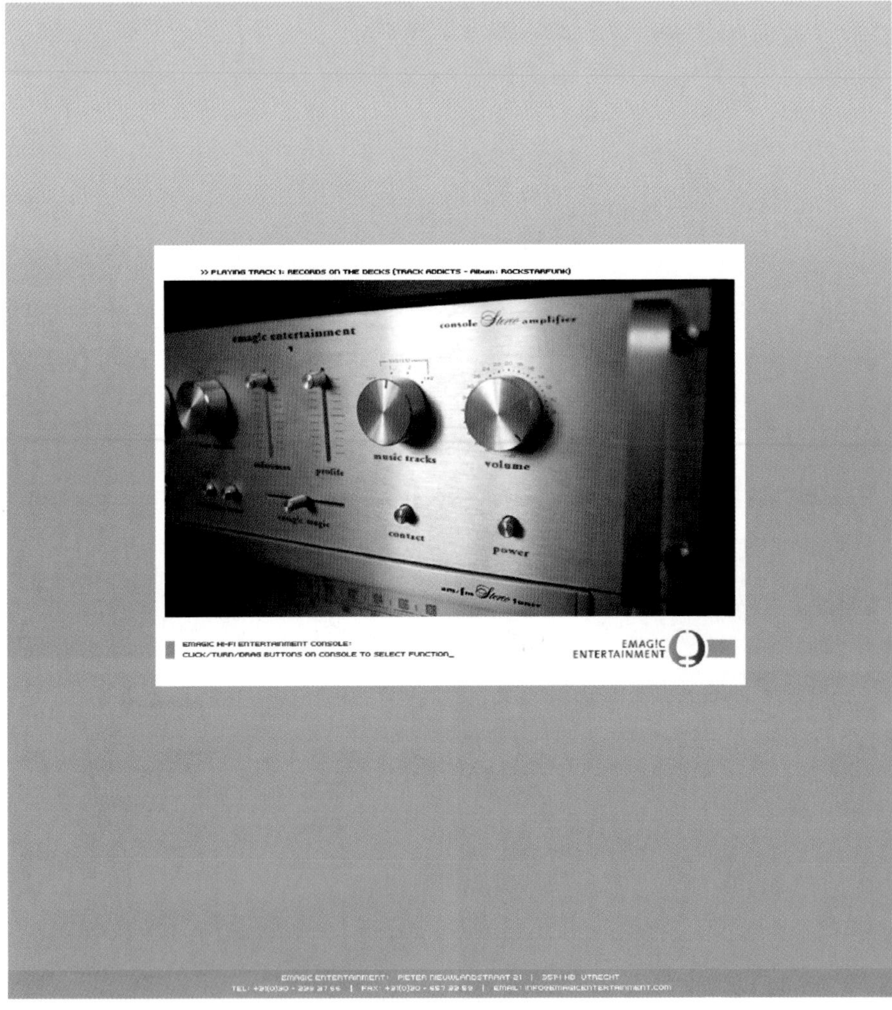

Info

DESIGN: Emilio van Wanrooij [GAZZ] <www.gazz.nl>. /// **PROGRAMMING**: Emilio van Wanrooij & Bas van Hout. /// **TOOLS**: Adobe Photoshop, Macromedia Flash, ASP, CMS. /// **CONTENTS**: animation, music, games. /// **COST**: 160 hours.

ESCAPE ROUTE

www.escapelab.com.au

AUSTRALIA
2004

Concept

A Travelogue of almost 1500 photos organized by the geographical location where they were taken. Users can navigate the photos using a 3D globe or 2D map, or view them in chronological order. /// Un Travelogue de presque 1 500 photos organisées selon le lieu où elles ont été prises. Les utilisateurs peuvent naviguer entre les photos à l'aide d'un globe en 3D ou d'une carte en 2D, ou les voir en ordre chronologique. /// Ein Fotoalbum mit fast 1500 Reisefotos, die nach der geographischen Lage des Ortes, an dem sie gemacht wurden, geordnet ist. Die Benutzer können die Fotos mit Hilfe eines 3D-Globus oder einer 2D-Karte aufrufen oder diese in chronologischer Reihenfolge einsehen.

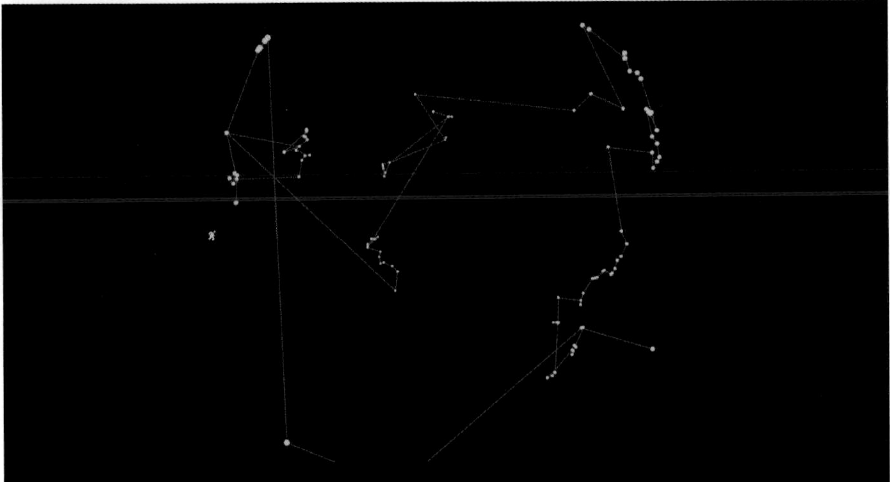

Info

Design and Programming: Henry Dawson (Escape Laboratories) <www.dphoto.com>; <www.dfunct.com>. /// **Tools:** Macromedia Flash, PHP, MySQL. /// **Contents:** travel photos. /// **Awards:** Yahoo (Pick of the day), FWA, Design TAXI (site of the day), Golden Web Award. /// **Cost:** 1 year.

EXTROVERSE

ITALY

www.extroverse.it

2005

Concept

Extroverse is the integration of illustrations, photos, motion graphics... at the best level... We hope. /// Extroverse, c'est l'intégration d'illustrations, de photos, de graphismes animés... du meilleur niveau... Nous l'espérons. /// **Die Website von Extroverse verbindet Bilder, Fotos, bewegliche Grafiken.... auf höchstem Niveau.... hoffen wir.**

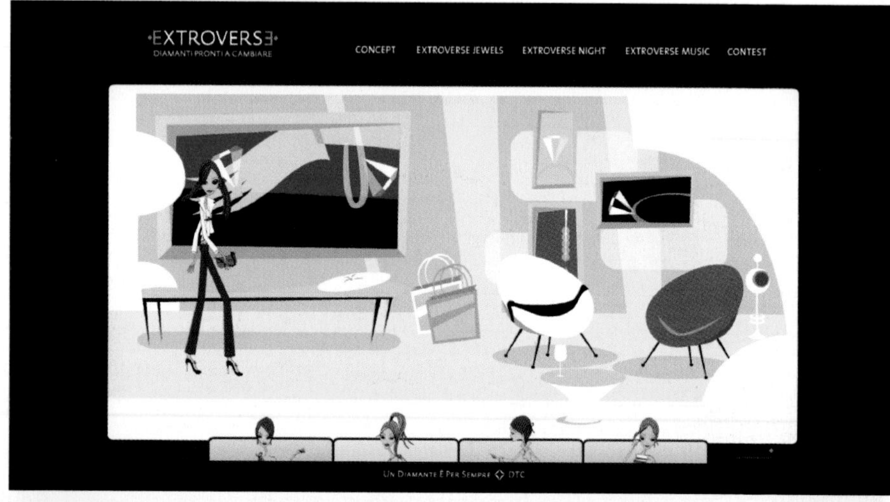

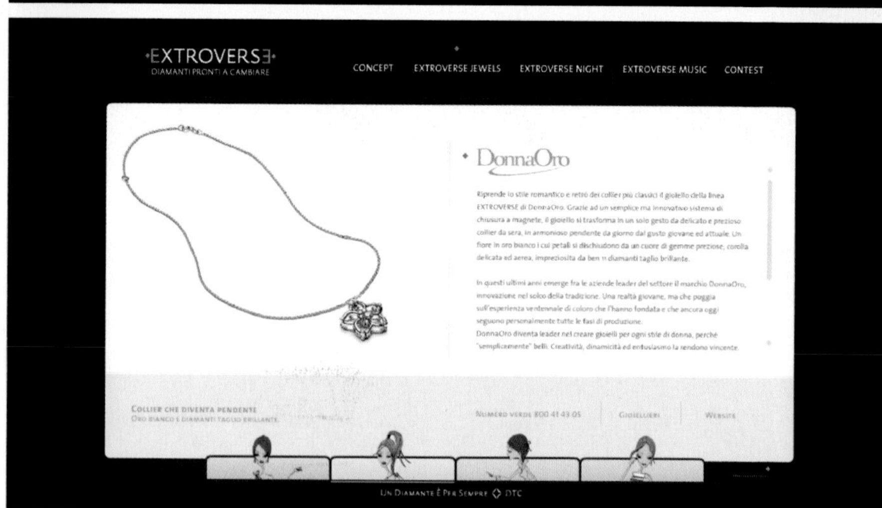

Info

DESIGN: Alessandro Orlandi & Matteo Giuricin (FISHOUSE) <www.fishouse.net>. /// **TOOLS:** Macromedia Flash, Adobe Photoshop, Adobe Illustrator. /// **CONTENTS:** photo, music, animation. /// **COST:** 300 hours.

F1 PLAY

CANADA

www.f1play.com

2005

Concept

The client wanted a "technical" look and we also had to deal with tons of content. again a site that gives the user a lot to explore. /// Le client voulait un look « technique » et nous avons aussi dû gérer des tonnes de contenu. Encore un site qui donne à l'utilisateur beaucoup à explorer. /// Einerseits wünschte der Kunde einen „technischen" Look, andererseits sollten unzählige Inhalte untergebracht werden. Wieder eine Website, auf der es viel zu erforschen gibt.

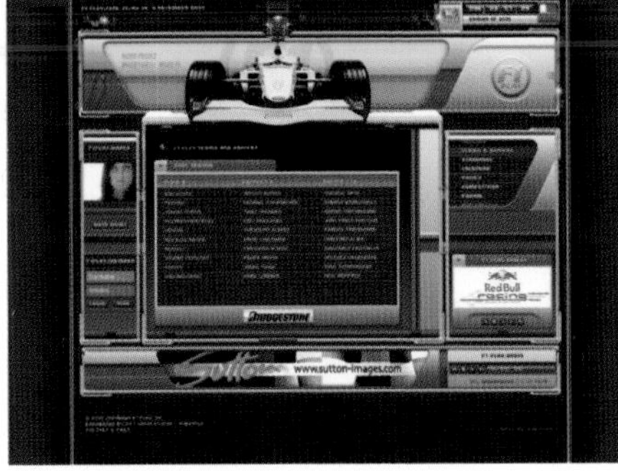

Info

Design: 247 Media Studios <www.24-7media.de>. /// **Programming**: 247 Media Studios; Amberfly <www.amberfly.com>. /// **Tools**: Adobe Photoshop, Macromedia Flash, PHP, XML. /// **Contents**: video, pictures, games. /// **Awards**: FWA. /// **Cost**: 2 months.

F6 CREATIONS

BELGIUM

www.f6creations.com

2004

Concept

Turn off the light, time stops, a flame wakes up and the contents appear. Welcome. /// Éteignez la lumière, le temps s'arrête, une flamme s'allume et les contenus apparaissent. Bienvenue. /// **Schalte das Licht aus! Die Zeit bleibt stehen, eine Flamme brennt und der Inhalt erscheint. Willkommen.**

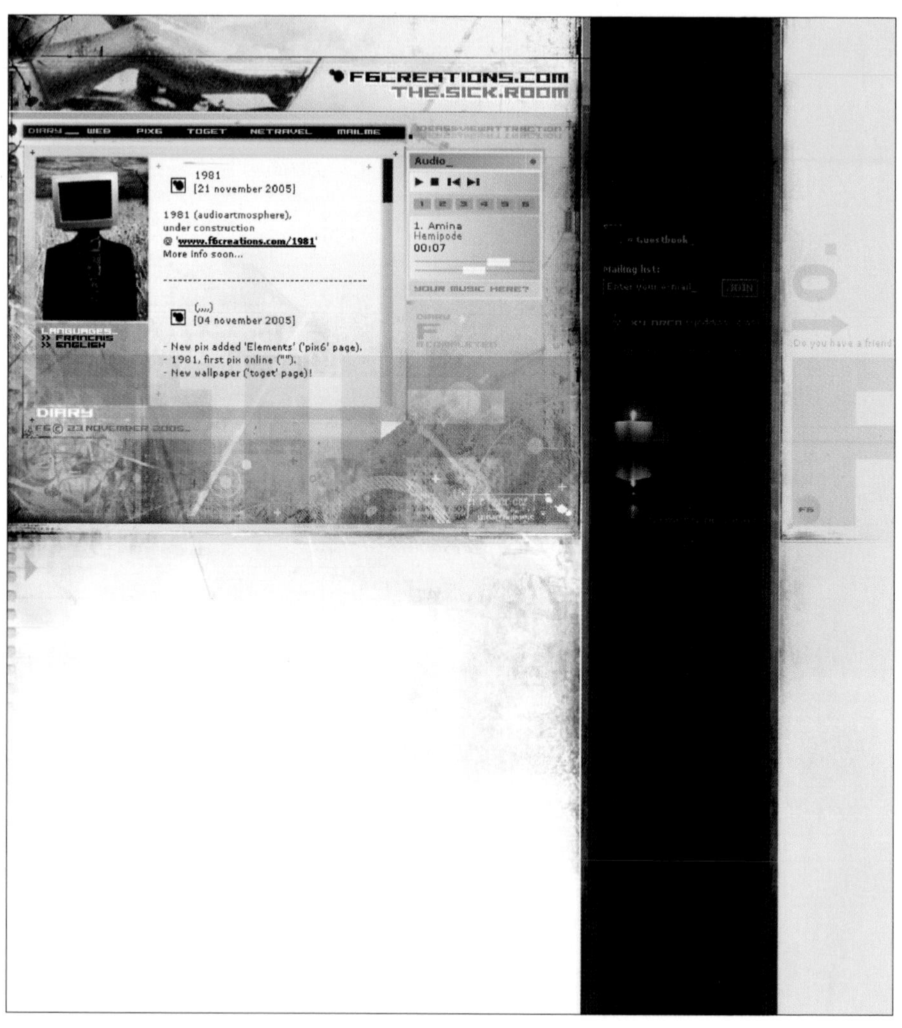

Info

Design and Programming: Fx. Marciat <www.xyarea.com>. /// **Tools**: Macromedia Flash, Macromedia Dreamweaver, Macromedia Fireworks, php, xml, video, music. /// **Contents**: news about various personnal projects, friends projects, music, photo, artwork and painting. /// **Awards**: WDA, MWA, EWA, Platic Pilots, e-Creative, Coolest Designs, DOPE Awards, and various other notifications. /// **Cost**: 4 weeks.

FAHRSCHULE LANDECK

AUSTRIA

www.fahrschule-landeck.at

2004

Concept

Users navigate from the driver's seat. Looking out through the windscreen they catch a glimpse of what it might be like when they will drive their own car. /// Les utilisateurs naviguent depuis le siège du conducteur. En regardant par le pare-brise, ils voient ce qu'ils pourront voir quand ils conduiront leur propre voiture. /// **Der Benutzer navigiert vom Fahrersitz aus. Durch die Windschutzscheibe bekommt er einen ersten Eindruck davon, wie es sein könnte, wenn er sein eigenes Auto fahren würde.**

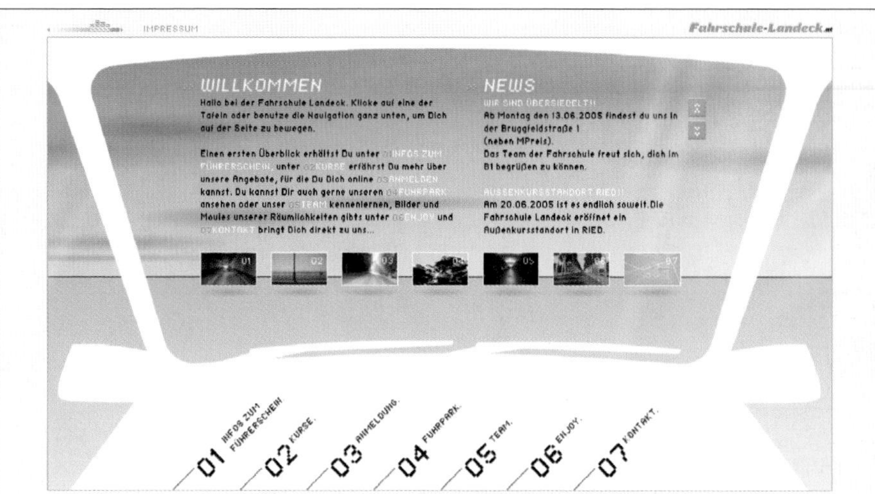

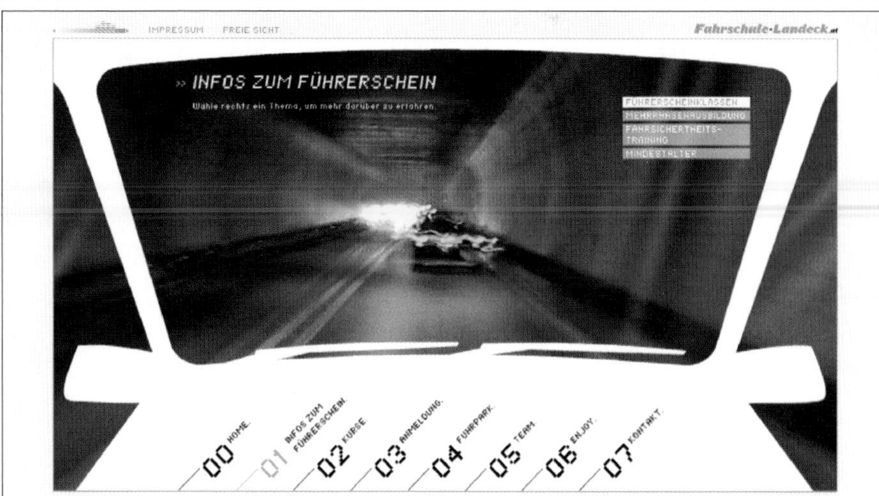

Info

DESIGN: transporter* <www.transporter.at>. /// **PROGRAMMING**: Rainer Fabrizi (transporter*). /// **TOOLS**: Macromedia Flash, Macromedia Dreamweaver, Adobe Photoshop, Macromedia Freehand, Soundedit, PHP, mySQL, cargo*CMS, Javascript, Transmit. /// **CONTENTS**: photos done with a digicam, sound effects recorded on the powerbook, background images animated in Flash. /// **COST**: 175 hours.

FILMWORKS COLLECTIVE

INTERNATIONAL

www.filmworkscollective.com

2005

Concept

Filmworks is refreshingly unconventional both in its navigation and creative approach. Exploring these pages gives the user the illusion of being in a film studio, as if looking at snippets of film. /// Filmworks est rafraîchissant et non conventionnel à la fois dans sa navigation et dans son approche créative. L'exploration de ces pages donne à l'utilisateur l'illusion de se trouver dans un studio de cinéma, comme s'il visionnait des fragments de film. /// Filmworks ist sowohl in der Navigation als auch im kreativen Ansatz erfrischend unkonventionell. Bei der Erforschung dieser Seiten hat der Benutzer den Eindruck, er befände sich in einem Filmstudio und sähe sich dort einige Filmpassagen an.

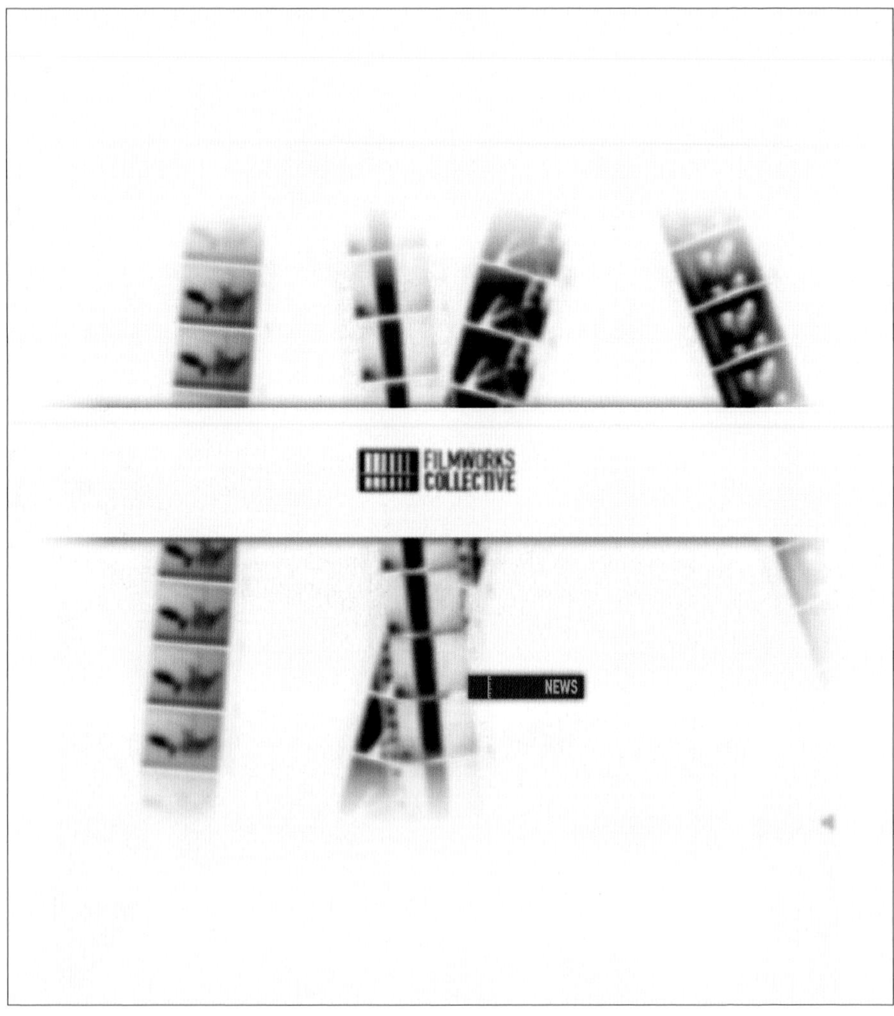

Info

Design: Isaac Wong, Kenny Choo (Kinetic) <www.kinetic.com.sg>. /// **Programming**: Isaac Wong (Kinetic). /// **Tools**: Adobe Photoshop, Adobe After Effects, Adobe Illustrator, Macromedia Freehand, Macromedia Flash, CMS, php, RSS XML. /// **Contents**: Film showreels. /// **Cost**: 200 hours.

FISH'N'CHIPS

www.fish-n-chips.net

FRANCE
2005

Concept

Having the same homepage for more than two weeks may be boring. To avoid this problem, our site has a minimal interface, with several different skins that can be updated daily. /// Garder la même page d'accueil plus de quinze jours peut être monotone. Pour éviter ce problème, notre site a une interface très simple, avec plusieurs habillages différents qui peuvent être mis à jour quotidiennement. /// Wenn man ein und dieselbe Homepage länger als zwei Wochen lang besitzt, kann es langweilig werden. Um das zu vermeiden, verfügt unsere Website über eine minimalistische Oberfläche mit mehreren verschieden Schalen, die täglich aktualisiert werden können.

Info

Design: Simon Frankart (Fish). /// **Programming**: Sean Tempère (Chips). /// **Tools**: Macromedia Flash, Adobe Photoshop, Adobe Illustrator, PHP, MySQL, Notepad, Autodesk 3ds Max, audio and music softwares. /// **Contents**: animations, websites, T-shirt design, music. /// **Awards**: FWA (site of the day), Paris Flash Festival (finalist), DOPE Awards, iBlog (site of the week), Uailab (site of the month), e-Creative (site of the day). /// **Cost**: 120 hours.

FOCUSTYLE

JAPAN
2005

www.focustyle.jp

Concept

New Life-style with Ford FOCUS. /// Un nouveau style de vie avec la Ford FOCUS. /// Neuer Life-Style mit Ford FOCUS.

Info

DESIGN: Shun Kawakami [artless Inc.] <www.artless.gr.jp>. /// PROGRAMMING: Kiyokazu Ohno. /// TOOLS: Adobe Photoshop, Macromedia Flash. /// CONTENTS: car, lifestyle.

FOSTER ARCHITECTS

NEW ZEALAND

www.fosterarchitects.co.nz

2004

Concept

Motion based navigation introduces you to beautifully animated architectural projects. The image specific transitions customized for each project develop an immersive and seamless flow. /// La navigation basée sur le mouvement vous présente des projets architecturaux superbement animés. Les transitions entre images, personnalisées pour chaque projet, donnent un flux enveloppant et sans accroc. /// **Bewegungsbasierte Navigation führt Sie zu wunderschön animierten, architektonischen Projekten. Die bild- und projektspezifischen Übertragungen entwickeln einen eindringlichen und nahtlosen Fluss.**

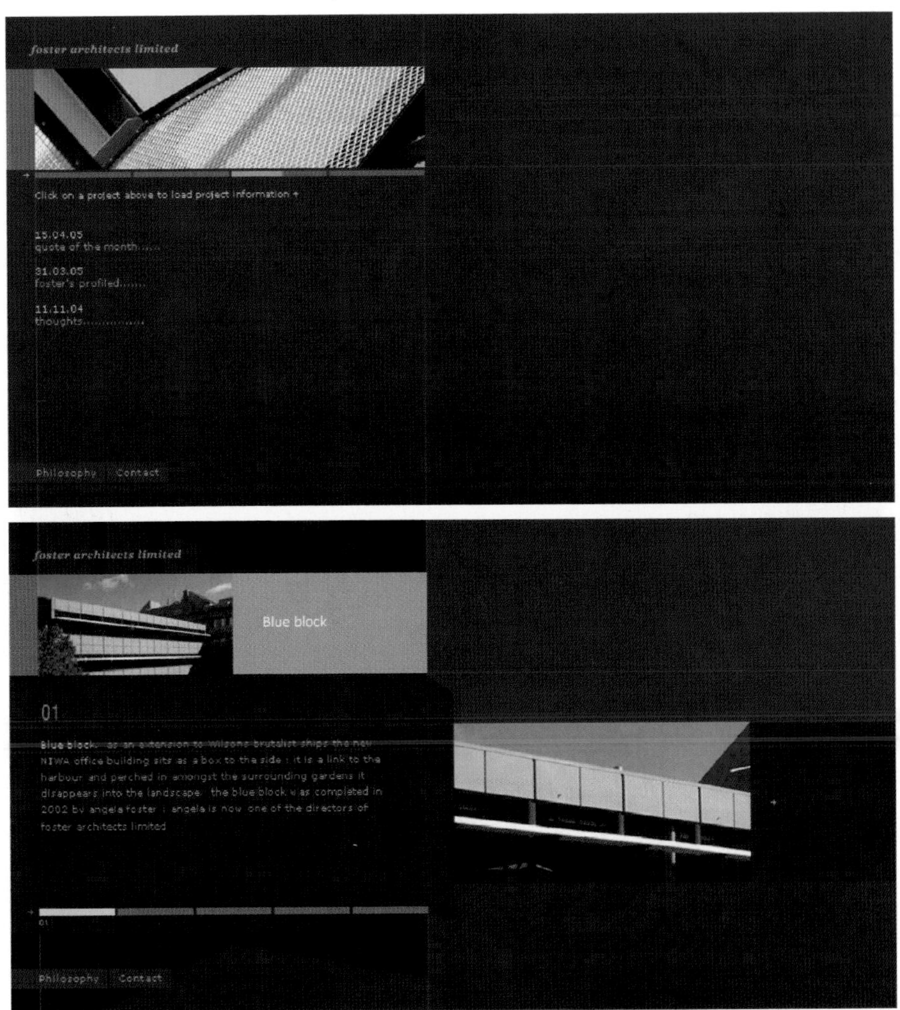

Info

Design and Programming: Resn <www.resn.co.nz>. /// **Tools:** Macromedia Studio MX, Adobe Photoshop, pencil & paper. /// **Contents:** architects portfolio, images, animation. /// **Awards:** DOPE Awards, TINY, Plasticpilots. /// **Cost:** 400 hours.

FREDDY FUSION

CANADA

www.freddyfusion.com

2005

Concept

Freddy Fusion features custom graphic design, Action-scripted easing and tweens, original sound composition and a multi-user live chat application to deliver a rich, entertaining and engaging user experience. /// Freddy Fusion présente une conception graphique sur mesure, des interpolations et de l'easing en ActionScript, une composition sonore originale et une application de chat multi-utilisateurs, ce qui en fait un site très riche, ludique et captivant. /// Das Hauptmerkmal der Website von Freddy Fusion ist das maßgeschneidertes Grafik-Design, die kinderleichte Bedienung, der originelle Ton und eine live Multiuser-Chat-Anwendung. Die Website bietet dem Benutzer ein reiches, unterhaltsames und aufregendes Erlebnis.

Info

DESIGN: Marco Di Carlo (Velocity Studio & Associates) <www.velocitystudio.com>. /// **PROGRAMMING:** Jonathan Coe (Velocity Studio & Associates) <www.velocitystudio.com>. /// **TOOLS:** Adobe Photoshop, Adobe Illustrator, Macromedia Fireworks, Macromedia Flash, Ableton Live 4, Native Instruments Kontakt, Native Instruments Reaktor 4, Bias Peak 4.0, Robert Penner's Tween, Easing Prototypes. /// **COST:** 5 months including photo shoot, site layout/design/IA and flash build/integration.

GEORGINA GOODMAN

UK/USA/DENMARK

www.georginagoodman.com

2003

Concept

This site was conceptualized in London, designed in Copenhagen and built in New York. The Georgina site is an extraordinary fairy-tale experience that takes place in a foreign and magical world. It's a defining piece of interactive art. /// Ce site a été conçu à Londres, dessiné à Copenhague et construit à New York. Le site de Georgina vous emmène dans un conte de fées extraordinaire, dans un monde étrange et magique. C'est une pièce maîtresse de l'art interactif. /// Diese Website von Georgina wurde in London konzipiert, in Kopenhagen entworfen und in New York erstellt. Sie bietet ein außergewöhnliches Märchenerlebnis, welches in einer fremden und zauberhaften Welt stattfindet. Es handelt sich um eine Vorzeigewebsite für interaktive Kunst.

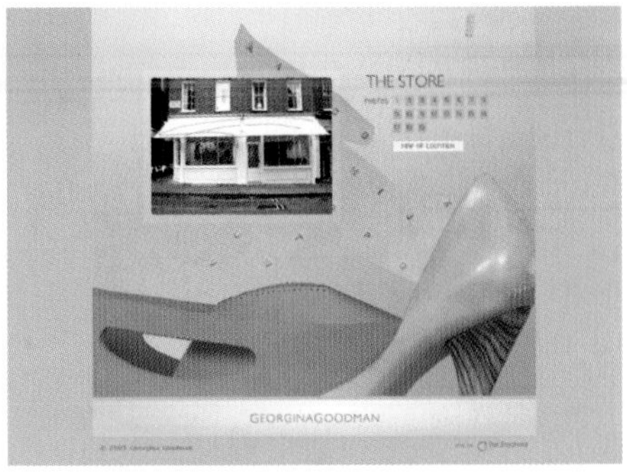

Info

DESIGN AND PROGRAMMING: Diet Strychnine Corp. <www.dietstrychnine.com>. /// **TOOLS:** Adobe Creative Suite, Macromedia Flash, PHP. /// **CONTENTS:** flash, original score music, Quicktime film. /// **AWARDS:** Communication Arts. /// **COST:** over 1000 hours and counting...

GOOQ

GERMANY

www.gooq.de

2005

Concept

My website isn't just my portfolio... it is also a platform for my friends. Never struggle alone! /// Mon site web n'est pas seulement mon portfolio... c'est aussi une plateforme pour mes amis. Ne luttez jamais seul ! /// Meine Website ist nicht nur mein Portfolio... sie stellt auch eine Plattform für meine Freunde dar. Kämpfe niemals alleine!

Info

Design and Programming: Huy Dieu (GOOQ). /// **Tools**: Adobe Photoshop, Macromedia Freehand, Macromedia Flash, CMS, XML, PHP. /// **Contents**: graphics, photos. /// **Awards**: DOPE Awards, Moluv, e-Creative (site of the day), quandnet.de, NewWebPick, Pixelmakers (site of the week), Website Design Awards. /// **Cost**: 45 days.

CIRCULO CREATIVO

MEXICO

www.grupow.com/circulo

2005

Concept

It is an abstract experience based in a simple circle, composed by several sections. Inside each one, the user can access diverse content like news, articles, tv spots, etc. /// C'est une expérience abstraite basée sur un simple cercle, composé de plusieurs sections. Dans chaque section, l'utilisateur a accès à différents types de contenus, comme des informations, des articles, des spots tv, etc. /// Es handelt sich hierbei um ein abstraktes Gebilde in Form eines einfachen, aus mehreren Segmenten bestehenden Kreises. Die einzelnen Segmente enthalten diverse Inhalte, wie z.B. Nachrichten, Artikel, Fernseh-Spots usw.

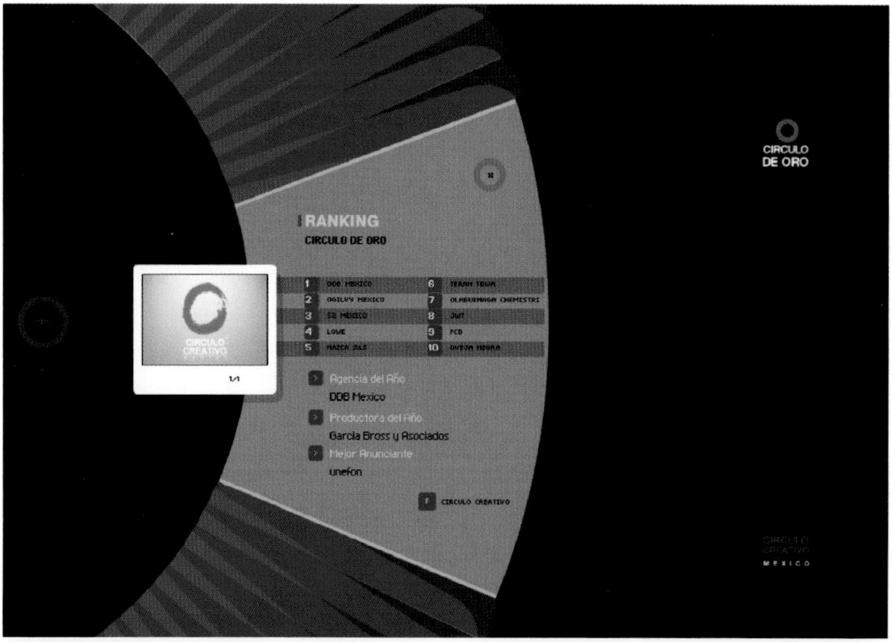

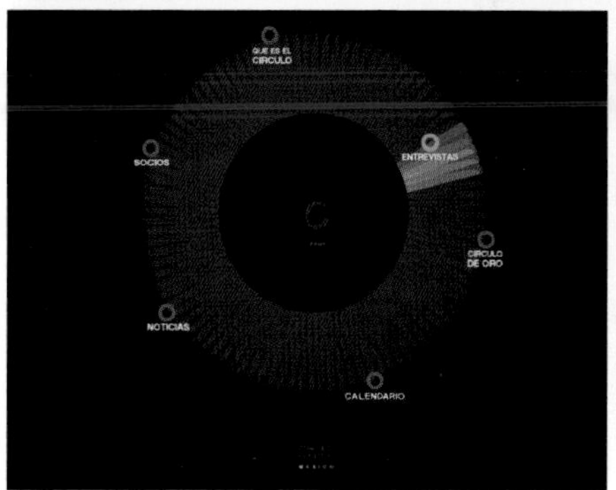

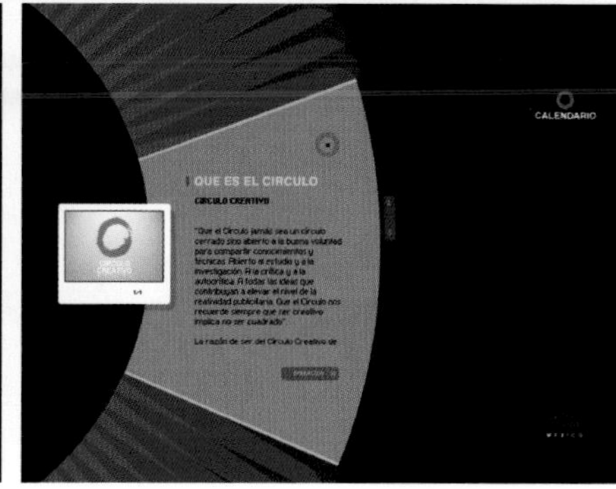

Info

Design: Miguel Calderon (GRUPO W). /// **Programming:** Raul Uranga, Homero Sousa (GRUPO W). /// **Tools:** Macromedia Flash, PHP Database, Xml, Fractal Painter. /// **Contents:** rich media like video, sound and pictures. /// **Awards:** FWA, a! Design International Award, Iberoamerican Advertasing Festival, TINY, Wow Factor, Crossmind, Styleboost. /// **Cost:** 450 hours.

MI VIDA COMO UN 10

MEXICO

www.grupow.com/nike10

2005

Concept

The power of the strategy was based on create a digital film with a funny story about a guy who looks exactly like Ronaldinho, the most important soccer player in the world. /// Le pouvoir de la stratégie était basé sur la création d'un film numérique avec une histoire amusante, sur un type qui ressemble trait pour trait à Ronaldinho, le plus grand joueur de foot du monde. /// Die Strategie bestand in der Erstellung eines digitalen Films mit einer witzigen Geschichte über einen jungen Mann, der genauso aussieht wie Ronaldinho, der beste Fußballspieler der Welt.

Info

Design: GRUPO W: Ulises Valencia, Miguel Calderon. /// **Programming**: Raul Uranga, Homero Sousa. /// **Tools**: Macromedia Flash, Fractal Painter, Autodesk 3ds Max, Adobe Premiere, Adobe After Effects, Adobe Audition, Javascript. /// **Contents**: rich media website and a digital short film. /// **Awards**: FWA, a! Design International, Moluv, Crossmind, DOPE Awards, WellVetted, Style Awards. /// **Cost**: 2 months.

HAVAIANAS

BRAZIL

www.havaianas.com.br

2005

Concept

The major difference between Havaianas' website and other Flash sites is an unique brazilian style of colorful illustrations combined with a outstanding animation and world music effects. /// La principale différence entre le site de Havaianas et les autres sites en Flash, c'est le style brésilien unique de ses illustrations colorées, avec une animation exceptionnelle et des effets de world music. /// Der Hauptunterschied zwischen der Website von Havaianas und anderen Flash-Websites besteht in den farbenreichen Bildern einzigartigen, brasilianischen Stils in Verbindung mit außergewöhnlicher Animation und Musikeffekten.

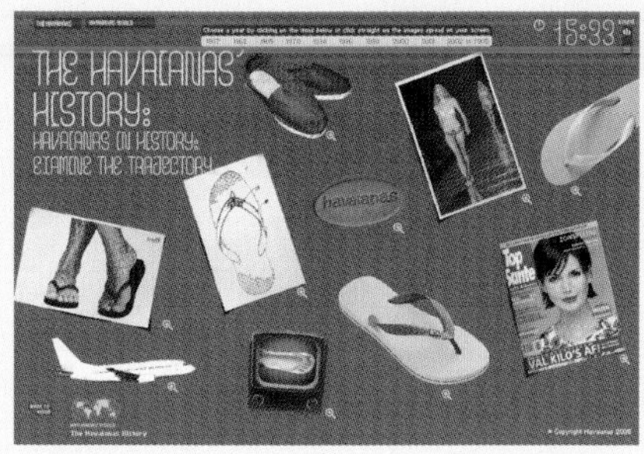

Info

Design: AlmapBBDO <www.almapbbdo.com.br>: Creative Director: Marcello Serpa; Sérgio Mugnaini. Art Director: Adhemas Batista. Copywriter: Luciana Haguiara. Motion Designer: Ricardo Martins. Illustration: Adhemas Batista. /// **Programming**: Fabricio Zuardi, Flavio Ramos. /// **Tools**: Adobe Photoshop, Macromedia Flash, php. /// **Contents**: film, animations, texts and illustrations. Sound track by Lua Web. /// **Awards**: London Festival 2005 (Finalist). MSN/MMonline Awards Product Website (Silver). /// **Cost**: 480 hours.

HEINEKEN INNOVATORS

SINGAPORE

www.heineken.com.sg/innovators

2005

Concept

The Heineken Innovators site was an event-oriented site that challenged the audience to take up the creative mantle. Users are alloted space online to develop some seriously creative virtual real estate. /// Le site Heineken Innovators est un site créé autour d'un événement, qui lance un défi à l'audience : prendre en main les rênes de la création. Les utilisateurs disposent d'un espace en ligne pour développer un univers sérieusement créatif. /// Die Website von Heineken Innovators ist eventorientiert und fordert den Besucher auf, seine eigene Kreativität auszuleben. Die Benutzer bekommen einen eigenen Online-Raum zur Verfügung gestellt und sollen ein kreatives Innendesign für eine virtuelle Immobilie entwickeln.

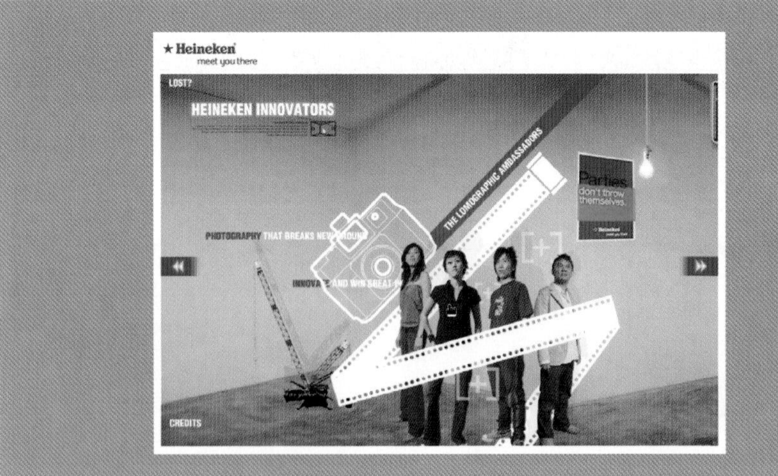

Info

Design: Sean Lam, Isaac Wong, Ken Choo, Jason Chan (Kinetic) <www.kinetic.com.sg>. /// **Programming**: Isaac Wong, Eng Sin Phang (Kinetic). /// **Tools**: Adobe Photoshop, Macromedia Flash, Macromedia Dreamweaver, Ultraedit, Macromedia Freehand, Adobe Illustrator. /// **Contents**: photos, music samples, customizable e-card engine, animation, video. /// **Cost**: 190 hours.

CODE

INTERNATIONAL

www.hellocode.com

2001

Concept

A place for experimentation where we try new things and challenge ourselves to think beyond the norm in terms of web interaction. /// C'est un lieu d'expérimentation où l'on peut essayer des choses nouvelles et se lancer le défi de penser au-delà des normes en termes d'interaction sur Internet. /// Ein Raum für Experimente, in dem wir neue Dinge ausprobieren und uns der Herausforderung stellen, die Denkmuster in Bezug auf Website-Interaktion zu sprengen.

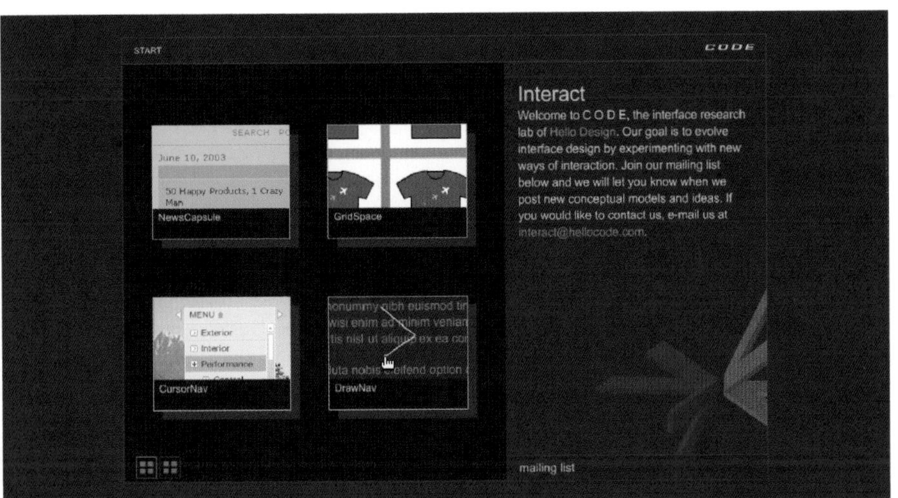

Info

Design and Programming: Hello Design <www.hellodesign.com>. /// **Tools:** CMS: Java, PHP. Adobe Photoshop, Adobe Illustrator, Macromedia Flash, BBEdit. /// **Contents:** there are eight experiments in C O D E: CursorNav, DrawNav, Global Communicator, Photospace, Calendar(cubed), Contentscope. /// **Awards:** Communication Arts Interactive Design Annual, Flashforward Flash Film Festival (Finalist), Macromedia.com (Site of the Day), AIGA Grown in California Exhibition, Pirelli Award (Finalist).

AIWAWORLD

INTERNATIONAL

www.hellodesign.com/aiwa

2004

Concept

The site's activities encourage kids to develop critical life skills such as critical thinking, problem solving, and visual literacy. /// Les activités de ce site encouragent les enfants à développer des compétences vitales telles que la pensée critique, la résolution de problèmes, et l'alphabétisation visuelle. /// Durch die Funktionen der Website werden Kinder animiert, wesentliche Fähigkeiten zu entwickeln. Dazu gehören: kritisches Denken, Problemlösungskraft und visuelle Fertigkeiten.

Info

Design: Hello Design, THE_GROOP, Oceanmonsters, Wieden+Kennedy. /// **Tools**: Adobe Photoshop, Adobe Illustrator, Macromedia Flash, Macromedia Dreamweaver. /// **Contents**: videos, music. /// **Awards**: Cannes Cyber Lion (Silver), Art Directors Club Interactive Award, D&AD Digital Crafts Nomination, Communication Arts Interactive Design Annual. /// **Cost**: 3 months.

HELLO SEXY

USA

www.hello-sexy.com

2004

Concept

Portfolio site for designer/developer Ian Coyle; it is an experiment in organic motion, designed to break the mold of traditional portfolio sites. /// Portfolio du concepteur/développeur Ian Coyle. C'est une expérience sur le mouvement organique, conçue pour casser le moule des portfolios traditionnels. /// Portfolio-Website des Designers/Entwicklers Ian Coyle; Es ist ein Experiment mit organischer Bewegung, die mit dem Ziel entwickelt wurde, aus der Norm der traditionellen Portfolio-Websites auszubrechen.

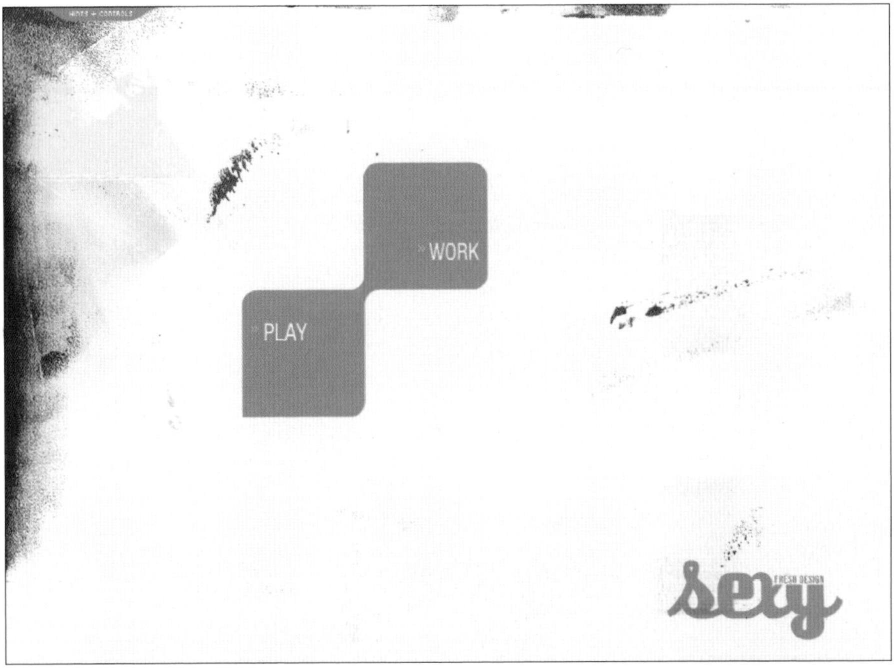

Info

Design and Programming: Ian Coyle (Hello Sexy). /// **Tools:** Macromedia Flash, Adobe Photoshop, asp.net, xml. /// **Contents:** portfolio. /// **Awards:** FWA (Site of the Day), South by Southwest Interactive 2005 (Finalist), American Design Awards (Gold), Flash In The Can 2005 (Finalist), Step Inside Design Magazine (Best of Web 2005), Art Director's Club of Denver 2005 (Silver).

HORLICKS

UK

www.horlicks.co.uk

2004

Concept

Illustration, animation and sound creates a calm, atmospheric website where users drift seamlessly from section to section on a journey to 'Sweet Dreams'. /// Illustrations, animation et son créent un site calme, évocateur, où les utilisateurs se laissent porter en douceur d'une section à l'autre, dans un voyage vers le pays des « beaux rêves ». /// **Hier wurde mit Hilfe von Illustration, Animation und Ton eine ruhige und stimmungsvolle Website erstellt. Der Benutzer kann übergangslos von einem Bereich zum anderen gleiten, auf seiner Reise in die „süße Welt der Träume".**

Info

Design: Matt Rice, Hege Aaby [Sennep] <www.sennep.com>. /// **Programming:** Matt Rice, Thomas Poeser [Sennep]. /// **Tools:** Macromedia Freehand, Macromedia Flash, Adobe Photoshop. /// **Contents:** interactive illustrations, animation, horlicks products. /// **Cost:** 425 hours.

HOTMONKEY DESIGN

UK

www.hotmonkeydesign.com

2004

Concept

The difference between our site and other flash sites is that we wanted to have fun... And we did. /// La différence entre notre site et d'autres sites Flash, c'est que nous voulions nous amuser... Et c'est ce que nous avons fait. /// Der Unterschied zwischen unserer Website und anderen Flash-Websites besteht darin, dass wir Spaß haben wollten... Und den hatten wir auch.

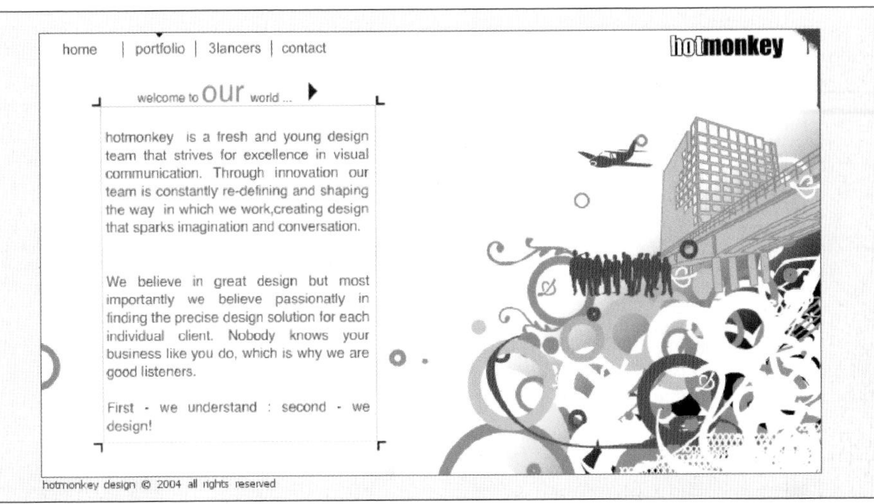

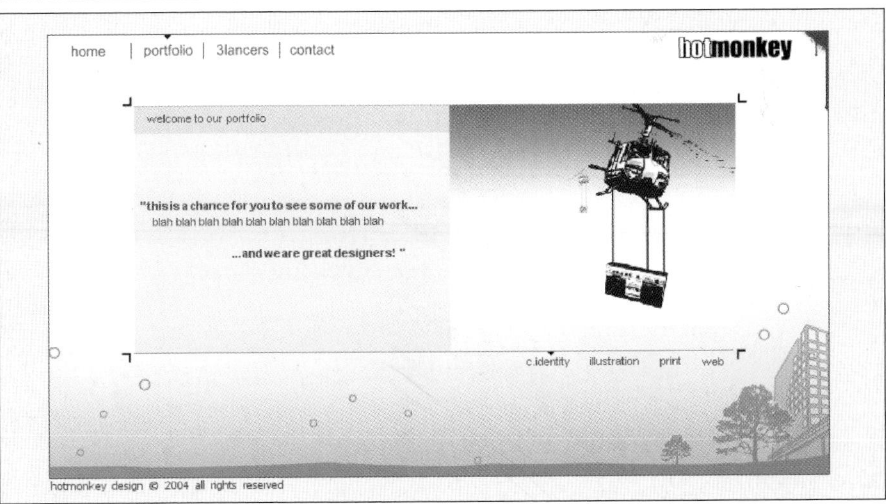

Info

Design and Programming: hotmonkey design. /// **Tools:** Adobe Photoshop, Macromedia Flash. /// **Contents:** web graphics, animations, graphic design for print and web. /// **Awards:** NewWebPick, Websmarty, Progressive Design, Pixelmakers, Coolest Websites, iTraffic Boost. /// **Cost:** 3 weeks.

HSTEC

CROATIA

www.hstec.hr

2005

Concept We wanted to present this (not so usual theme) for FLASH website in minimalist and most user friendly way but at the same time we wanted to keep our artistic style. /// Nous voulions présenter ce thème assez inhabituel pour un site Flash de manière minimaliste et conviviale tout en gardant notre style artistique. /// Wir wollten dieses (nicht ganz gewöhnliche) Thema für eine Flash-Website in einer minimalistischen Weise und so benutzerfreundlich wie möglich präsentieren. Gleichzeitig wollten wir aber auch unserem künstlerischen Stil treu bleiben.

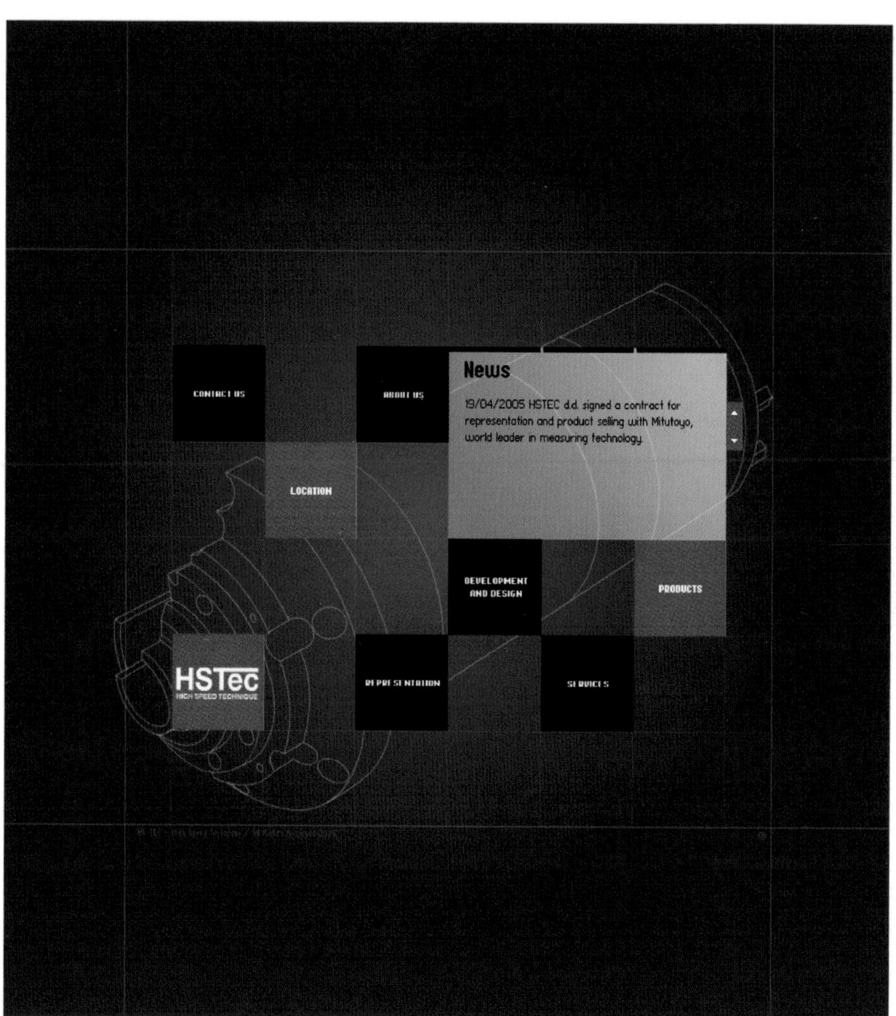

Info DESIGN AND PROGRAMMING: Rootylicious.inc <www.rootylicious.com>. /// TOOLS: Macromedia Studio, Adobe Studio Creative Suite. /// CONTENTS: photography by Thomas Kohnle. /// COST: 10 working days.

GRAPHIC MERCENARY

BELGIUM

www.hypnotized.org

2005

Concept

This website is about Image-Manipulations, Graphic Design & Illustrations, it shows many "see the steps" animations to explain the image-building evolution. /// Ce site traite des manipulations d'images, de la conception graphique et des illustrations. Il montre de nombreuses animations décomposées en étapes pour expliquer l'évolution de la construction d'une image. /// Diese Website beruht auf Bildbearbeitung, Grafikdesign und Illustrationen. Sie zeigt viele Zwischenstufen der Animationen und erklärt somit die Evolution der Bilder.

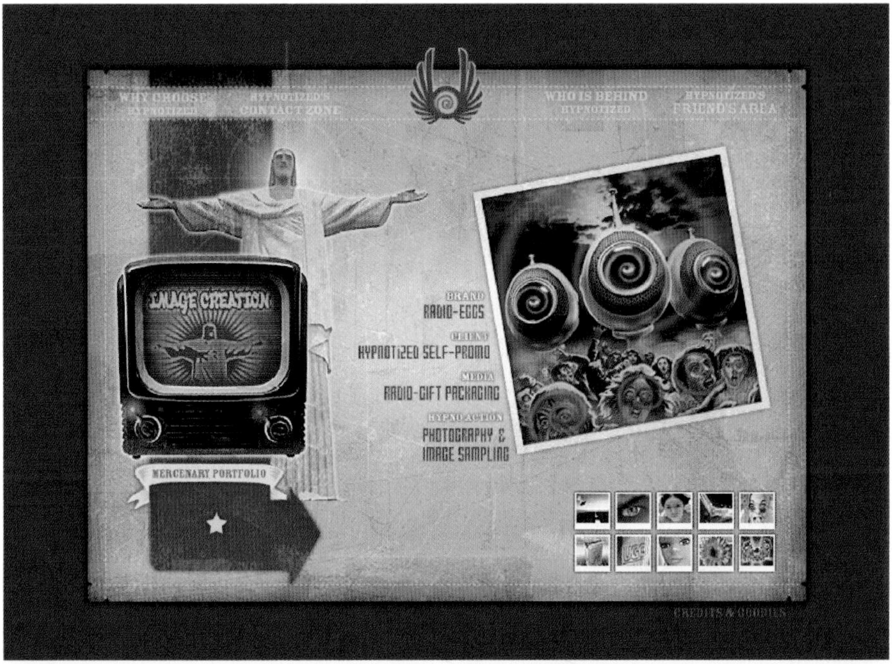

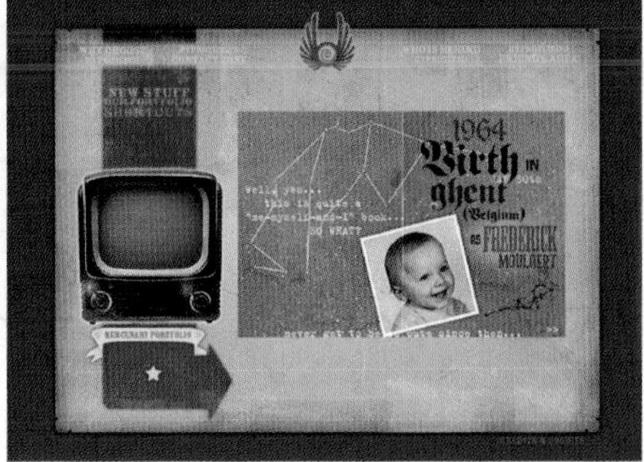

Info

Design: Frederick Moulaert (Hypnotized). /// **Programming**: Olivier De Martino <www.root7.org>. /// **Tools**: Macromedia Flash, Javascript, Adobe Photoshop, Adobe Illustrator. /// **Contents**: photo, image manipulations, animations, music. /// **Awards**: American Design Award, Ultraweb, Plasticpilots, Coolhomepages (Site of the Week), e-Creative, Yellowpimento, Ades Design, Website Design Awards, Strangefruits, Wow Organicpixel, Pixelmakers, NewWebPick, Digital Refueler, Crossmind, Media Inspiration. /// **Cost**: 225 hours.

INCA CORP

USA

www.inca-tvlifts.com

2004

Concept

The entire interface operates using 4 minimal pieces of geometry. These pieces reconfigure to frame the content of the entire site, a myriad of product; vendor and customer data from a PHP based CMS. /// Toute l'interface fonctionne grâce à 4 pièces de géométrie minimalistes. Ces pièces se reconfigurent pour encadrer le contenu de tous les sites, une myriade de produits, et les données des fournisseurs et des clients viennent d'un CMS en PHP. /// Die gesamte Oberfläche arbeitet mit vier einfachen geometrischen Figuren. Die Figuren dienen als Bilderrahmen für die Inhalte der gesamten Website: unzählige Produkte und Kundendaten eines auf PHP basierten CMS.

Info

Design and Programming: CRIMSON Design Group <www.crimsonmade.com>. /// **Tools:** Macromedia Flash, XML, PHP, MySQL, Maya. /// **Contents:** photography, renderings, animation, video and web-based forms. /// **Cost:** 150 hours.

INTERONE WORLDWIDE

GERMANY

www.interone.de

2005

Concept

The reduced and focused Look & Feel of the site combined with dynamic transitions and asymmetric layouts allows the user an exciting look at the agency and the agencies work. /// Son esprit minimaliste et direct, combiné à des transitions dynamiques et à un agencement asymétrique, donne à l'utilisateur un point de vue fascinant sur l'agence et sur son travail. /// **Das reduzierte und fokussierte Look & Feel der Website in Verbindung mit dynamischen Übergängen und asymmetrischen Layouts verschafft dem Benutzer einen aufregenden Einblick in die Agentur und ihre Arbeit.**

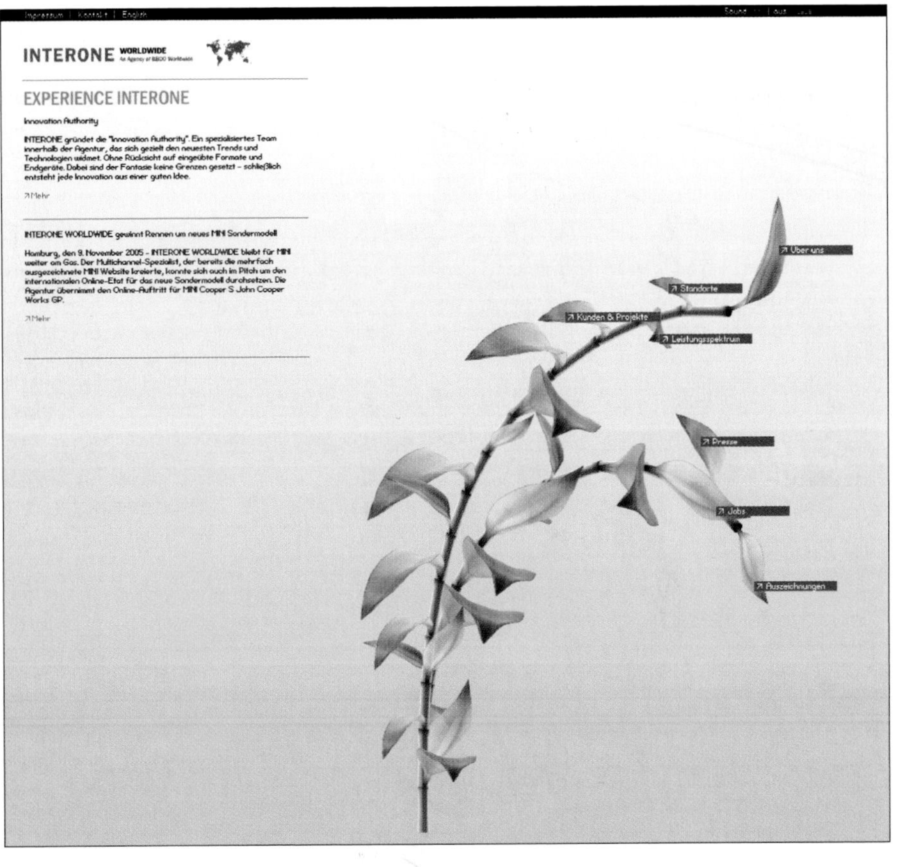

Info

Design: [INTERONE] Creative Directors: Mike John Otto & Chris Bauer. Art Director: Torben Cording. Flash Designer: Lars Gercke, Andrew Sinn. 3D: David Löhr. /// **Tools:** Xhtml, Macromedia Flash, Cinema 4D, Adobe Photoshop, php. /// **Contents:** photos, music, animations. /// **Awards:** FWA, Lookom, Netdiver, Res72, Highflooter, and various other magazines. /// **Cost:** 2 months.

PHAMOUS HAIR & MAKEUP

UK

www.isphamous.com

2004

Concept

The early hours of London's Old Street is brought to life with sights and sounds. A billboard provides a novel way of displaying artist's portfolios. /// L'environnement visuel et sonore évoque les premières heures de l'Old Street londonienne. Un panneau d'affichage présente les portfolios des artistes de manière originale. /// Die Londoner Old Street wird in den frühen Morgenstunden durch neue Aktionen und durch Ton zum Leben erweckt. Die Reklametafel stellt eine neue Möglichkeit dar, das Portfolio des Künstlers zu präsentieren.

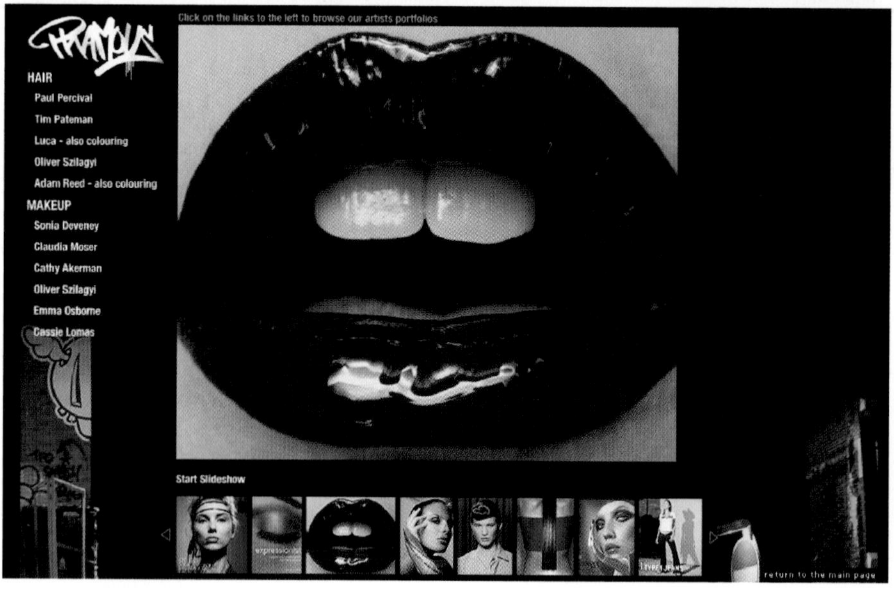

Info

DESIGN and **PROGRAMMING**: Ten4 Design <www.ten4design.co.uk>. /// **TOOLS**: Macromedia Flash, Adobe Photoshop, xml, php. /// **CONTENTS**: artist's animated photographic portfolios. /// **COST**: 1 month.

FLASHTV

USA/BRAZIL

www.iwantmyflashtv.com

2000

Concept

FlashTV features four channels of digital content produced by independent artists worldwide for visitors to enjoy online including the option to pay to download content to go on devices such as the PSP and the iPod. /// FlashTV présente quatre chaînes dont les contenus numériques sont produits par des artistes indépendants internationaux. Les visiteurs peuvent les voir en ligne et ont l'option de payer pour télécharger des contenus sur des appareils comme la PSP ou l'iPod. /// FlashTV bietet vier Programme mit digitalen Inhalten, die von unabhängigen Künstlern weltweit angeboten werden. Sie können online angesehen oder aber bezahlt und für die Benutzung über Geräte wie PSP und iPod heruntergeladen werden.

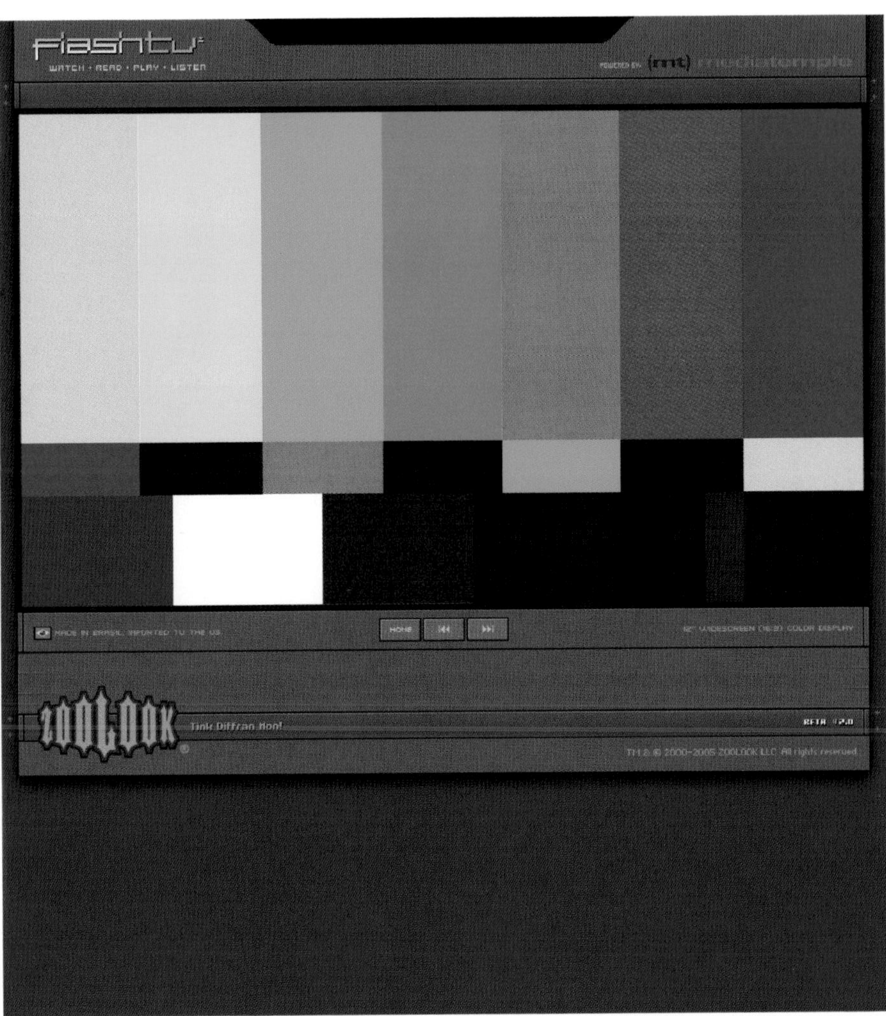

Info

Design: ZOOLOOK <www.zoolook.com>. /// **Programming**: Nicholas Da Silva (ZOOLOOK). /// **Tools**: Adobe Illustrator, Adobe Photoshop, Macromedia Flash, Macromedia Dreamweaver, Macromedia Fireworks, php, Apple Quicktime. /// **Contents**: animation and films, games, digital comic books and music. /// **Awards**: Macromedia (Site of the Day); FWA; Cool Homepages (Site of the Week); Ultrashock Bombshock. /// **Cost**: 7 months from concept to site launch.

JAQUELYN A. GUEVARRA

USA

www.jguevarra.com

2005

Concept

This page emulates what an interior designers desk would look like, cluttered but well managed. This site allows the user to go through her work while giving them a hands on experience. /// Cette page simule un bureau d'architecte d'intérieur, encombré mais bien organisé. Elle permet à l'utilisateur d'explorer le travail de l'artiste de façon active et directe. /// Diese Website ahmt einen typischen Innenarchitekten-Schreibtisch nach. Darauf herrscht ein gut organisiertes Chaos. Die Website ermöglicht dem Benutzer, in die Arbeiten der Architektin Einblick zu nehmen und damit in Berührung zu kommen.

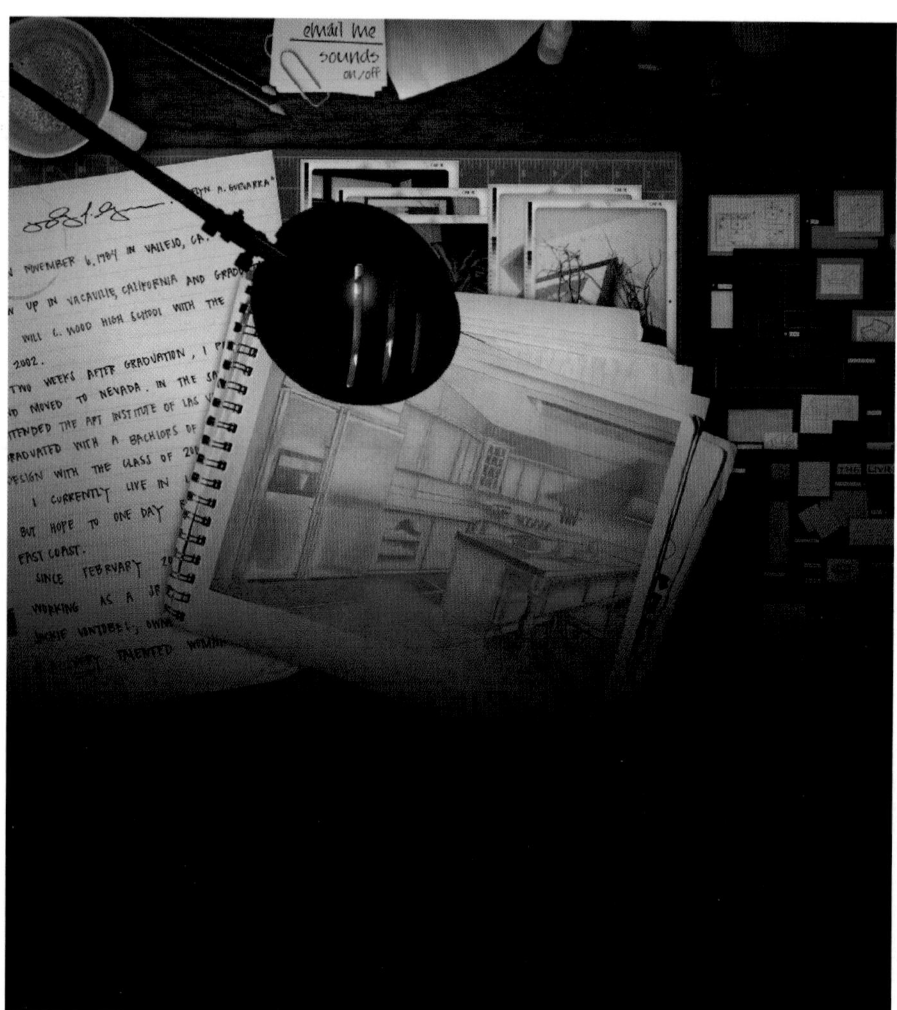

Info

Design and Programming: Chris Pierantozzi <chrispierantozzi@hotmail.com>. /// **Tools:** Adobe Photoshop, Adobe After Effects, Macromedia Flash. /// **Contents:** sketches, layouts and pictures. /// **Awards:** TINY, DOPE Awards. /// **Cost:** 200 hours.

JOHN VEGA & ASSOCIATES

USA

www.johnvega.com

2005

Concept

John Vega & Associates was designed to be an engaging interactive experience with the idea of "immersive travel" guiding the design. Use of an XML layer allows for easy edits and re-organization of the site. /// John Vega & Associates a été conçu comme une expérience interactive captivante, et c'est l'idée de « voyage en immersion » qui a guidé le design. Un calque en XML permet de modifier et de réorganiser facilement le site. /// John Vega & Associates wurde entwickelt mit dem Ziel, ein einbeziehendes, interaktives Erlebnis von „beeindruckender Reise" zu erschaffen. Der Einsatz einer XML-Schicht ermöglicht ein einfaches Editieren und Reorganisieren der Website.

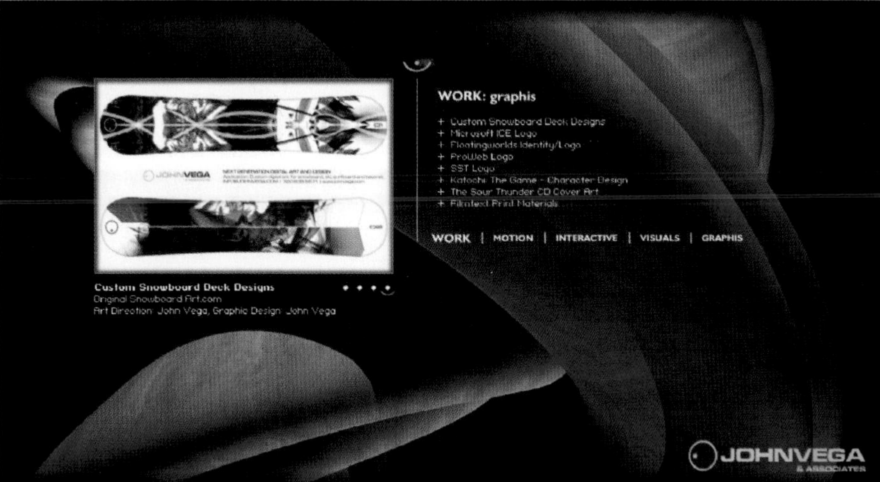

Info

DESIGN: John Vega <www.johnvega.com>. /// **PROGRAMMING**: Aaron Wilson <www.technic9.com>. /// **TOOLS**: Macromedia Flash, XML, HTML, Adobe Photoshop, Autodesk 3ds Max. /// **AWARDS**: TINY, 4EFX, NewWebPick, DOPE Awards, Design Firms, Web Smarty, e-Creative, Blue Idea, Design Pop, 2-Inside, Pixel Gangster. /// **CONTENTS**: Text, Flash Animation, QT Video, Digital Audio. /// **COST**: 92 hours.

KARMA PRODUCTION

BELGIUM

www.karma-production.com

2005

Concept

In this work we had to make feel the video production atmosphere. This Website also had to be sober, intuitive and built with dynamic content. /// Pour ce travail, nous devions rendre l'atmosphère de la production vidéo. Ce site devait également être sobre, intuitif, et son contenu devait être dynamique. /// Bei dieser Arbeit mussten wir die Atmosphäre einer Video-Produktion schaffen. Die Website sollte nüchtern wirken, aber gleichzeitig intuitiv und mit dynamischem Inhalt sein.

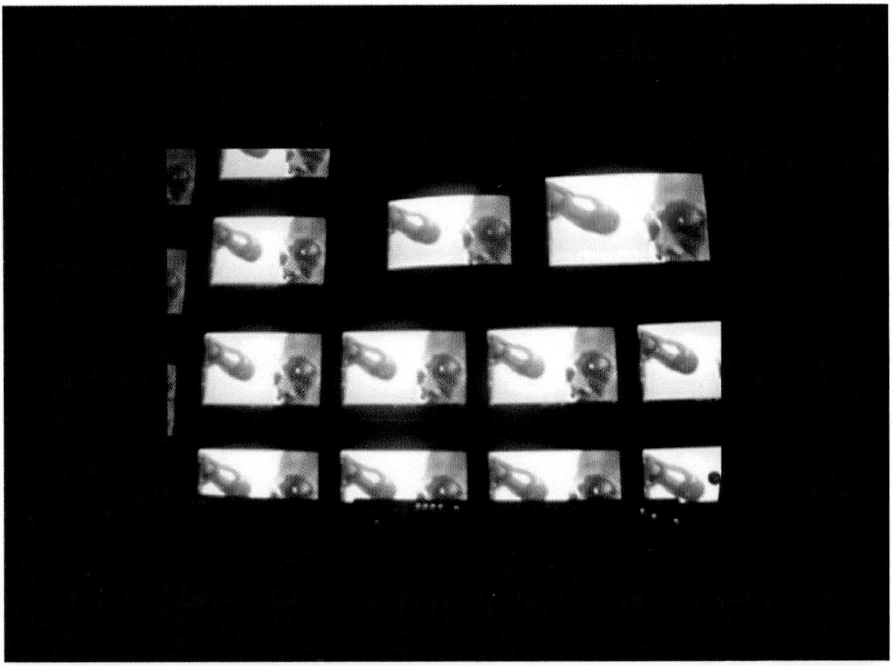

Info

Design and Programming: Fx. Marciat (xy area) <www.xyarea.com>. /// **Tools:** Macromedia Flash, Macromedia Dreamweaver, Macromedia Fireworks, php, xml, video, MySQL. /// **Contents:** video, music, photo, shop. /// **Awards:** e-Creative and various other notifications. /// **Cost:** 7 weeks.

KINETIC VERSION 4

SINGAPORE

www.kinetic.com.sg

2005

Concept

The site is done with a tongue-in-cheek approach and is entirely hand drawn to give it an edgy, less than perfect look. Other than the body copy, everything else is constantly in motion. /// Ce site a été fait avec beaucoup d'humour et est entièrement dessiné à la main pour lui donner une image plus nerveuse, imparfaite. À part le fond de l'écran, tout le reste est toujours en mouvement. /// Die Website wurde mit einem ironischen Ansatz konzipiert und ist von Hand gezeichnet, damit ein unebener, nicht ganz perfekter Look entsteht. Im Gegensatz zum Rahmentext sind alle anderen Elemente stets in Bewegung.

Info

DESIGN: Sean Lam & Kinetic Team. /// **PROGRAMMING**: Kinetic Team. /// **TOOLS**: Adobe Photoshop, Macromedia Flash, Macromedia Dreamweaver, Adobe Audition. /// **CONTENTS**: animation, video, photos. /// **AWARDS**: FWA, fcukstar.com. /// **COST**: 220 hours.

KOHN PEDERSEN FOX

USA

www.kpf.com

2005

Concept

This site is an immersive experience comprised of over 400 images from the firms greatest projects. By viewing "full screen" shots of every image, the site comes to life as an interactive and informative portfolio book. /// Ce site propose une immersion dans plus de 400 images des meilleurs projets de la société. En visionnant les clichés « plein écran » de chaque image, le site devient un portfolio interactif et informatif. /// Diese beeindruckende Website besteht aus über 400 Bildern der größten Projekte des Unternehmens. Beim Betrachten der Bilder unter Ausnutzung der vollen Bildschirmgröße wird die Website zu einem interaktiven und informativen Portfolio-Buch.

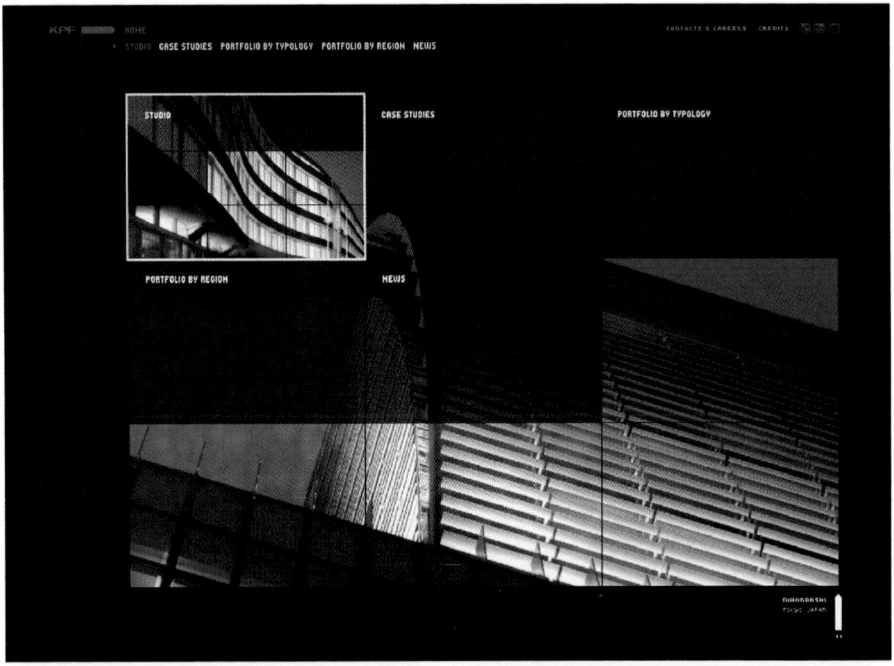

Info

Design: Vas Sloutchevsky (Firstborn) <www.firstbornmultimedia.com>. /// **Programming**: Joon Yong Park, Gicheol Lee (Firstborn). ///
Tools: Adobe Photoshop, Macromedia Flash, Macromedia Dreamweaver/ ASP, Visual Studio/ ASP.NET, SQL Server 2000. /// **Contents**: photographs. ///
Cost: 2.400 hours.

KRISTINA DRAGOMIR

ROMANIA

www.kristinadragomir.com

2005

Concept

Being multidisciplinary artist, Kristina had a lot of work to present. We had to come up with a way of presenting everything in an exciting way. The navigation system became the site's real novelty. /// Comme c'est une artiste multidisciplinaire, Kristina avait beaucoup de travail à présenter. Nous avons dû trouver une manière de présenter tout cela d'une manière intéressante. Le système de navigation est devenu la vraie originalité du site. **/// Da Kristina eine fachübergreifende Künstlerin ist, hatte sie sehr viele Arbeiten zu präsentieren. Wir mussten ihr einen Vorschlag für eine aufregende Darstellung unterbreiten.**

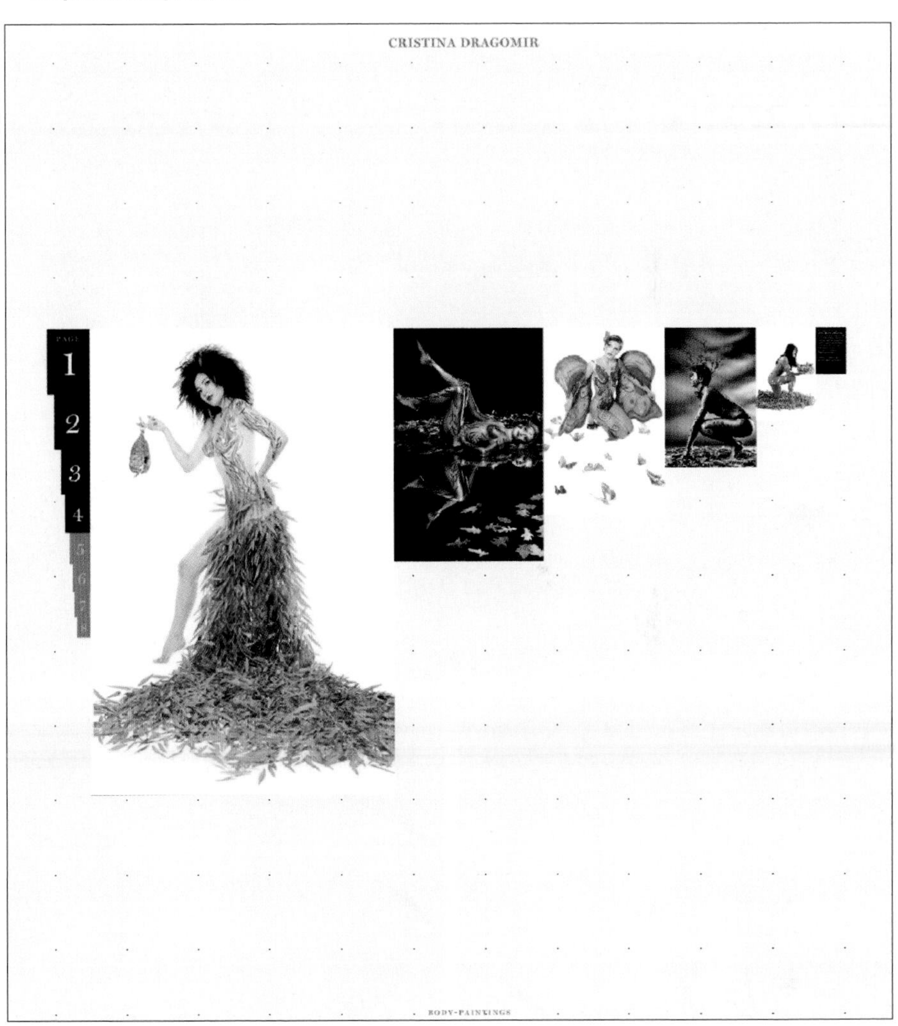

Info

Design and Programming: It's Everyday media <www.itseveryday.ro>. /// **Tools:** Macromedia Flash, Adobe Photoshop. /// **Contents:** photo, painting, art. /// **Awards:** FWA, Newstoday. /// **Cost:** 8 weeks.

LA FANO

ITALY

www.lafano.it

2005

Concept

The only way to bring the feeling of the firm, the product and the people of La Fano, is to do a hi impact flash site. /// La seule manière de rendre l'esprit de la société, du produit et des employés de La Fano, c'est de faire un site qui exploite Flash généreusement. /// **Die einzige Möglichkeit, ein Gefühl für das Unternehmen, die Produkte und die Mitarbeiter von La Fano zu vermitteln, war, eine „hi impact"-Flash-Website zu erstellen.**

Info

Design and Programming: Extera <www.extera.com>. /// **Tools**: Xhtml, Asp, Adobe Photoshop, Macromedia Flash. /// **Contents**: photo, text. /// **Awards**: Netdiver, Moluv, Pixelgangster.de, e-Creative. /// **Cost**: about 35 working days (client briefing, conceptual design, project design, implementation and testing).

LESS RAIN

UK/GERMANY

www.lessrain.com

2005

Concept

The Less Rain portfolio, updated to work on large resolutions, with a new showcase section, and our propaganda: "Say No to bad weather! Less Rain!" /// Le portfolio de Less Rain, mis à jour pour fonctionner avec de meilleures résolutions, avec une nouvelle section de présentation, et notre propagande : « Dites non au mauvais temps ! Moins de pluie ! ». /// Das Portfolio von Less Rain ist angepasst an hohe Auflösungen, verfügt über einen neuen Präsentationsbereich und unseren Slogan: „Say No to bad weather! Less Rain!"

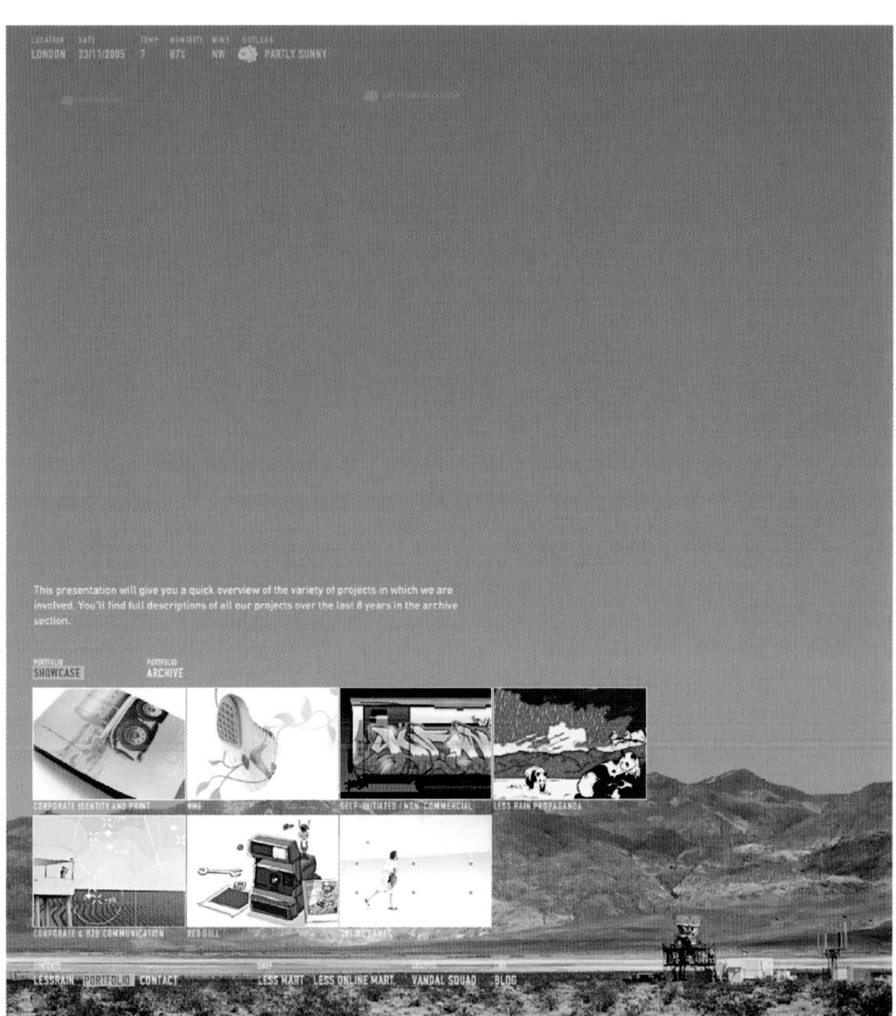

Info

Design: Lars Eberle, Matthias Netzberger, Carsten Schneider (Less Rain). /// **Programming**: Torsten Härtel, Thomas Meyer (Less Rain). /// **Tools**: Macromedia Flash (AS2), Adobe Photoshop, Macromedia Freehand, PHP / XML, XHTML, Eclipse. /// **Contents**: portfolio site with description, images of our work, team, etc. /// **Cost**: ongoing process.

LEVEN THUMPS

USA

www.leventhumps.com

2005

Concept

This new fantasy-adventure series is presented in a texture-rich interactive environment. The site's ambience and experience market the brand as a major player in its niche. /// Cette nouvelle série d'aventures fantasmatiques est présentée dans un environnement interactif aux textures riches. L'atmosphère du site positionne la marque comme un acteur important dans sa niche. /// Diese neue Fantasy-Abenteuer-Serie wurde in einer interaktiven texturreichen Umgebung präsentiert. Das Ambiente und die Erfahrung, die auf der Website zur Geltung kommen, lassen die Marke als die Wichtigste in ihrem Segment erscheinen.

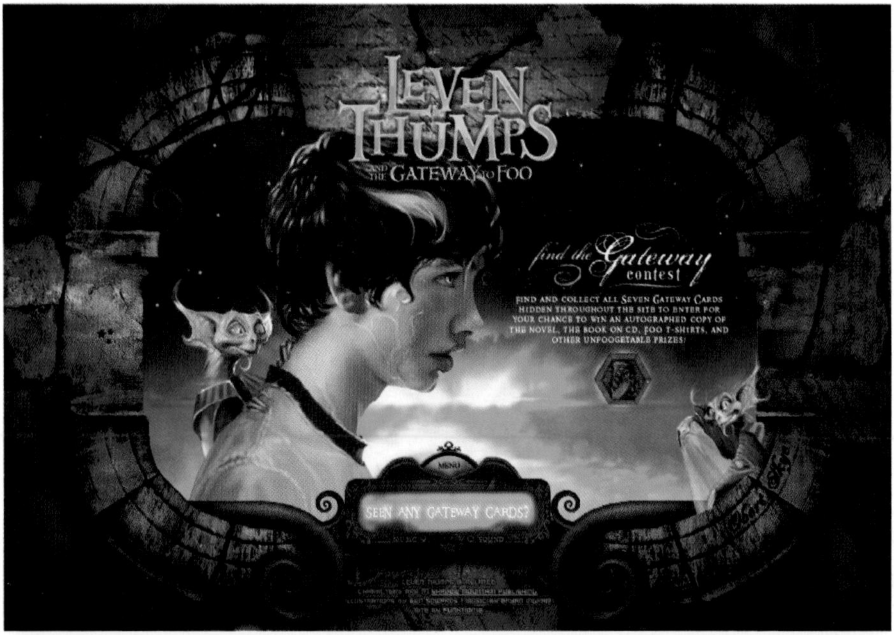

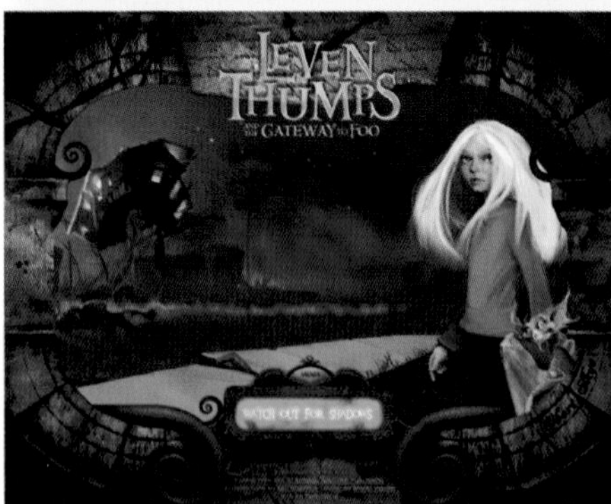

Info

Design: Funktion12 <www.funktion12.com>. /// **Tools**: Adobe Photoshop, Macromedia Flash. /// **Contents**: animation, music, text. Music by Bryan Ingram <www.bryaningrammusic.com>. /// **Awards**: FWA, Bombshock, TINY (Site of the Month).

LIBERONLINE HOLOGRAM

ITALY

www.liberonline.com

2005

Concept

LIBEROnline seeks to provide a harmony between design and experimentation in its creative approach. /// LIBEROnline, c'est la recherche de l'harmonie du design et de la dynamique à travers l'expérimentation d'une interface créative. /// **LIBEROnline versucht auf ihrer kreativen Oberfläche eine Harmonie zwischen Design und Experiment herzustellen.**

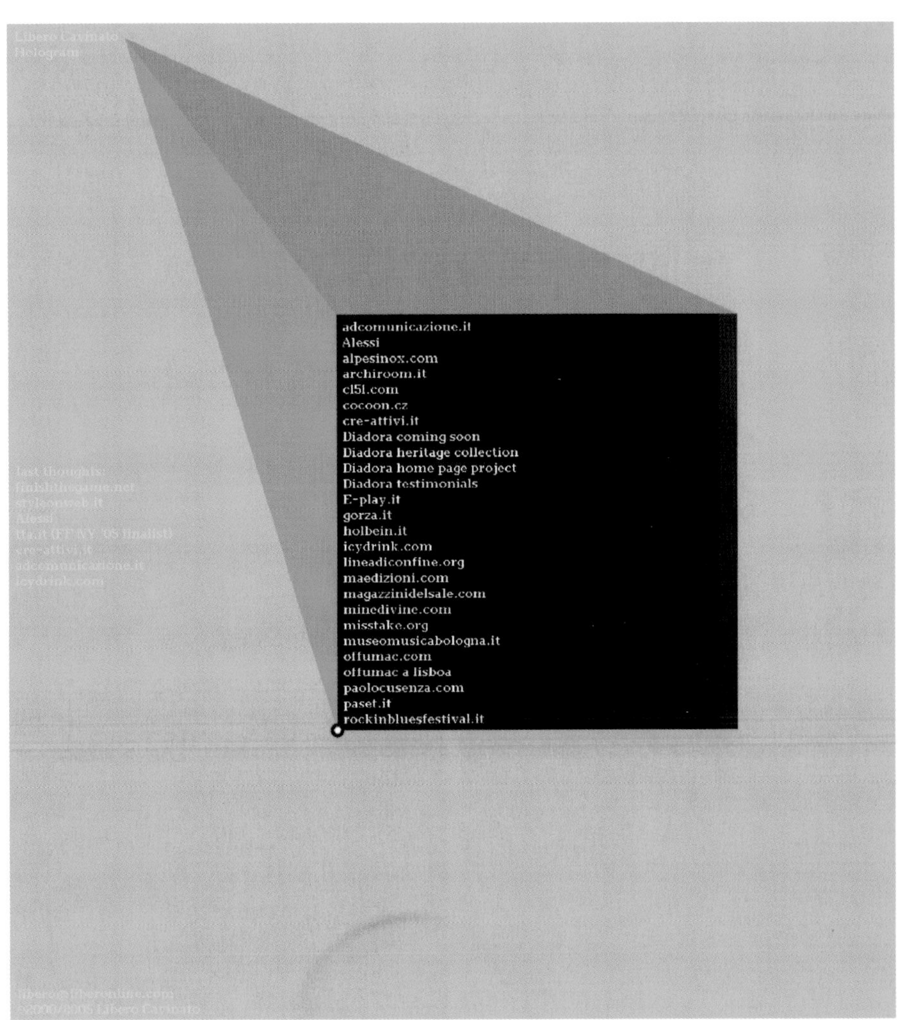

Info

Design and Programming: Libero Cavinato <www.liberonline.com>. /// **Tools:** Macromedia Flash, Adobe Photoshop, Remoting PHP. /// **Contents:** animation, programming, photo. /// **Awards:** Flashforward 2005 San Francisco Experimental Section (Finalist), FWA. /// **Cost:** 21 hours.

LIFEVISUALS

CANADA

www.lifevisuals.com

2005

Concept

Creating a "room of dreams" filled with the clients items. /// Créer une « chambre des rêves » remplie des objets des clients. /// Die Website ist ein „Raum der Träume", voller Elemente der Kunden.

Info

Design: 247 Media Studios. /// **Programming**: 247 Media Studios; Amberfly <www.amberfly.com>. /// **Tools**: Adobe Photoshop, Macromedia Flash, Cinema 4D, PHP, XML. /// **Contents**: pictures. /// **Awards**: FWA. /// **Cost**: 3 months.

LILLI PIOVESAN

BRAZIL

www.lillipiovesan.com.br

2005

Concept

The main difference is the combination of the modern flash animation with classic design elements. This provides the site its cozzy feeling. /// La principale différence, c'est la combinaison de l'animation Flash moderne avec des éléments de design classique. Cela donne au site son esprit douillet. /// Das Besondere an dieser Website ist die Kombination zwischen moderner Flash-Animation und klassischen Designelementen. Das verleiht der Website ihren harmonischen Charakter.

Info

Design: 6d Estúdio <www.6d.com.br>. /// **Programming**: Marlus Araújo & Gabriel Marques (6d Estúdio). /// **Tools**: Adobe Photoshop, Adobe Illustrator, Macromedia Flash. /// **Cost**: 90 hours.

LIVING DIVANI

ITALY

www.livingdivani.it

2005

Concept

You can jump to any part of the site at any point of the navigation because every voice of the menu is always available. /// Vous pouvez accéder à n'importe quelle partie du site à n'importe quel moment de la navigation, parce que chaque section du menu est toujours disponible. /// Man kann zu jedem Teil der Website und zu jedem Navigationspunkt springen, weil jeder Menüpunkt jederzeit erreichbar ist.

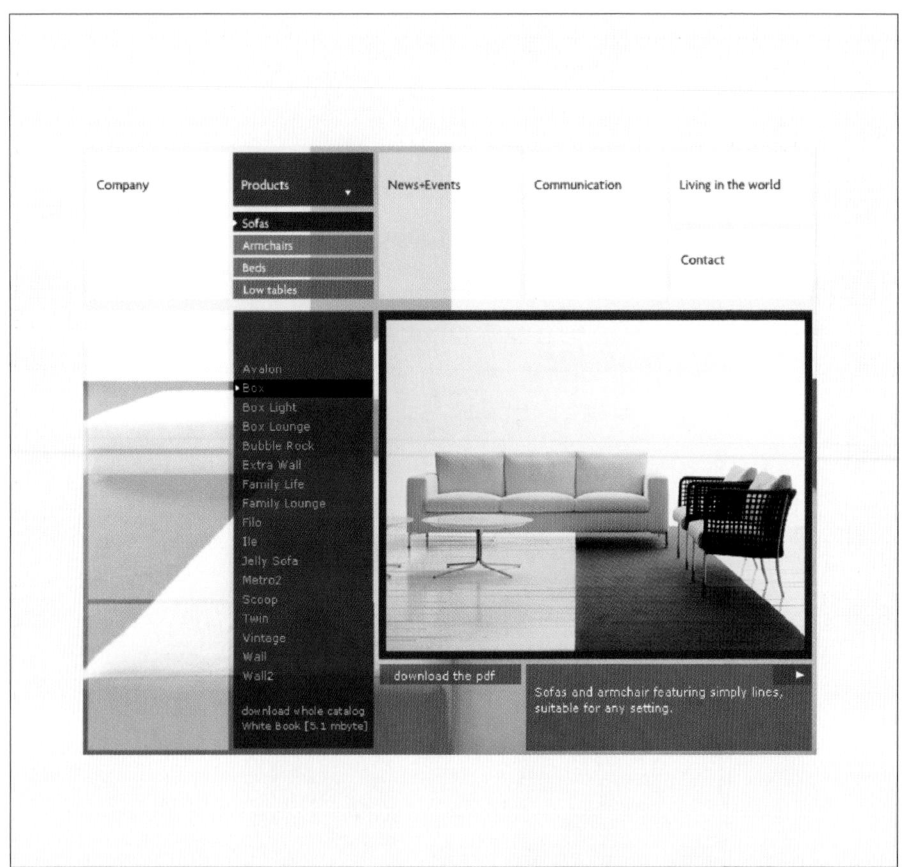

Info

Design: studio FM milano <www.studiofmmilano.it>. /// **Programming**: Parkmedia <www.parkmedia.com>. /// **Tools**: Adobe Illustrator, Macromedia Flash, Macromedia Dreamweaver. /// **Contents**: photo and text.

LOWEBULL

SOUTH AFRICA

www.lowebull.com

2005

Concept

Content within the site is accessed via interaction with the various floors of a virtual Lowe Bull Headquarters building. The unconventional execution reflects the culture of the ad agency - unorthodox, original and creative. /// On peut accéder au contenu du site en interagissant avec les différents étages d'un bâtiment virtuel du siège de Lowe Bull. L'exécution non conventionnelle reflète la culture de l'agence de publicité : non orthodoxe, originale et créative. /// **Der Inhalt der Website ist über Interaktion mit verschiedenen Stockwerken des virtuellen Hauptsitzgebäudes von Lowe Bull zugänglich. Die unkonventionelle Vorgehensweise spiegelt die Kultur der Werbeagentur wider – unorthodox, originell und kreativ.**

Info

Design and Programming: STONEWALL+ <www.stonewall.co.za>. /// **Tools:** XHTML/CSS, Bespoke PHP CMS, XML, Macromedia Flash with Flash Remoting. /// **Contents:** corporate information brought to life! /// **Cost:** 3 months.

LOWORKS

www.loworks.org

JAPAN

2005

Concept

This site is graphical and interactive. The navigation of this site has assimilated with the illustration. /// Ce site est graphique et interactif. La navigation du site se confond avec l'illustration. /// Es handelt sich hierbei um eine grafische und interaktive Website. Die Navigation ist in die Illustration eingebunden.

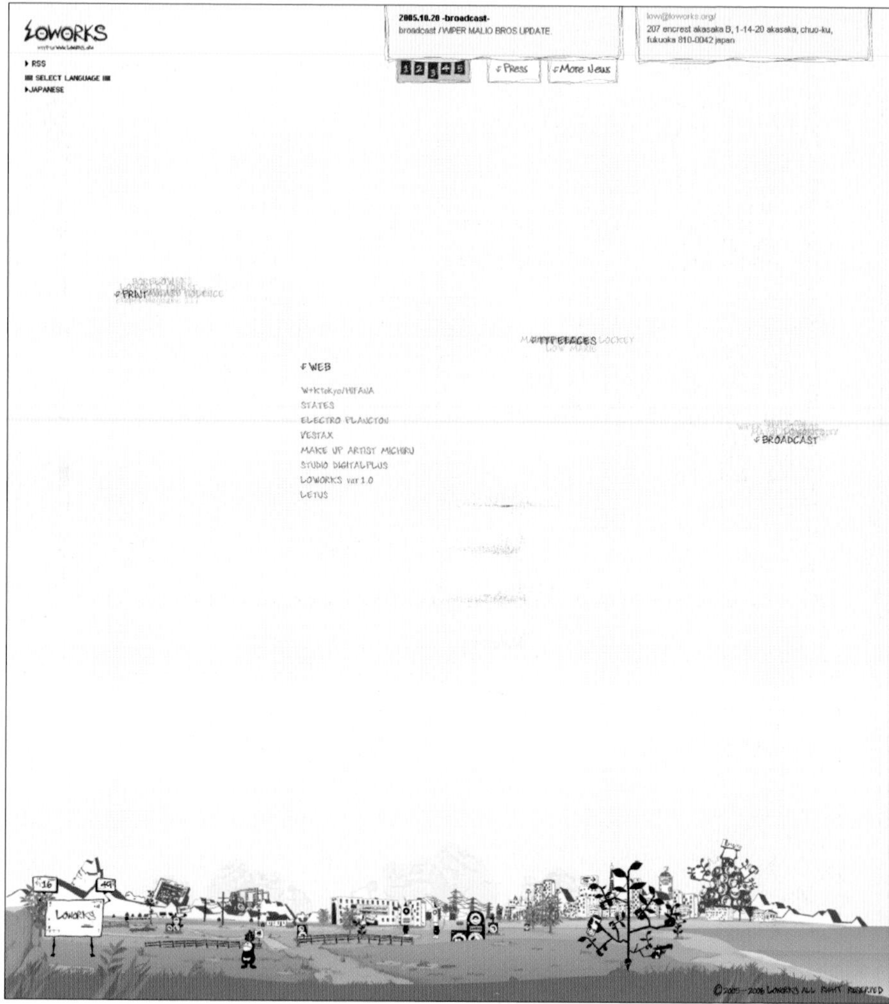

Info

Design and Programming: Haruki Higashi (Loworks). /// **Tools:** xhtml, Macromedia Flash, Adobe Illustrator, Autodesk 3ds Max. /// **Contents:** print, web, film, typefaces. /// **Awards:** Netdiver, FWA, WellVetted, Moluv, fcukstar.com. /// **Cost:** 3 months.

LUVGALZ

www.luvgalz.com

FRANCE
2005

Concept An edgy graphical environment using exclusively black, white and pink colors. A gallery showcasing works of various artists sharing a common goal: paying tribute to women. /// Un environnement graphique nerveux qui utilise exclusivement le noir, le blanc et le rose. Une galerie qui présente les travaux de différents artistes partageant un but commun : rendre hommage aux femmes. /// Die Website bietet eine prickelnde Umgebung, für die nur die Farben schwarz, weiß und pink benutzt werden. Eine Galerie mit Arbeiten von verschiedenen Künstlern, die ein gemeinsames Ziel haben: Frauen zu ehren.

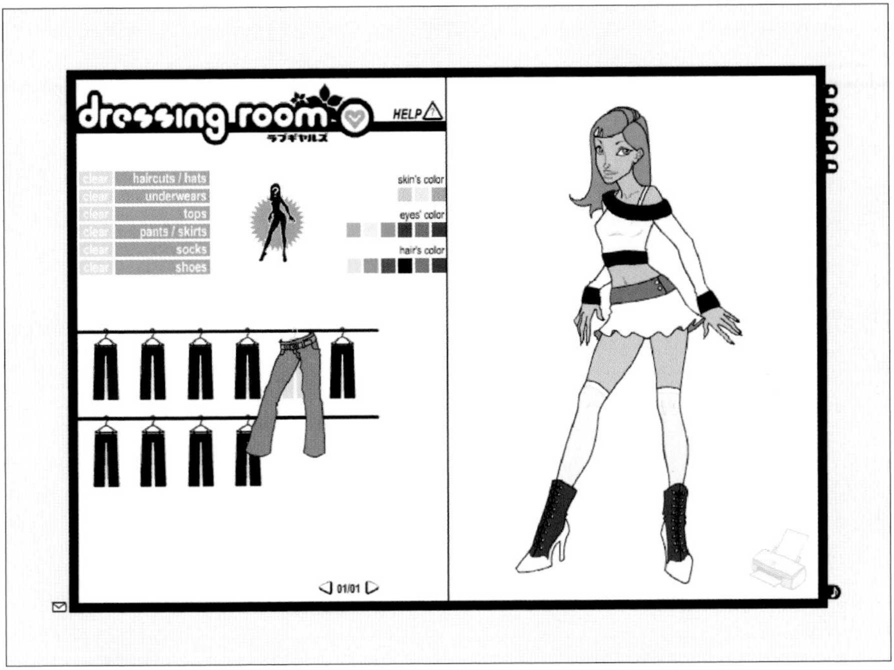

dressing room
HELP
clear haircuts / hats
clear underwears
clear tops
clear pants / skirts
clear socks
clear shoes
skin's color
eyes' color
hair's color
01/01

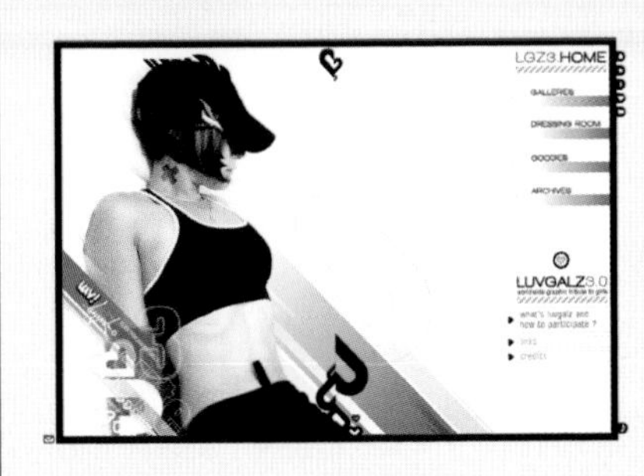

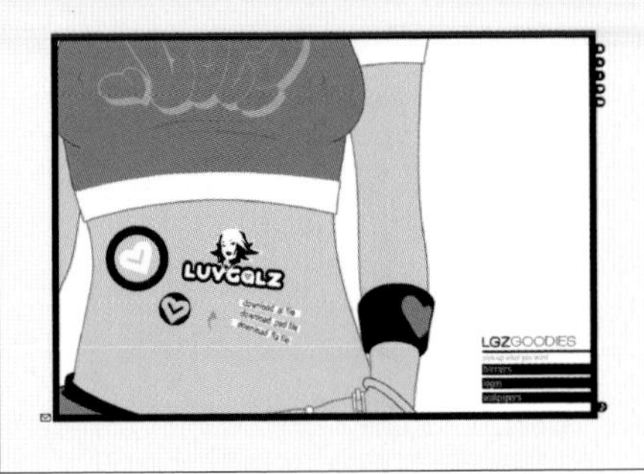

Info DESIGN: Stenkat <www.stenkat.com>. /// PROGRAMMING: Franck Sinatra <www.flasheur.com>. /// TOOLS: Macromedia Flash, Adobe Photoshop, Adobe Illustrator, CMS, php, Scite|Flash. /// CONTENTS: graphic design, illustration, photo, music, animation. /// AWARDS: Beautifully-Webdesign.net; DOPE Awards; NewWebPick; European Web Award; Ultrashock; Web Design Awards; TINY. /// COST: 8 months.

MAGICSOCKET

ITALY

www.magicsocket.com

2005

Concept **This websites is either a random 3d gallery about computer history either the showcase of magicsocket's works. Every cube and their movements are code-generated.** /// Ce site est soit une galerie 3D aléatoire sur l'histoire des ordinateurs, soit la présentation des travaux de magicsocket. Les cubes et leurs mouvements sont générés par code. /// **Diese Website stellt sowohl eine zufallsgenerierte 3D-Gallerie über Computer-Geschichte als auch die Präsentation der Arbeiten von magicsocket dar. Jeder Würfel und seine Bewegungen sind Code-generiert.**

Info **Design:** magicsocket. /// **Programming:** Mario Ballario, Marco Corti (magicsocket). /// **Tools:** MySQL, PHP, AmfPHP, Macromedia Flash, Adobe Photoshop, Autodesk 3ds Max. /// **Contents:** photo, animation. /// **Awards:** fcukstar.com. /// **Cost:** 480 hours.

MAGWERK

NORWAY

www.magwerk.com

2004

Concept

Not relevant - Our focus; We have declared war against the paper-industry to make the world a better place. MagWerk - No More Paper-cuts. /// Notre mission : nous avons déclaré la guerre à l'industrie du papier, pour donner naissance à un monde meilleur. MagWerk – On ne se coupera plus les doigts avec du papier. /// **Nicht relevant – nicht unser Schwerpunkt; Wir haben der Papier-Industrie den Krieg erklärt, damit die Welt besser wird. MagWerk – Schluss mit dem Papierschneiden!**

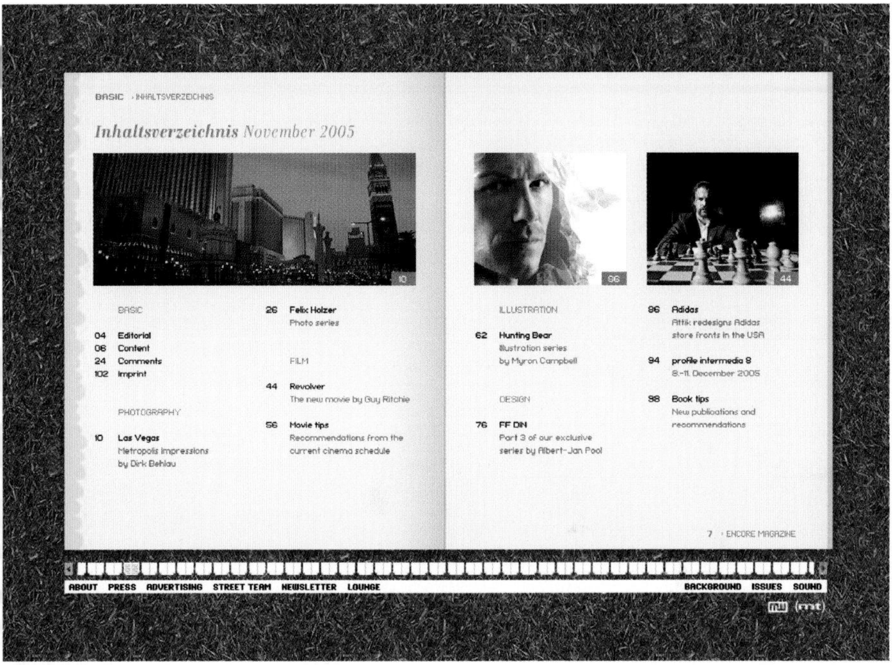

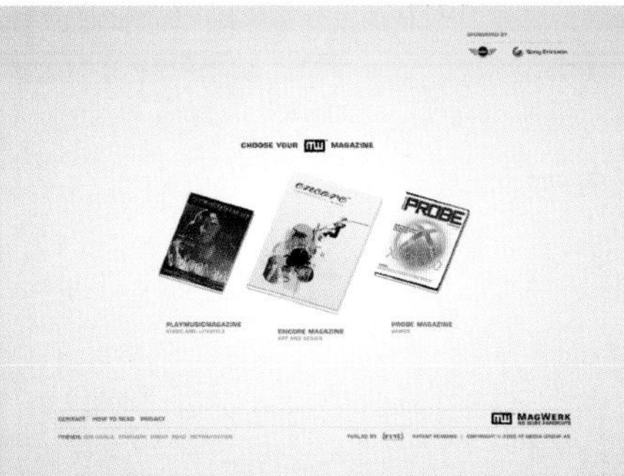

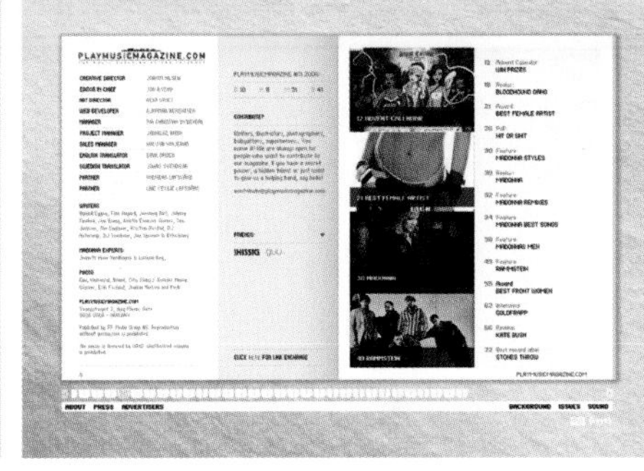

Info

DESIGN: (FF Media Group) Joakim Nilsen, Kent Loset, Paul Holliday, Per Kristian Stoveland, Jonas Svensson, Daniel Harrington, Pascal Jeschke. /// **PROGRAMMING:** Bjornar Berentsen. /// **TOOLS:** Macromedia MX, Adobe Photoshop, CMS MagWerk Engine™, xhtml, php, Adobe Illustrator, Sorenson Squeeze. /// **CONTENTS:** photo, music, games, films, animations, art, illustrations, blogs, communities. /// **AWARDS:** Macromedia (Site of The Day), Lead Award, Ultrashock BombShock, fcukstar.com, WellVetted. /// **COST:** 24 hours everyday.

MAKINE STUDIOS

USA

www.makinestudios.com

2005

Concept

Mecano's job was to develop a design in harmony with their style, and create a immersive, fun yet futile experience so the user will spend more time as possible exploring their universe. /// Le travail de Mecano était de développer une conception graphique en harmonie avec leur style, et d'immerger l'utilisateur dans leur univers ludique afin qu'il passe le plus de temps possible à l'explorer. /// Mecanos Aufgabe bestand in der Entwicklung eines Designs im Einklang mit ihrem Stil und in der Kreation eines interessanten, witzigen und doch unsinnigen Erlebnisses, damit der Benutzer so viel Zeit wie möglich bei Erforschung ihres Universums verbringt.

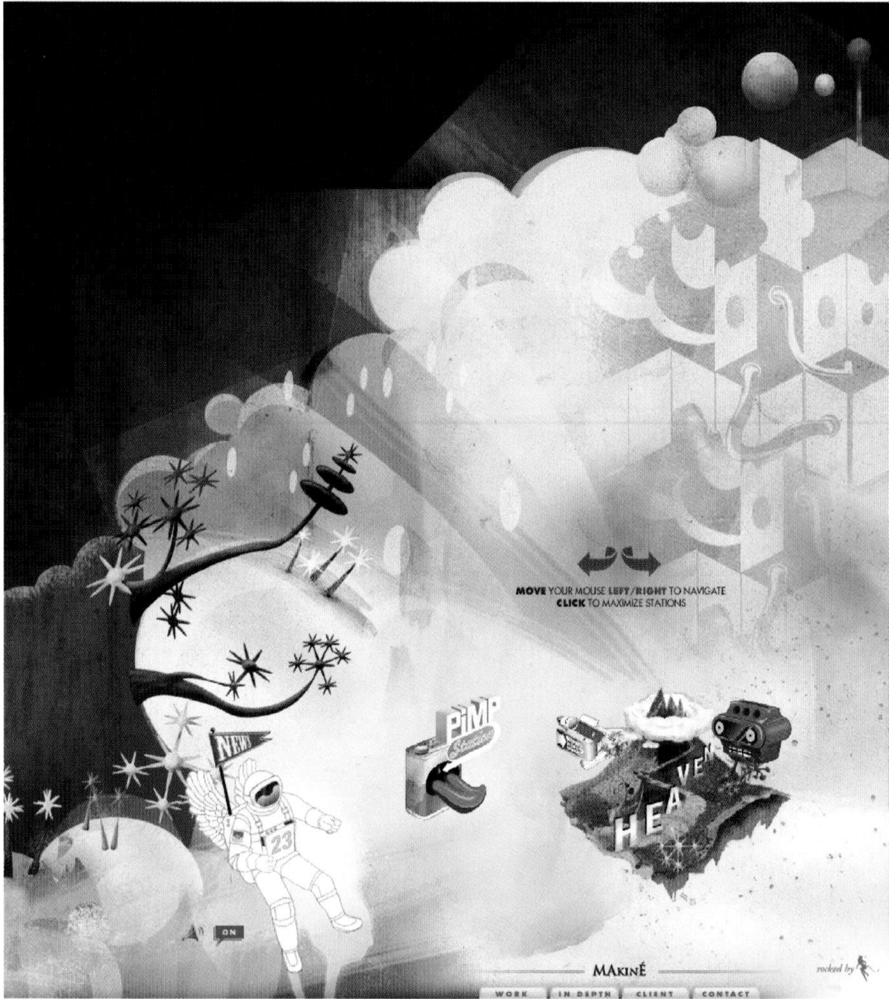

Info

Design and Programming: Mecano <www.mecano.ca>. /// **Tools**: Adobe Photoshop, Adobe Illustrator, Macromedia Flash, Sorenson Squeeze, AmfPHP, paper, pencil & brushes. /// **Contents**: photo, music, movies, games, animation. /// **Awards**: Lounge 72, Ventilate. /// **Cost**: 500 hours.

MARINA PENNO

ITALY

www.marinapenno.com

2005

Concept

While moving the mouse around the user can reach the site contents "swimming" among fishes, corals and shells, the menu ensures a quick access to each section of interest. /// En promenant sa souris, l'utilisateur peut accéder aux contenus du site en « nageant » au milieu des poissons, des coraux et des coquillages, mais le menu assure un accès rapide à chaque section. /// Während sich der Benutzer mittels Maus hin und her bewegt, „schwimmt" er unter Fischen, Korallen und Muscheln und kommt so an die Website-Inhalte. Das Menü ermöglicht einen schnellen Zugriff auf alle interessanten Bereiche.

Info

DESIGN: Marina Penno Advertising & Graphic Design. /// **PROGRAMMING**: Magicsocket <www.magicsocket.com>. /// **TOOLS**: MySQL, PHP, Macromedia Flash, Adobe Photoshop, Autodesk 3ds Max, Macromedia Freehand. /// **CONTENTS**: photo, animation. /// **AWARDS**: fcukstar.com. /// **COST**: 320 hours.

MARQUEENY

USA

www.marqueeny.com

2003

Concept

When the site came out in 2003, it was the hottest site in the industry and still is today. Good and simple design stays. /// Lors de sa publication en 2003, c'était le site le plus sensationnel du secteur, et c'est toujours le cas aujourd'hui. Un bon concept est une valeur sûre. /// Als die Website 2003 publiziert wurde, galt sie als die aufregendste Website. Gutes und einfaches Design setzt sich eben durch.

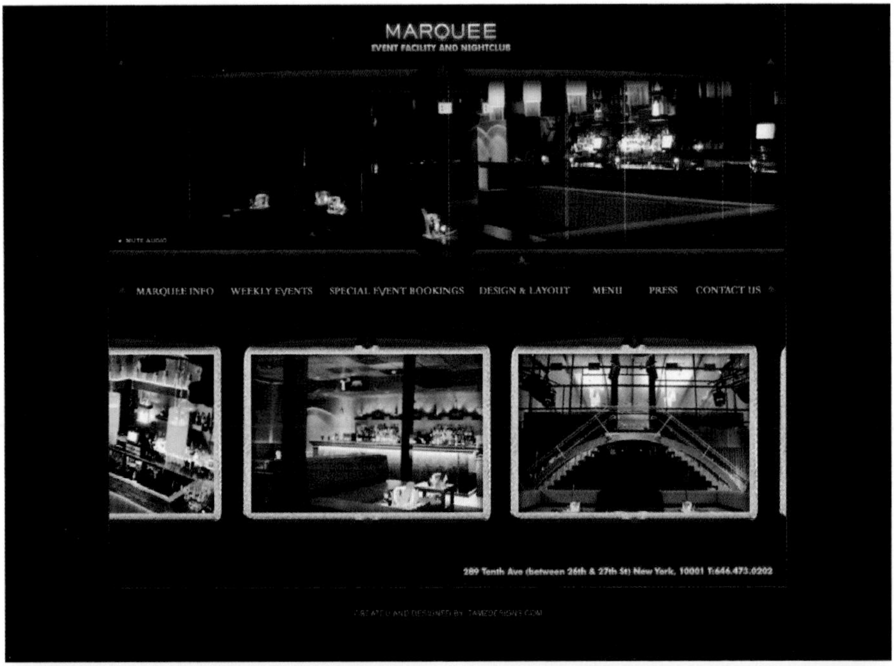

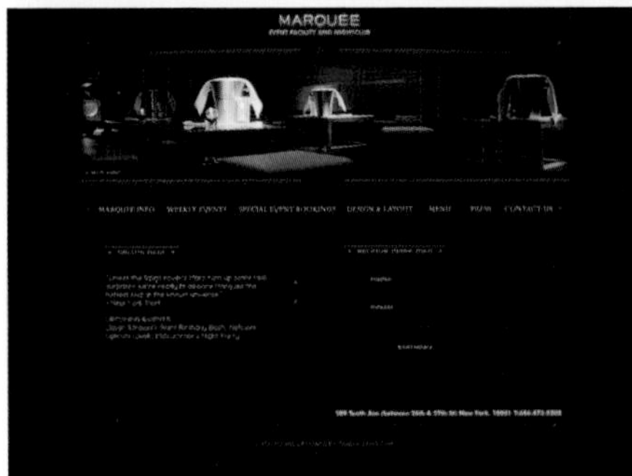

Info

DESIGN: Tamzdesigns >www.tamzdesigns.com>. /// PROGRAMMING: Scott Cook. /// TOOLS: Macromedia Flash, Macromedia Dreamweaver, Adobe Photoshop. /// CONTENTS: photo, music, animation, text. /// COST: 2 Weeks.

MATTHEW MAHON

USA

www.matthewmahon.com

2005

Concept

Wefail created me one of the most dynamic photography website on the internet today. They created a site that is not only compelling and ballsy, but entertaining as well. /// Wefail a créé pour moi l'un des sites de photographie les plus dynamiques d'Internet aujourd'hui. Ils ont créé un site qui est non seulement fascinant et gonflé, mais aussi divertissant. /// **Wefail konzipierte für mich eine der dynamischsten, fotografischen Websites, die heutzutage im Internet zu finden sind. Sie hat eine Website erschaffen, die nicht nur fesselnd und mutig ist, sondern auch unterhaltsam.**

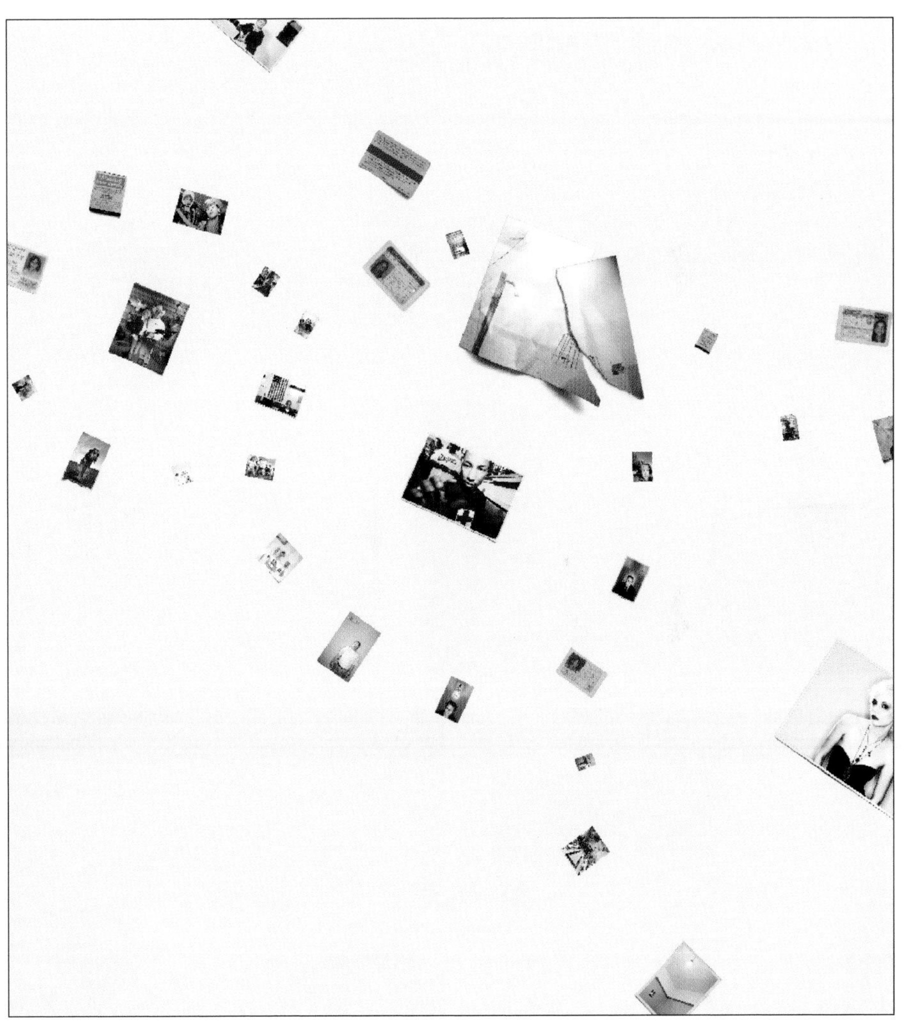

Info

DESIGN: We Fail <www.wefail.com>. /// **TOOLS**: Adobe Photoshop, Macromedia Flash, and a sound editing program . /// **CONTENTS**: photography. /// **COST**: 8 weeks.

MUSEUM OF CONTEMPORARY ART USA

www.mcartdenver.org 2005

Concept

The site is designed to convey the feeling of being in the museum, moving from room to room, interiors complete with "visitors" serving as the site backdrop, providing the illusion of a shared museum experience. /// Le site est conçu pour donner l'impression de se trouver dans le musée, d'aller de salle en salle. Des intérieurs garnis de « visiteurs » servent d'arrière-plan, et donnent l'illusion de visiter le musée en compagnie d'autres personnes. /// Die Website wurde so entworfen, dass sie das Gefühl vermittelt, als wäre man in einem Museum und würde sich von einem Raum zum anderen bewegen. In den Innenräumen befinden sich Menschen, die als Hintergrund dienen und der Website die Atmosphäre eines gemeinsamen Museumsbesuches geben.

we are the
MUSEUM OF
CONTEMPORARY
ART | DENVER

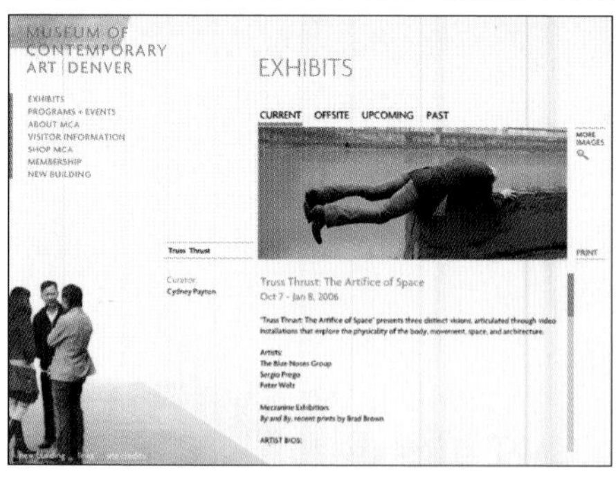

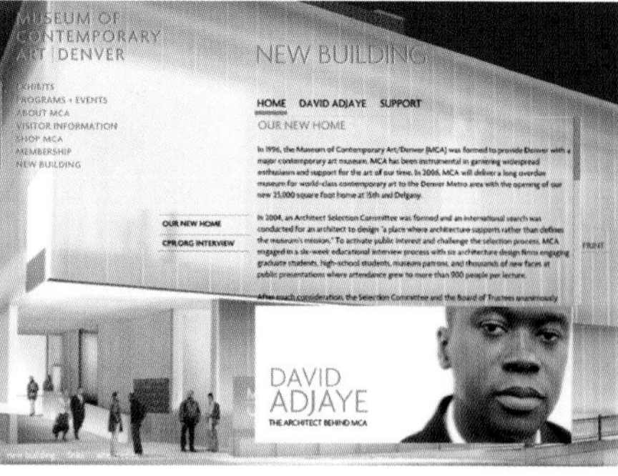

Info

DESIGN: Ian Coyle (FL2) <www.fl-2.com>; <www.hello-sexy.com>. /// **PROGRAMMING**: Ian Coyle & Nathan Kurach (FL2). /// **TOOLS**: Macromedia Flash, Adobe Photoshop, asp.net, Xhtml, css. /// **CONTENTS**: photo, 3d renderings. /// **AWARDS**: Communication Arts (Site of the Week), American Design Awards (Platinum).

MÉCHANT CHOCO

CANADA

www.mechantchoco.com

2005

Concept

The navigation concept uses broken pieces of static images to emulate a 3D video panoramic. Somehow like stop-motion. /// Le concept de navigation utilise des morceaux d'images statiques pour simuler un panoramique vidéo en 3D. Un peu comme en stop-motion. /// Das Navigationskonzept nutzt Stücke von gebrochenen, statischen Bildern, um ein 3D-Videopanorama zu erhalten, ähnlich wie die „stop motion"-Technik.

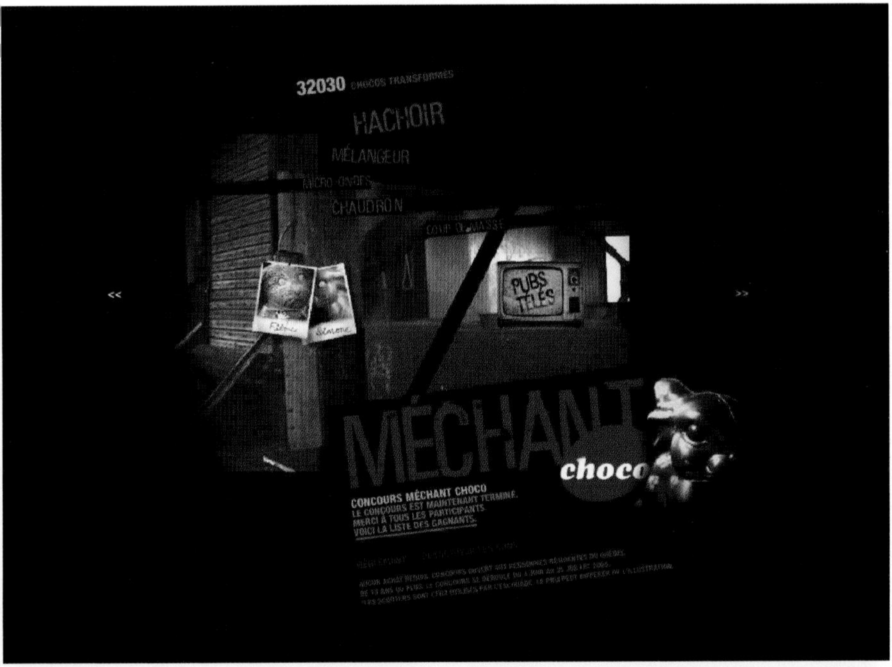

Info

DESIGN: BBDO Montreal <www.bbdo-montreal.com> in collaboration with Mecano <www.mecano.ca>. /// **PROGRAMMING**: Mecano. /// **TOOLS**: Adobe Photoshop, Adobe Illustrator, Macromedia Flash, PHP. /// **CONTENTS**: photo, music, movies, animation. /// **COST**: 250 hours.

MINORITY

SPAIN

www.minority.es

2005

Concept

A new agency without a portfolio. We had to attract viewers with almost zero content. Zoom in - zoom out and sliding navigation plus nice illustrations make it work. /// Une nouvelle agence sans portfolio. Il fallait attirer les visiteurs, presque sans aucun contenu. Le zoom avant et arrière et la navigation par glissement, ainsi que de bonnes illustrations, font que notre site fonctionne. /// **Eine neue Agentur ohne Portfolio. Wir mussten Zuschauer fast ohne Inhalte gewinnen. Mit Zoom und gleitender Navigation, und mit netten Bildern ist es gelungen.**

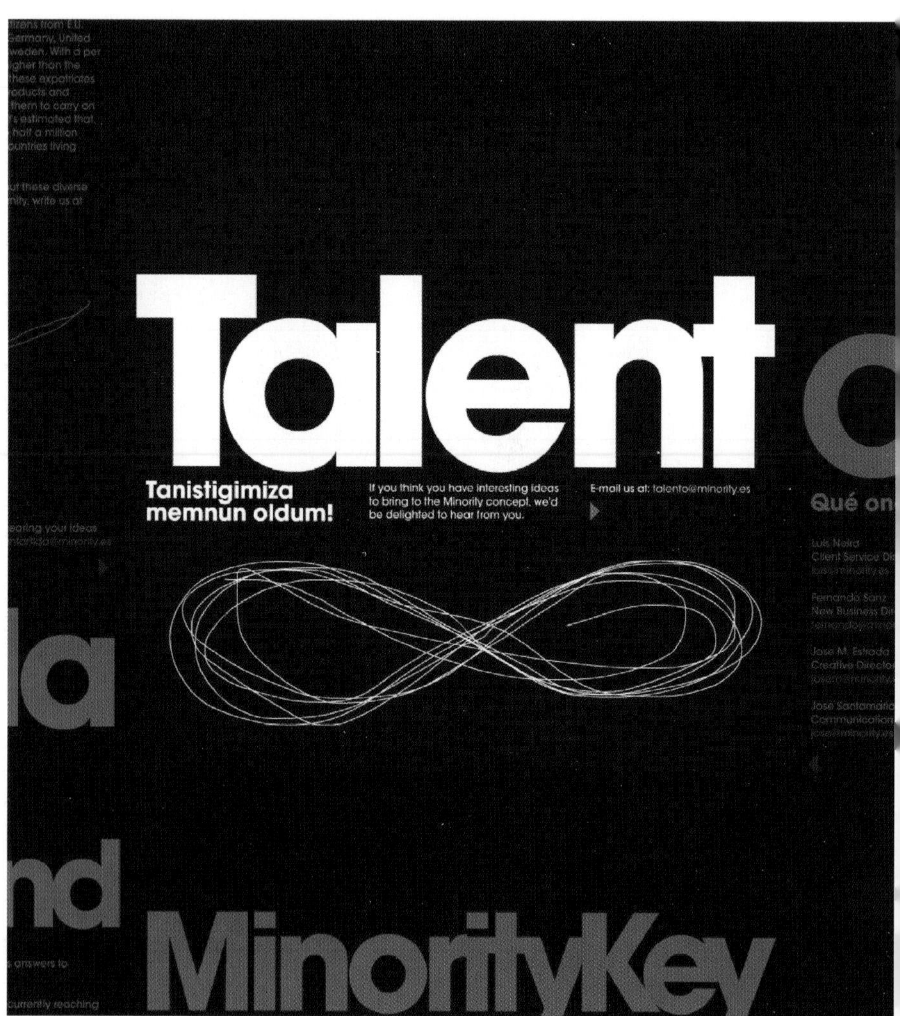

Info

Design and Programming: It's Everyday media <www.itseveryday.ro>. /// **Tools:** Macromedia Flash, Adobe Illustrator. /// **Contents:** illustration meets BoldFatType and a bit of script. /// **Cost:** 2 weeks.

MODE

UK

www.mode-online.co.uk

2005

Concept

Mode didn't want to be just another design company with a portfolio, this site focuses on the elegance of typography and pacing. /// Mode ne voulait pas être une simple société de design avec un portfolio. Ce site se concentre sur l'élégance de la typographie et sur le rythme. /// Mode wollte nicht einfach nur ein weiteres Design-Unternehmen mit Portfolio sein. Die Website konzentriert sich auf die Eleganz der Typografie und des Tempos.

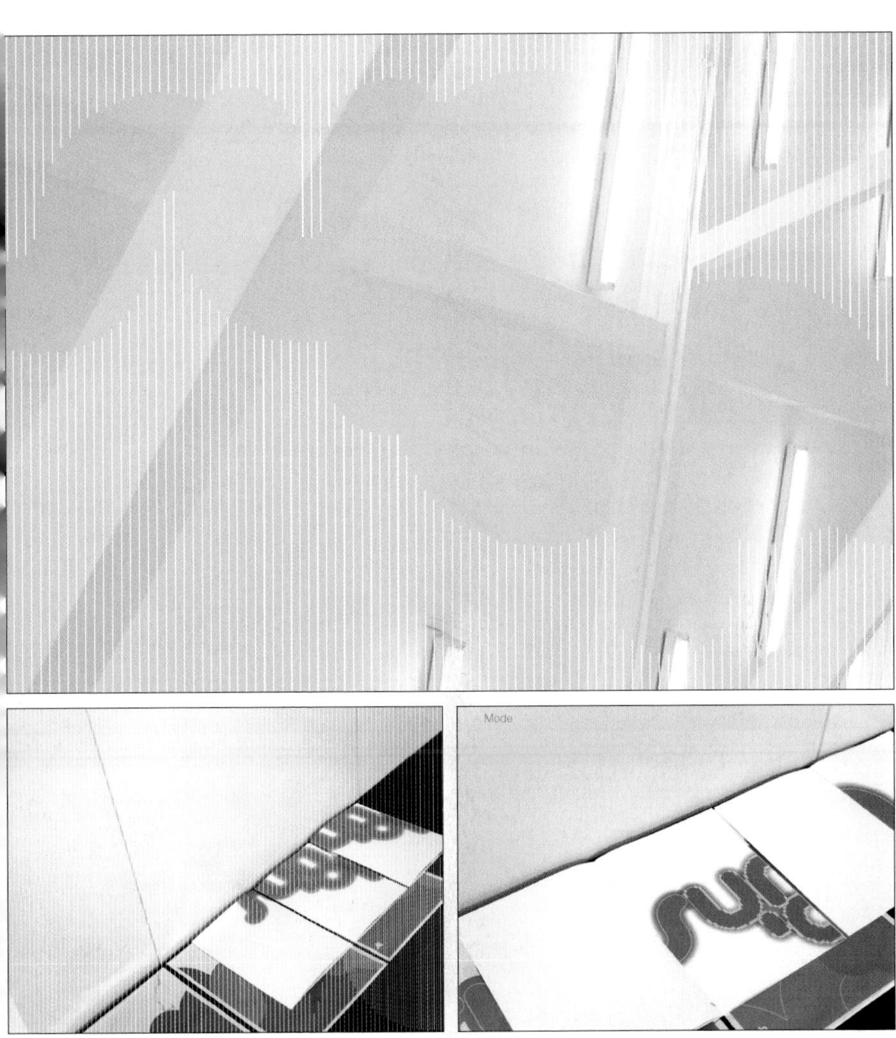

Info

Design: Engage <www.engagestudio.com>, and Mode. /// **Programming**: James Stone (Engage). /// **Tools**: Macromedia Flash and custom made animation tools. /// **Contents**: portfolio. /// **Cost**: 1 month.

MOLSON USA

USA

www.molsonusa.com

2005

Concept

Tongue-in-cheek humor with interactivity that shows Molson is more than a beer, it also helps you connect with others. /// De l'humour, de l'ironie et de l'interactivité, pour montrer que Molson c'est plus qu'une simple bière. Elle vous aide aussi à entrer en contact avec les autres. /// Ironie in Verbindung mit Interaktivität in der Form, in Molson sie einsetzt, ist mehr als nur ein Bier. Sie hilft auch, in Verbindung mit anderen zu treten.

Info

Design and Programming: Hello Design <www.hellodesign.com>. /// **Tools:** PHP, XML, Macromedia Flash, Adobe Photoshop, Adobe Illustrator. /// **Contents:** browse, search, or filter by themes. Training & tools. /// **Awards:** HOW Interactive Design Competition. /// **Cost:** 4 months.

MOONCRUISE

CANADA

www.mooncruise.com

2004

Concept

We wanted to maintain a rich user experience by capturing the essence of a magazine, without resorting to mimicking print magazines. /// Nous voulions capturer l'essence d'un magazine, sans pour autant imiter les magazines imprimés. /// Wir wollten ein intensives Erlebnis für die Benutzer erzeugen, indem wir die wesentlichen Züge einer Zeitschrift erfassten, und zwar ohne die gedruckten Zeitschriften zu imitieren.

Info

DESIGN: Trevor Brady <www.trevorbrady.com>. /// **PROGRAMMING**: Aleksander Katusenko. /// **TOOLS**: Macromedia Flash, Macromedia Dreamweaver, Adobe Photoshop, xml, .NET. /// **CONTENTS**: photography, music. /// **AWARDS**: Yahoo (site of the day), Design TAXI (site of the day). /// **COST**: the initial design and framework took about 80 hours. Each issue takes about 10-15 hours of development.

FALLEN VODKA

UK

www.moresoul.com

2005

Concept

Layered content loads in randomly and disintegrates while user input adds to the structured chaos and reinforces the central theme - that there is 'more soul in imperfection'. /// Les contenus sur plusieurs calques se chargent de façon aléatoire et se désintègrent, pendant que les actions de l'utilisateur nourrissent le chaos structuré et renforcent le thème central : il y a un supplément d'âme dans l'imperfection. /// Geschichtete Inhalte werden nach dem Zufallsprinzip geladen und zerfallen, sobald der Benutzer seinen Beitrag zum strukturierten Chaos macht. Dies verstärkt die zentrale These – dass „Unvollkommenheit mehr Seele enthält"

Wabi-sabi
"The true gourmet, like the true artist, is one of the unhappiest creatures existent. His trouble comes from so seldom finding what he constantly seeks: perfection."
Ludwig Bemelmans

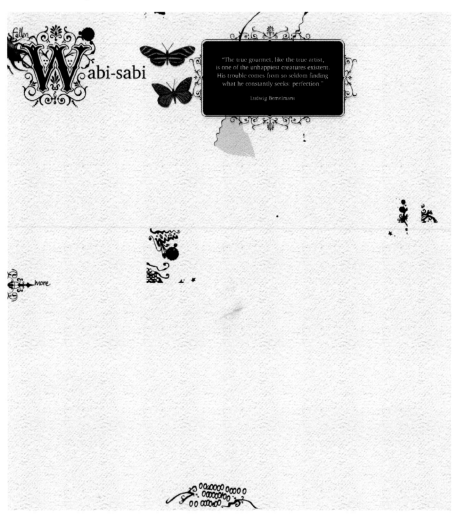

Info

DESIGN: Matt Rice, Hege Aaby (Sennep) <www.sennep.com>. /// **PROGRAMMING**: Matt Rice, Mikkel Askjær (Sennep). /// **TOOLS**: Macromedia Freehand, Macromedia Flash, Adobe Photoshop, PHP, MySQL, pen & paper. /// **CONTENTS**: illustration, text, animation and user input relating to the overall concept that there is "more soul in imperfection". /// **COST**: 390 hours.

MYST V GAME

USA

www.mystvgame.com

2005

Concept

Thanks to his innovative widescreen format, the Myst V website keeps up with web trends. We have tried to create the best atmosphere for a real attractive user experience. /// Grâce à ce format d'écran large innovant, le site Myst V évolue avec les tendances d'Internet. Nous avons essayé de créer la meilleure atmosphère possible pour que la visite du site soit vraiment intéressante. /// Dank ihres innovativen Panorama-Bildschirm-Formats, ist es der Myst V-Website gelungen mit den neuesten Trends Schritt zu halten. Wir haben versucht, das beste Ambiente für ein wirklich attraktives Erlebnis zu schaffen.

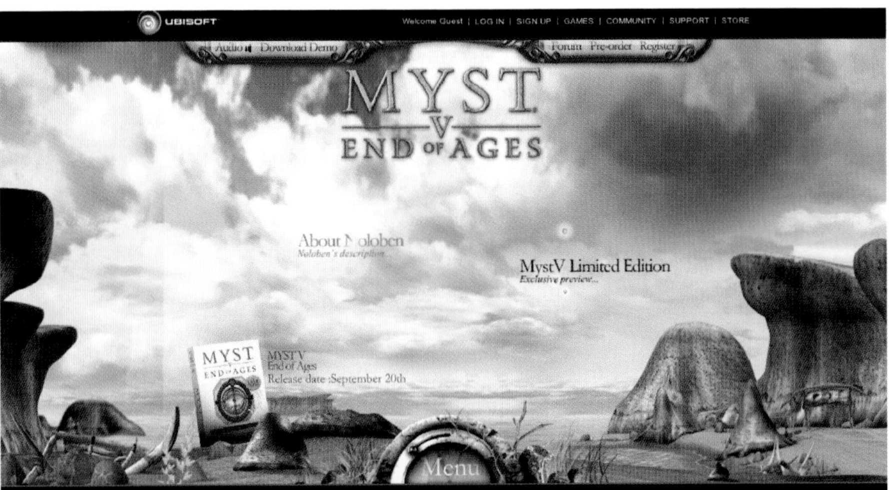

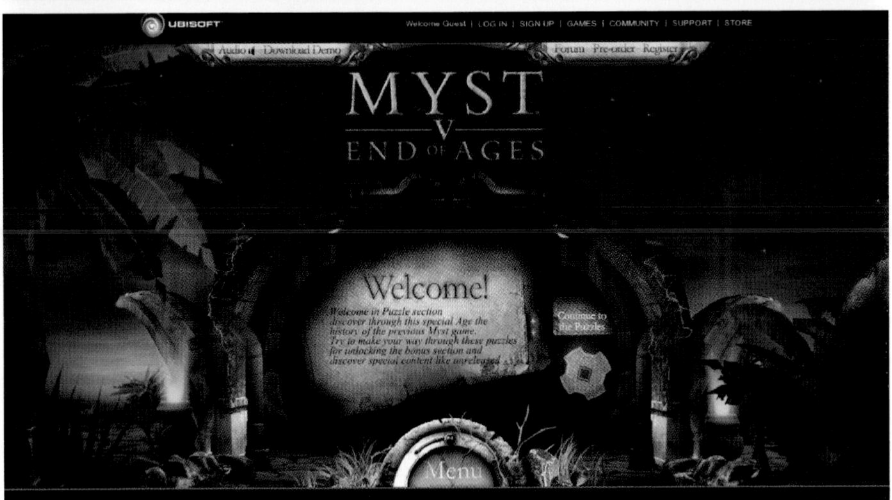

Info

Design: Aster <www.synthesis01.com> [Soleil Noir] <www.soleilnoir.net>. /// **Programming**: Mx. <www.montegnies.net> [Soleil Noir] <www.soleilnoir.net>. /// **Tools**: localised website using XML content, Macromedia Flash using shared objects function. /// **Contents**: text content, pictures, video, animated content. /// **Awards**: FWA. /// **Cost**: 21 days of development [every backgrounds have been made by ourself and are mixing different graphic contents of the game].

NATSMASH

USA

www.natsmash.com

2005

Concept

NatSmash.com was designed the way any portfolio piece should be — as a memorable experience. The site proves to be as interactive and entertaining as the work it was built to display. /// NatSmash.com a été conçu comme tout portfolio devrait l'être : une expérience mémorable. Le site se révèle être aussi interactif et ludique que le travail qu'il présente. /// NatSmash.com wurde so konzipiert, wie eine Portfolio-Website sein sollte —unvergesslich. Die Website hat sich als genauso interaktiv und unterhaltsam bewährt, wie der Inhalt, der präsentiert wird.

Info

Design and Programming: Nathaniel (NATSMASH). /// **Tools:** Macromedia Flash, Adobe Photoshop, Adobe Photoshop, Alien Skin's Machine Wash. /// **Contents:** design, illustration, animation, advertising. /// **Awards:** designsnack Golden Cookie, Design Firms, Flashpearls, Creative Public (designer of the month), Mars Moon, Kokonut, Website Design Awards, Internet Vibes, Atlantis Media, Flashloaded, Coolwebsites, Gouw, Design Collector, Carldesigns, Funkbuilders, Pixelmakers. /// **Cost:** 120 hours.

NESTEA COOL

INTERNATIONAL

http://nesteacool.com

2004

Concept

I quick but fun interactive experience that lets users interact directly with the brand mascot. /// Une visite rapide mais amusante qui permet aux utilisateurs d'interagir directement avec la mascotte de la marque. /// Bei dieser Website handelt es sich um eine schnelle, witzige und interaktive Flash-Animation. Der Benutzer kann mit dem Marken-Maskottchen spielen.

Info

DESIGN AND PROGRAMMING: Juxt Interactive <www.juxtinteractive.com>. /// **TOOLS**: Adobe Photoshop, Adobe Illustrator, Macromedia Freehand, Macromedia Flash. /// **CONTENTS**: interactive music video maker, tons of animation. /// **AWARDS**: Step Interactive Design Awards. /// **COST**: 2 months.

NESTEA ICE

INTERNATIONAL

http://nesteaice.com

2005

Concept

This site presents users with a very unique and entertaining brand experience that is full of great content. The tee shirt designer is quite a robust application. /// Ce site présente aux utilisateurs une visite vraiment unique et amusante autour d'une marque, avec beaucoup de contenus intéressants. L'application de personnalisation de tee-shirt est une application robuste. /// Diese Website bietet dem Benutzer ein einzigartiges und unterhaltsames Marken-Erlebnis voller außergewöhnlicher Inhalte. Eine amüsante Anwendung ist der „Tea-Shirt"-Designer.

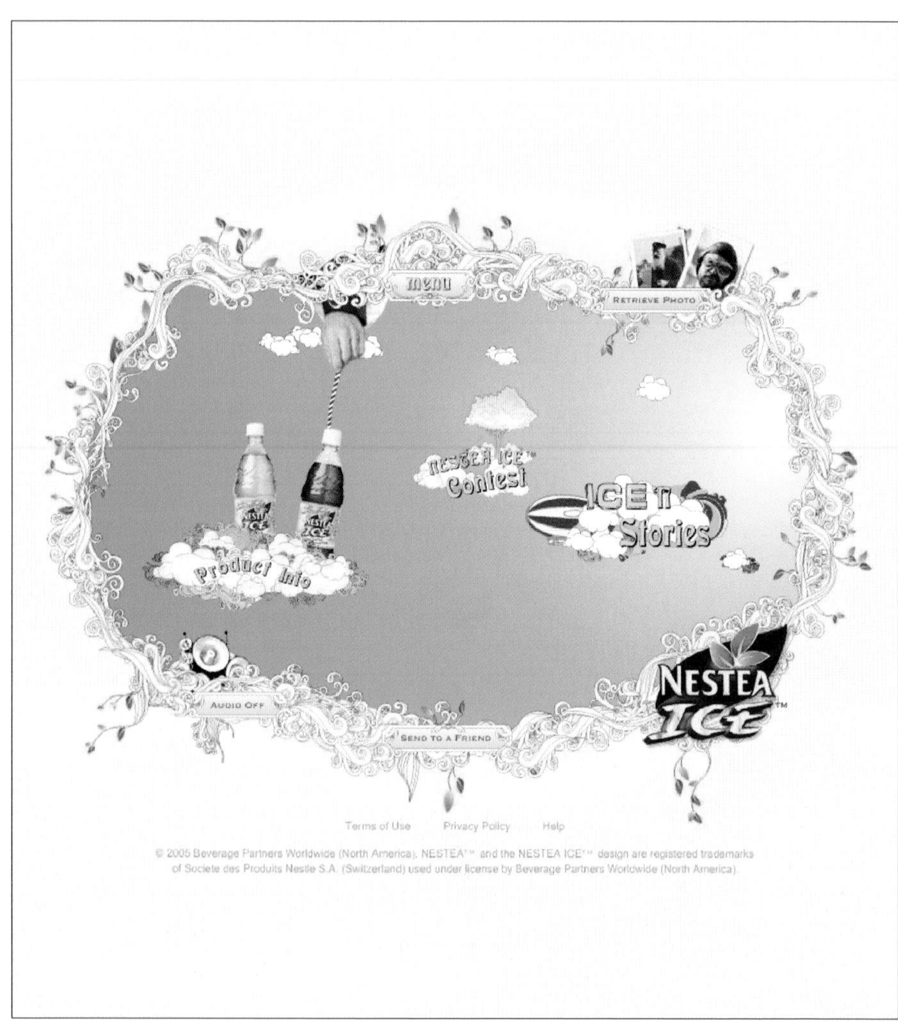

Info

Design and Programming: Juxt Interactive <www.juxtinteractive.com>. /// **Tools:** Adobe Photoshop, Adobe Illustrator, Macromedia Freehand, Macromedia Flash, Finalcut, Adobe After Effects, Swift 3d. /// **Contents:** brand entertainment featuring videos games, polls and a T-shirt design application. /// **Awards:** London International Design Awards, Design Interact (Site of the Week). /// **Cost:** 4 months.

NEWPANIC

USA

www.newpanic.com

2004

Concept

Other flash sites don't make cool forts, boxes do. /// Les autres sites Flash ne font pas de bons forts, mais les cartons, si. /// **Selbst mit Paketen kann man Geld machen, wie die Website zeigt.**

Info

DESIGN: Giancarlo Yerkes (Newpanic). /// **TOOLS**: CMS, PHP, XML, Adobe Photoshop, Adobe Illustrator, Macromedia Flash. /// **CONTENTS**: bubble wrap, portfolio, photos, packing peanuts, animations, drawings, information. /// **AWARDS**: American Design Awards, NewWebPick, DOPE Awards, Crossmind, Blue Idea, Netdiver, Res72.

NIKE.JP

JAPAN
2004

www.nike.jp

Concept

Rich AD graphic. Uncluttered Menu. Modifiability by Movable Type. /// Des graphismes AD très riches. Le menu est clair. Modifiable par type d'élément mobile. /// Reichhaltiges, grafisches Werbematerial. Nicht überladenes Menü. Veränderbar durch verschiedene Schrifteffekte.

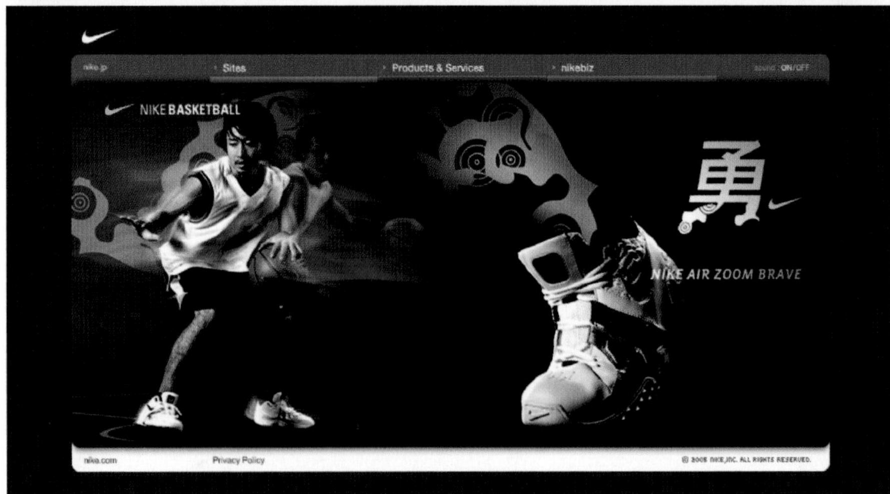

Info

Design: Shun Kawakami (artless Inc.) <www.artless.gr.jp>. /// **Programming:** Takashi Kamada (spfdesign) <www.spfdesign.com>. /// **Tools:** Adobe Photoshop, Macromedia Flash. Movable Type, xml. /// **Contents:** Nike, sports.

THE NOBLE SURFER

POLAND

www.noblesurfer.com

2005

Concept

Flash technology, video sequences, animations, perfectly matching music and sound effects together give a unique result - see it for yourself. /// Technologie Flash, séquences vidéo, animations, une musique en parfaite harmonie et des effets sonores. Tout cela donne un résultat unique. Voyez par vous-même. /// **Flash-Technologie, Video-Sequenzen, Animationen, perfekte Übereinstimmung von Musik und Toneffekten, alles zusammen führt zu einem einzigartigen Ergebnis – sehen Sie selbst.**

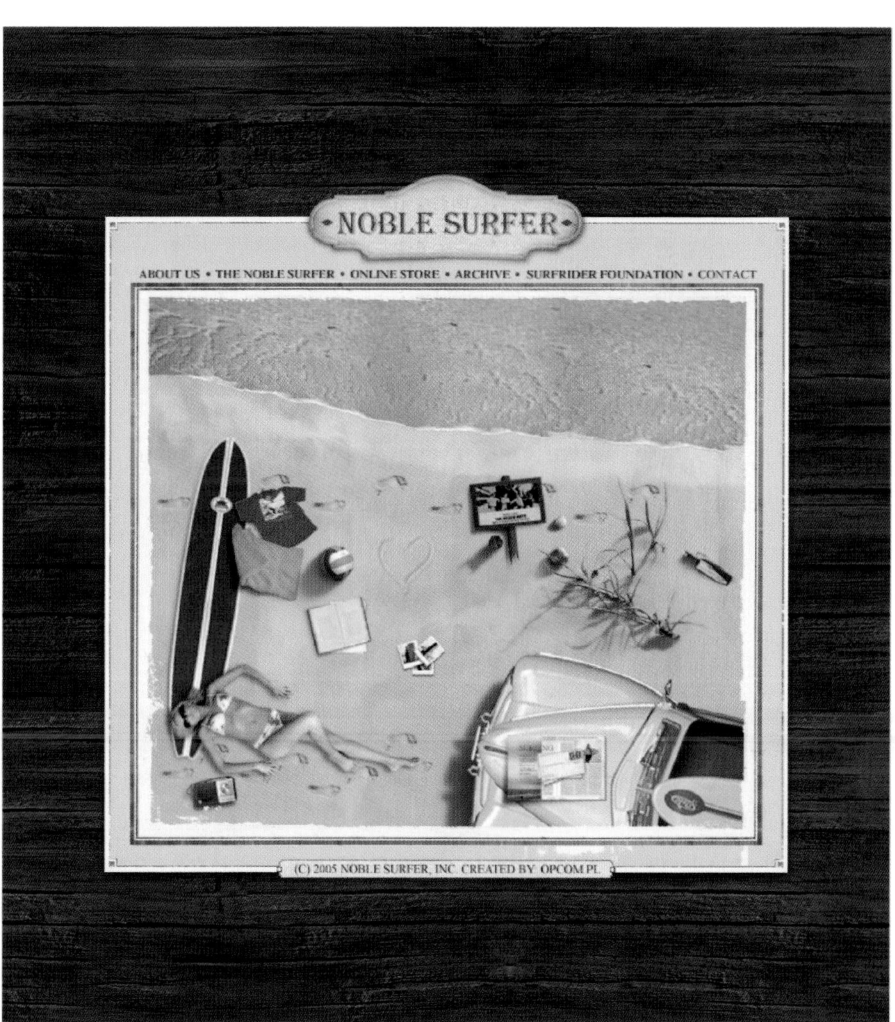

Info

Design: OPCOM.pl <www.opcom.pl>. /// **Tools**: Php, Macromedia Flash. /// **Contents**: photo, video, animation, music. /// **Awards**: Webesteem (Site of the Month), Pixelmakers (Site of the Week), Cult-Favorites. /// **Cost**: 250 hours.

NOREIGN STUDIOS

USA

www.noreign.com

2005

Concept

A site were the user could have every section open at once. /// Un site où l'utilisateur pourrait ouvrir toutes les sections en même temps. /// Es ist eine Website, bei der alle Bereiche gleichzeitig geöffnet werden.

Info

DESIGN: Giancarlo Yerkes <www.newpanic.com>. /// **PROGRAMMING:** Darren Cline <www.8mod.com>. /// **TOOLS:** CMS, PHP, XML, Adobe Photoshop, Adobe Illustrator, Macromedia Flash, Adobe After Effects, Cubase SX. /// **CONTENTS:** "the world won't wait".

NORTH KINGDOM

SWEDEN

www.northkingdom.com

2005

Concept

It is unusual that webdesign agencies put such great effort on their own portfolio site. This Flash site displays its work in a unique way. /// Il est inhabituel qu'une agence de design web investisse autant d'efforts dans son propre site de présentation. Ce site Flash présente son travail de façon exceptionnelle. /// Es ist ungewöhnlich für eine Webdesign-Agentur, so viel Mühe in die eigene Portfolio-Website zu investieren. Diese Flash-Website präsentiert die eigene Arbeit auf eine einzigartige Weise.

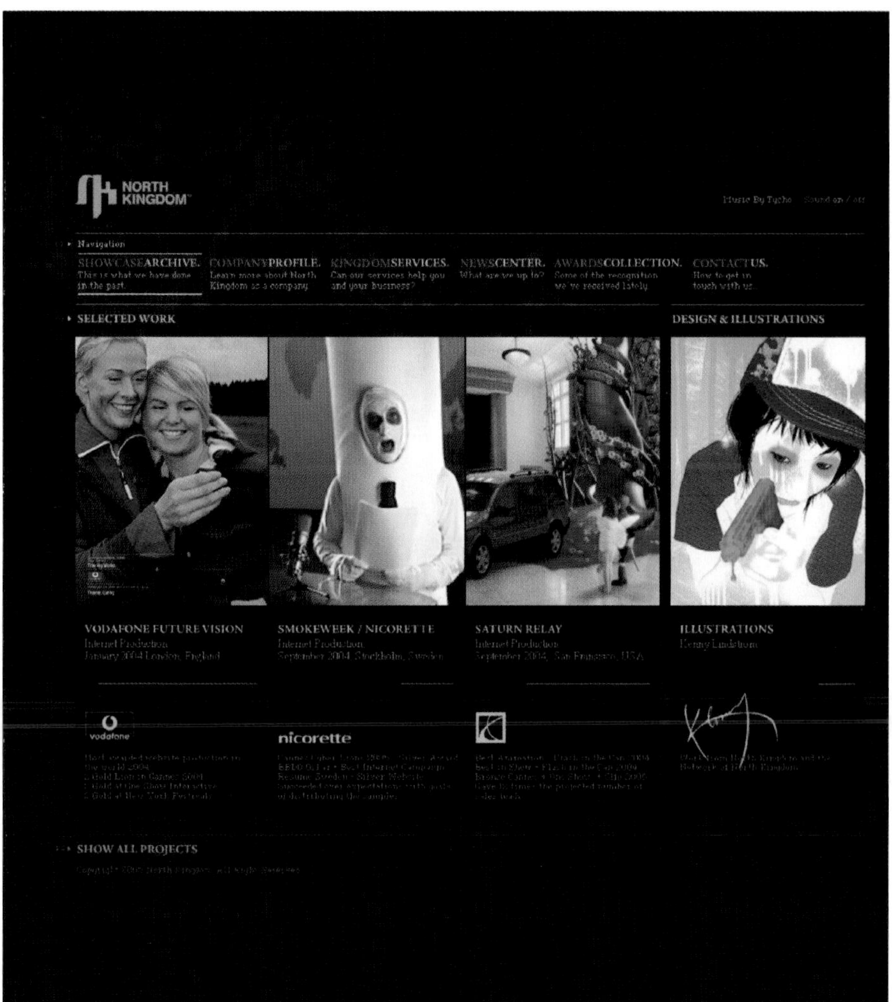

Info

Design and Programming: North Kingdom. /// **Tools:** Adobe Photoshop, Macromedia Flash. /// **Awards:** FWA (Site of the Day). /// **Cost:** 600 hours.

PAPER JAM DESIGN

NORTHERN IRELAND

www.paperjamdesign.com

2005

Concept

We designed this website with images in mind. The layout is completely 'liquid' and will work for any size of screen. The interaction drives discovery. /// Nous avons conçu ce site avec certaines images en tête. La présentation est complètement « liquide » et fonctionne avec toutes les tailles d'écran. L'interaction amène la découverte. /// Wir haben diese Website mit einer bestimmten Vorstellung entworfen. Das Layout ist absolut ‚flüssig' und wird bei jeder Bildschirmgröße funktionieren. Interaktion fördert Entdeckung.

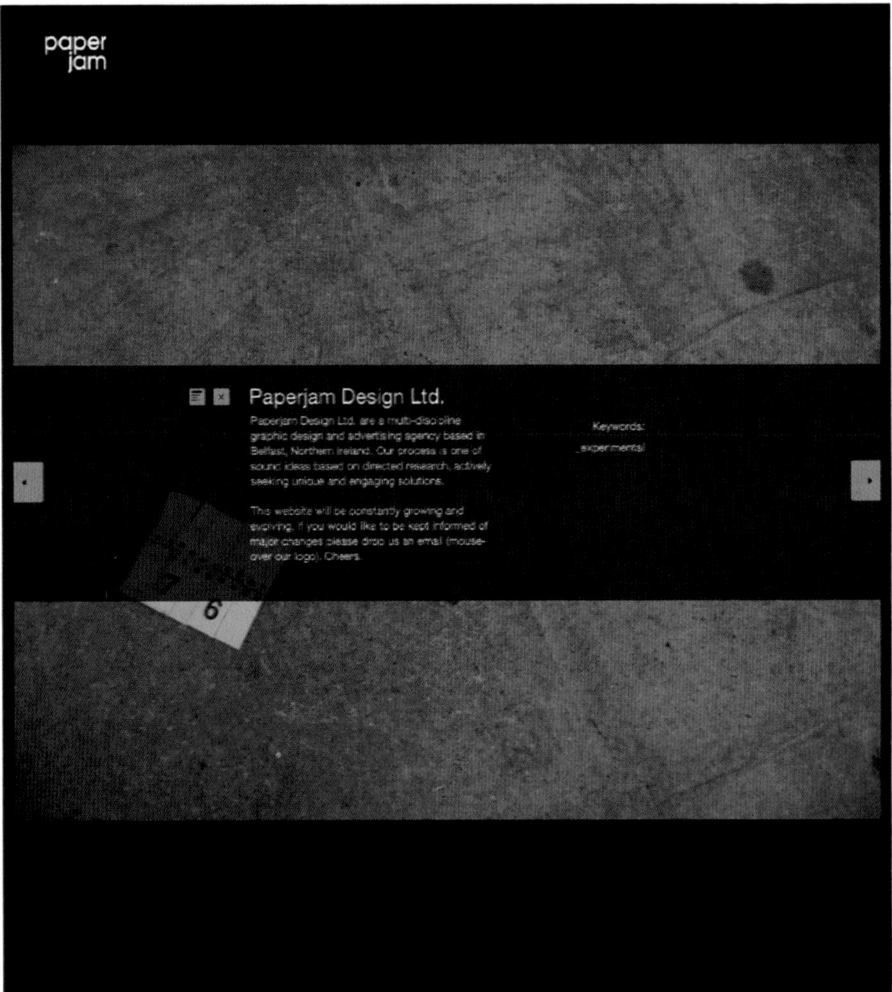

Info

Design: FRONT <www.designbyfront.com>. /// **Programming**: Matt Hutchinson (FRONT). /// **Tools**: Macromedia Flash, xml, php, CMS. /// **Contents**: photo, content managed information. /// **Awards**: Pixelsurgeon.

PARADISE GUEST RANCH

USA

www.paradiseranch.com

2004

Concept

Paradise Ranch's website creates a fun western adventure to excite and promote Paradise Guest Ranch in Wyoming. Filled with sounds, animation, and high quality photography, it brings the west to the web. /// Le site de Paradise Ranch recrée une drôle d'aventure western pour promouvoir le Paradise Guest Ranch, dans le Wyoming. Rempli de sons, d'animations, et de photographies de grande qualité, il fait vivre l'Ouest sur le web. /// Die Website von Paradise Ranch bietet ein witziges Western-Abenteuer, um für die Paradise Guest Ranch in Wyoming Interesse zu wecken und zu werben. Voller Animationen, Fotos und Toneffekte sehr guter Qualität bringt diese Website den Westen ins Internet.

Info

Design and Programming: Ian Coyle (FL2) <www.fl-2.com>. /// **Tools**: Macromedia Flash, Adobe Photoshop, asp.net, xml. /// **Contents**: photos, video, animation, music. /// **Awards**: South by Southwest Interactive 2005 (Finalist), American Design Awards (Gold).

PEEPSHOW

UK

www.peepshow.org.uk

2005

Concept

The photographic carousel and slides are manipulated in Flash to create a tactile, simple navigation that makes Peepshow's vast portfolio of illustration and animation easy to explore. /// Le panier et les diapositives sont manipulés en Flash pour créer une navigation simple et tactile, qui facilite l'exploration du vaste portfolio d'illustration et d'animation de Peepshow. /// Das Rundmagazin mit den Dias wird im Flash bedient und so entsteht eine berührungssensitive, einfache Navigation, die das riesige Portfolio aus Illustrationen und Animationen von Peepshow einfach zu erforschen macht.

Info

DESIGN: Matt Rice, Hege Aaby (Sennep) <www.sennep.com>; Spencer Wilson, Miles Donovan (Peepshow); Stephen Lenthall (photography). /// **PROGRAMMING**: Matt Rice, Mikkel Askjær (Sennep). /// **TOOLS**: Macromedia Flash, Macromedia Freehand, Adobe Photoshop, Sound Forge, PHP, MySQL, Cellotape & Glue. /// **CONTENTS**: illustration, animation, product design, set design, news, peepshop. /// **COST**: 140 hours.

PHAMOUS 69

UK

www.phamous69.com

2004

Concept

This magazine helps re-define sexual attitudes with bold design and perpetually expanding Flash content. /// Ce magazine contribue à redéfinir les attitudes sexuelles avec un graphisme audacieux et des contenus en Flash en perpétuelle expansion. /// Dieses Magazin hilft mit einem mutigen Design und sich ständig erweiterndem Flash-Inhalt, die sexuelle Einstellung neu zu definieren.

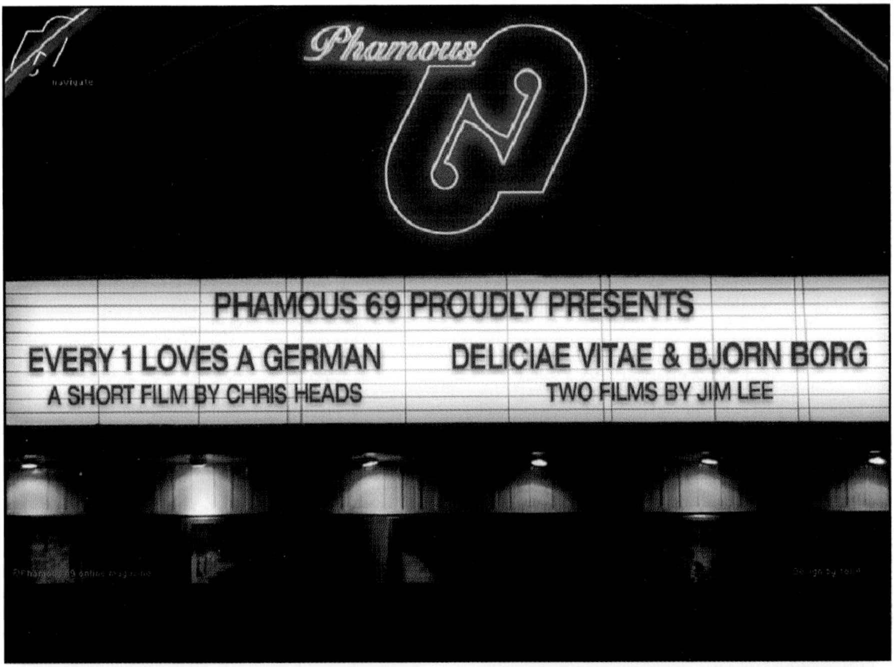

Phamous 69
PHAMOUS 69 PROUDLY PRESENTS
EVERY 1 LOVES A GERMAN
A SHORT FILM BY CHRIS HEADS
DELICIAE VITAE & BJORN BORG
TWO FILMS BY JIM LEE

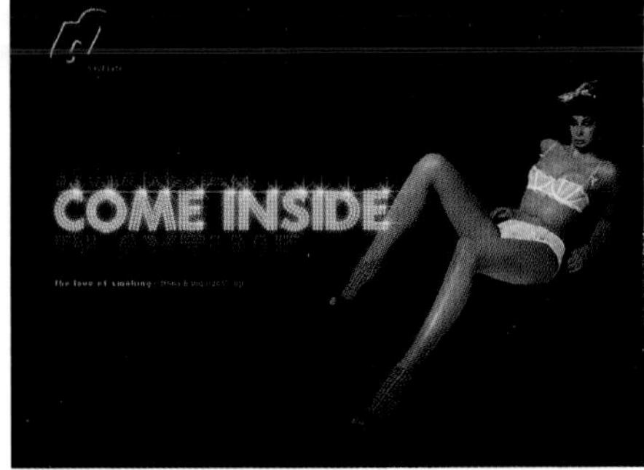

Info

Design and **Programming**: Ten4 Design <www.ten4design.co.uk>. /// **Tools**: Macromedia Flash, Adobe Photoshop, xml, php, CMS, Final Cut Pro. /// **Contents**: fashion photography, film, animation, music. /// **Cost**: ongoing project.

POWERBRIGHT

CANADA

www.powerbright.com

2005

Concept

The PowerBright website takes web surfers a notch higher in terms of 'Flash Intros'. It uniquely stands tall not only for its smooth vector animations but also famous with its 3D walking socket. /// Le site de Powerbright emmène les visiteurs un peu plus loin en termes « d'intros Flash ». Il se démarque non seulement par ses animations vectorielles fluides, mais aussi grâce à sa fameuse prise ambulante en 3D. /// Die Website von PowerBright ist noch eine Stufe besser als andere in Bezug auf ‚Flash Intros'. Sie ist nicht nur einzigartig wegen ihrer glatten Vektor-Animationen sondern auch durch ihre berühmte ‚laufende Steckdose' im 3D-Format.

Info

Design: DREAM Studio Design <www.dreamstudiodesign.com>. /// **Tools:** xml, php, Swift 3D, Macromedia Flash, Macromedia Dreamweaver. /// **Contents:** 3d vector animations. /// **Awards:** Flash Forward. /// **Cost:** 80 hours.

PSP-STYLE: A FAIRY TALE

KOREA

www.psp-style.co.kr

2005

Concept

In order to create a fairytale design concept, 3 different photographers were commissioned to plan and shoot specific images for the site. Finally, music and motion were applied to the finished design. /// Afin de créer un concept graphique de conte de fée, on a demandé à trois photographes différents de faire des photos spécifiques pour le site. Puis on a appliqué de la musique et du mouvement au résultat. /// Um ein Märchen-Design zu entwickeln, wurden drei voneinander unabhängige Fotografen damit beauftragt, die Fotos für die Website zu planen und zu schießen. Ganz zum Schluss wurden Musik und Bewegung hinzugefügt.

Info

Design: bandygarnet <www.bandygarnet.com>. /// **Programming**: DOFL Y.H. YUN <www.thedofl.com>. /// **Tools**: Adobe Photoshop, Adobe After Effects, Macromedia Flash, xml, php, etc. /// **Contents**: photo, film, music. /// **Awards**: FWA, DOPE Awards, Design TAXI. /// **Cost**: 3 months.

PUYOPOP

FRANCE/SPAIN

www.puyopop.com

2004

Concept

Really addictive. /// C'est vraiment comme une drogue. /// Man kann wirklich süchtig werden.

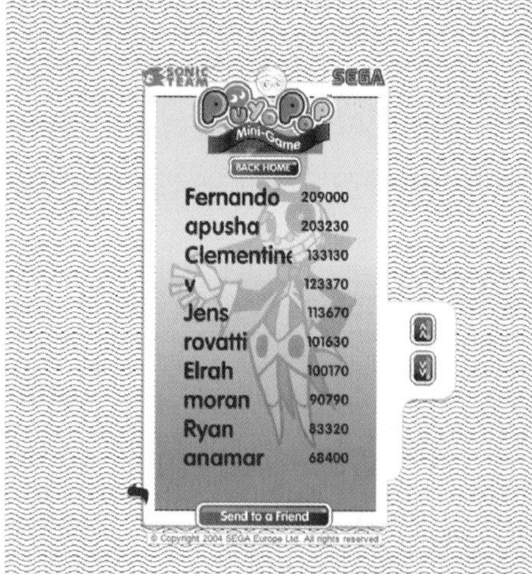

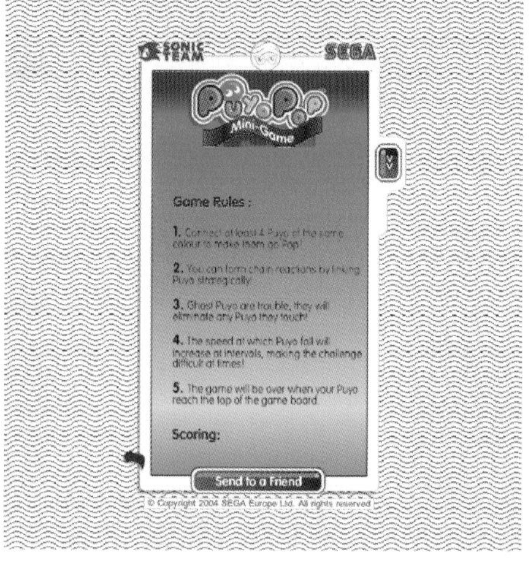

Info

DESIGN: Guillaume Fenwick "Guitz" (www.300k.com). /// **PROGRAMMING**: Guillaume Fenwick "Guitz" for game coding; Camille Ollier <www.carburant.fr> for PHP integration's. /// **TOOLS**: Macromedia Flash, Adobe Photoshop, Adobe Illustrator, PHP. /// **CONTENTS**: game contest. /// **AWARDS**: FWA (Site of the Day). /// **COST**: 1 month.

PZL PIECE COMPOSER

POLAND

www.pzl.pl

2005

Concept

The site is full of mysterious elements which compose unusual unlimited scenes. The website allows to each user uncovers his hidden potential of creativity and play with the graphic elements building original compositions. /// Il est rempli d'éléments mystérieux qui composent des scènes illimitées inhabituelles. Le site permet à l'utilisateur de découvrir son potentiel créatif caché et de jouer avec les éléments graphiques en construisant des compositions originales. /// Die Site ist voller geheimnisvoller Elemente, die ungewöhnliche, unendliche Szenen darstellen. Die Website ermöglicht jedem Benutzer, sein verstecktes kreatives Potenzial zu enthüllen und mit den grafischen Elementen spielerisch originelle Kompositionen zu erstellen.

Info

DESIGN: Adam Smereczynski, Rafał Górski, Sylwester Mielniczuk (Arc Warsaw) <www.arcww.com.pl/levis>, <www.przepraszam.com.pl>; Leo Burnett Group. /// **PROGRAMMING**: Sylwester Mielniczuk <www.mielniczuk.com>. /// **TOOLS**: Macromedia Flash, Adobe Photoshop, MySQL, PHP. /// **CONTENTS**: portfolio, self made sets, randomized music sound loops. /// **AWARDS**: Club of Advertising Creators (KTR) 2005 (Gold), Golden Drum 12th Advertising Festival finalist, FWA (Site of The Day). /// **COST**: 350 hours.

QUAKERSTATE

MEXICO

www.quakerstate.com.mx

2004

Concept

Corporative website in full Flash platform with rich visual & motion transitions, Big content and cool entertainment stuffs. /// Site d'entreprise avec une plateforme entièrement en Flash, avec des transitions visuelles et animées très riches, beaucoup de contenus et du divertissement. /// Offizielle Firmen-Website, vollkommen auf Flash basierend, mit prachtvollen visuellen, bewegten Übergängen, reichhaltigem Inhalt und tollen Unterhaltungselementen.

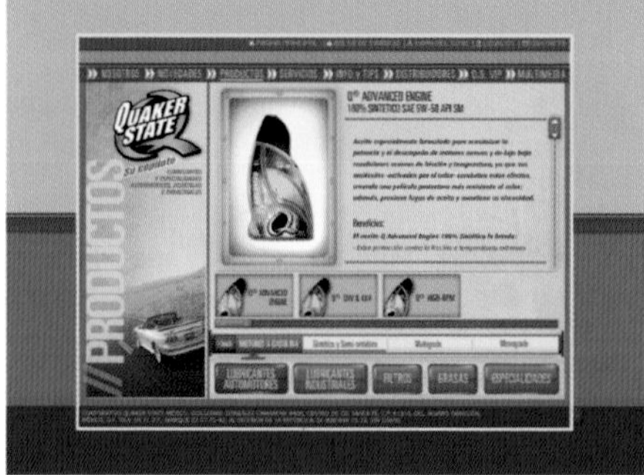

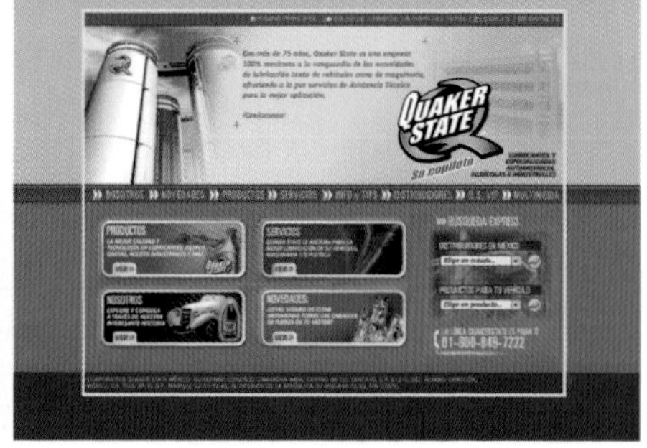

Info

Design and Programming: Alberto Cerriteno <www.albertocerriteno.com>. /// **Tools:** Macromedia Flash, Macromedia Dreamweaver, Adobe Photoshop, Adobe Illustrator, PHP, XML, MySQL. /// **Contents:** animation, commercial, products, games, info, photo, video. /// **Awards:** TINY (Site of the Day), Gold Portfolios, Pixelmakers (Site of the Month), Flash LA/Flavoritos (Site of the Week), Res 72 (Site of the Day). /// **Cost:** 450 hours.

RAG & BONE

USA

www.rag-bone.com

2005

Concept

The craftsmanship used to zoom-in and inspect the clothing is splendid. Plus we have enabled the user to feel like he or she is shopping amongst nature. A foreign feeling to anybody. /// Le travail de zoom avant pour inspecter les vêtements est splendide. De plus, nous permettons à l'utilisateur d'avoir l'impression de faire ses courses en pleine nature. Un sentiment étrange pour tout le monde. /// Die zum Zoomen und Untersuchen der Kleidung eingesetzte Technik ist ausgezeichnet. Darüber hinaus haben wir es dem Benutzer ermöglicht, sich zu fühlen, als ob er in der Natur einkaufen würde. Ein neuartiges Gefühl für jeden.

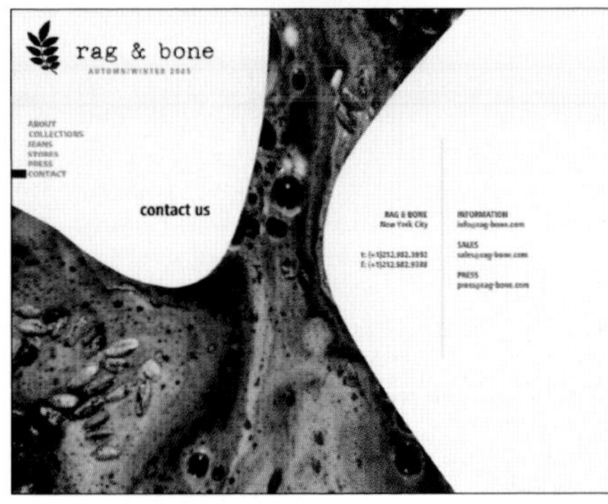

Info

Design and Programming: Diet Strychnine Corp. <www.dietstrychnine.com>. /// **Tools:** Adobe Creative Suite, Macromedia Flash. /// **Contents:** flash, audio track. /// **Cost:** 110 hours.

ROMAINGRUNER.COM

SWITZERLAND

www.romaingruner.com

2005

Concept

You are in a 100% realistic drawing website and there is no menu. All you have to do is to use the object like reality (CD for music, sofa for move the camera, remote control to see portfolio...). /// Vous vous trouvez sur un site de dessin 100 % réaliste, et il n'y a pas de menu. Tout ce que vous avez à faire c'est d'utiliser les objets comme dans la réalité (les CD pour la musique, le fauteuil pour déplacer la caméra, la télécommande pour voir le portfolio...). /// Sie befinden sich auf einer Website, die zu 100% aus echter Zeichnung besteht. Es gibt dort kein Menu. Alles, was Sie tun müssen, ist die Objekte gemäß ihrer wirklichen Funktion anzuklicken (CD für Musik, Sofa für Kamerabewegung, Fernbedienung, um das Portfolio anzusehen...).

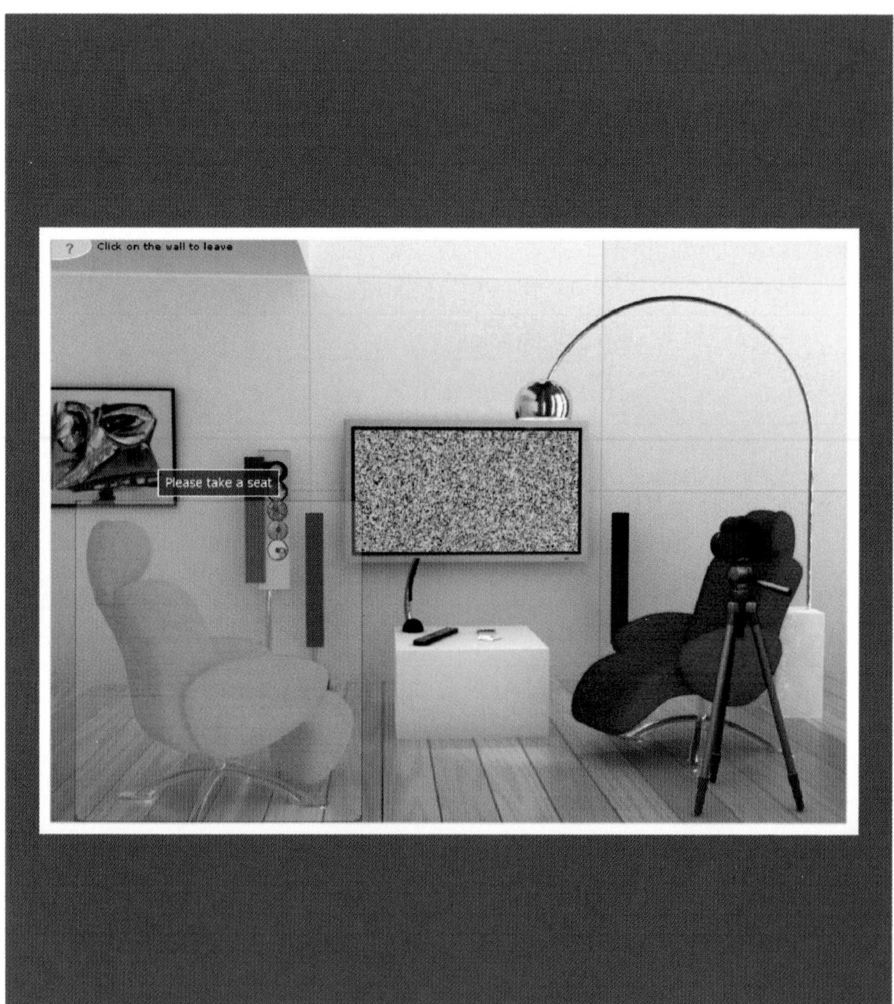

Info

Design: Romain Gruner. /// **Tools**: CMS (for updating) with PHP, Adobe Photoshop, Macromedia Flash, Autodesk 3ds Max, Final Render. /// **Contents**: music, animation, games, portfolio. /// **Cost**: 2 month (concept, 3d drawing and programming).

RON JONZO

UK

www.ronjonzo.com

2005

Concept

Ron Jonzo is London's "Man with Pen" 24/7 illustration emergency service. Fittingly, his site is based around a rusty minivan as an interface, and a billboard presenting his work. /// Ron Jonzo est « l'homme au stylo » de Londres, le service illustration d'urgence 24/7. Il est donc tout à fait approprié que ce site soit construit autour d'une interface en forme de minivan, et qu'un panneau d'affichage présente son travail. /// Ron Jonzo ist der Londoner „Man with Pen" - zeichnerischer Notdienst rund um die Uhr. Passenderweise basiert seine Website auf der Darstellung eines verrosteten Minivans und einer Reklametafel mit Beispielen seiner Arbeit.

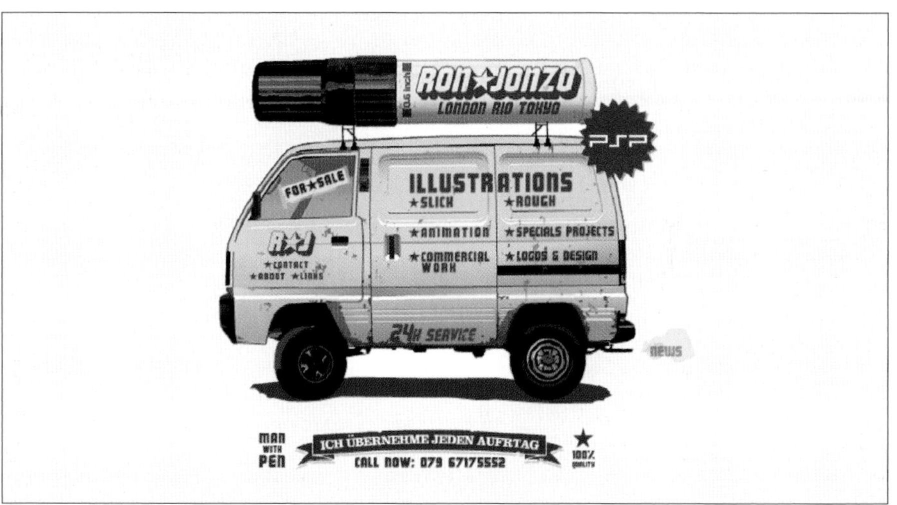

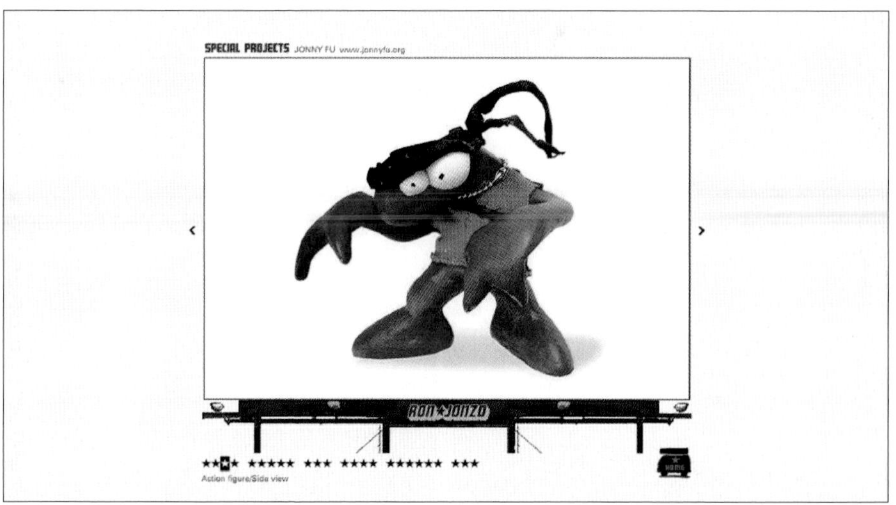

Info

Design: Ron Jonzo. /// **Programming**: Pär Stålberg, Isak Wiström <www.raspberryfall.com>. /// **Tools**: Macromedia Flash, Adobe Photoshop, Macromedia Freehand, XML. /// **Contents**: portfolio site with illustrations and animations by Ron Jonzo. /// **Cost**: 3 years.

SAVE YOURSELF

AUSTRALIA

www.saveyourself.com.au

2005

Concept

The object oriented navigation makes for an immersive and explorative experience. /// La navigation, basée sur les objets, fait de la visite du site une véritable exploration. /// **Die objektorientierte Navigation bietet ein interessantes Erforschungserlebnis.**

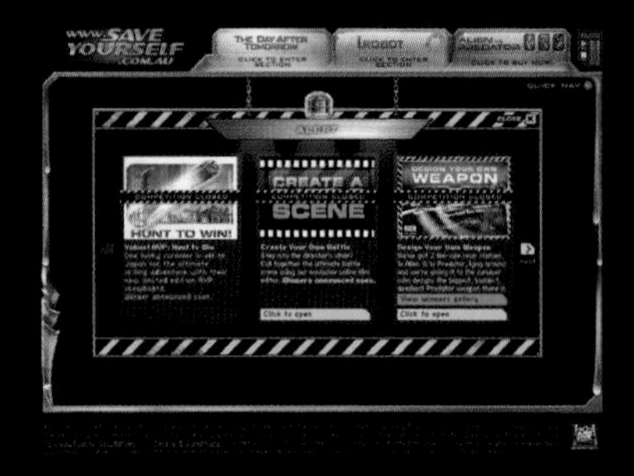

Info

Design: Robert Dennis, Ronald Kurniawan, David Brown, Brad Eldridge, Leonardo Zamboni (Soap Creative) <www.soapcreative.com.au>. /// **Programming:** Ashley Ringrose, Adam Johnson, Adam, Alan Gargett (Soap Creative). /// **Tools:** Adobe Photoshop, Adobe Illustrator, Macromedia Flash, xml. /// **Contents:** Film information for "The Day After Tomorrow", IRobot, Alien Vs Predator, trailers, competitions, games, trivia. /// **Cost:** 800 hours.

SEB JANIAK

FRANCE

www.sebjaniak.com

2005

Concept

Fast and progressive navigation, minimal design, we pay attention for the pictures quality, dynamic resizable screen (on thumbnails screen). /// Une navigation rapide et progressive, une conception minimaliste, des images soignées, un écran dynamique redimensionnable (sur l'écran des miniatures). /// Schnelle und fortschrittliche Navigation, minimales Design. Wir achten auf die Qualität der Bilder, dynamische und veränderbare Bildschirmgröße (Miniaturansicht).

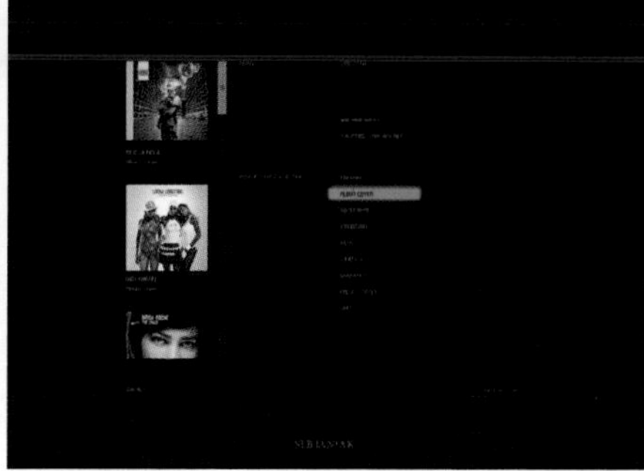

Info

DESIGN: Giuntini Philippe (Datakick) <www.datakick.com>. /// **PROGRAMMING**: Guillaume Barbaise (I-puzzle) <www.i-puzzle.fr>. /// **TOOLS**: xml, Macromedia Flash, Adobe Illustrator, Adobe Photoshop. /// **CONTENTS**: photo, film. /// **AWARDS**: FWA (Site of the Day), e-Creative (Site of the Week), fcukstar.com (Site of the Day), DOPE Awards, Digital Refueler. /// **COST**: 100 hours.

DESIO AE

JAPAN

www.sekisuiheim.com/desio-ae

2004

Concept

An interface design is incorporated that allows users to seamlessly experience the features of the SekisuiHeim three-story product in a way that differs from catalog sites. /// L'interface permet aux utilisateurs d'explorer les caractéristiques de la maison à trois étages de SekisuiHeim de manière fluide et bien différente des sites-catalogues. /// Das integrierte Design der Oberfläche ermöglicht es den Benutzern, die Merkmale des Produktes SekisuiHeim zu erforschen, anders als es im Katalog möglich wäre.

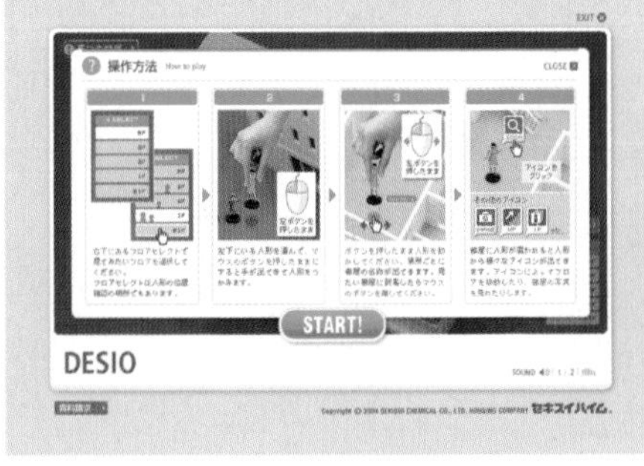

Info

Design: transcosmos inc. <www.trans-cosmos.co.jp/e/>. /// **Programming:** Mitsue-Links Co., Ltd. <www.mitsue.co.jp/english/>. /// **Tools:** Macromedia Flash. /// **Contents:** virtual space of "DESIO", Sekisui Heim's three-story house. /// **Awards:** FWA (Site Of The Month). /// **Cost:** 3 months.

SENSE TITOL

SPAIN

www.sensetitol.com

2005

Concept

This is an austere and simple website, equipped with great synthesis, based on the pixel philosophy. A wink to designers, with graphical resources as photoshop selections and images that pixelate. /// Voici un site austère et simple, très synthétique, et basé sur la philosophie du pixel. Un clin d'œil aux designers, avec des ressources graphiques en sélections Photoshop et des images qui se pixelisent. /// Es handelt sich hierbei um eine spartanische und einfache Website, die auf Pixel-Philosophie basiert. Ein Augenzwinkern in Richtung Designer, die mit grafischen Mitteln wie Photoshop-Anwendungen und Bildern arbeiten.

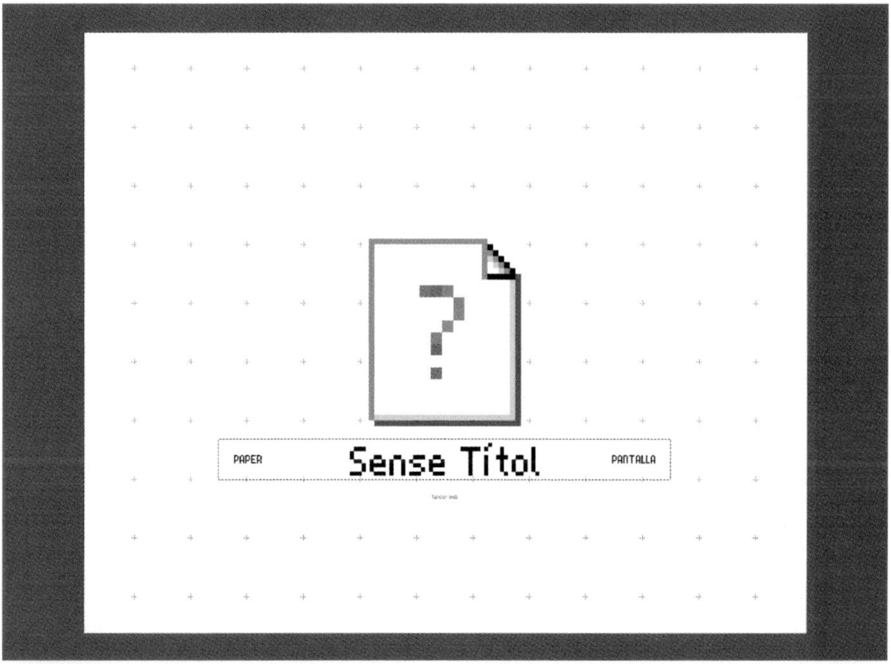

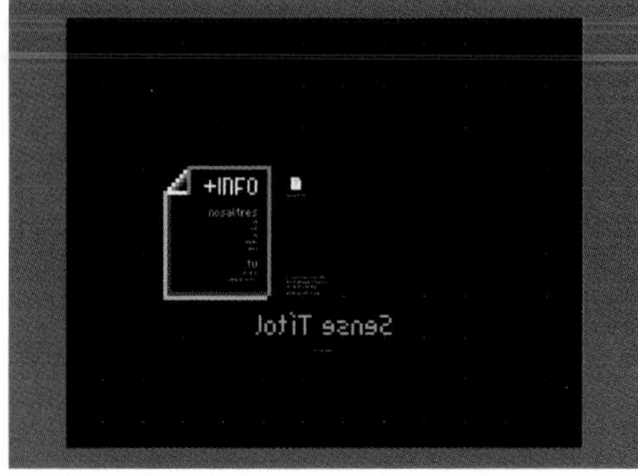

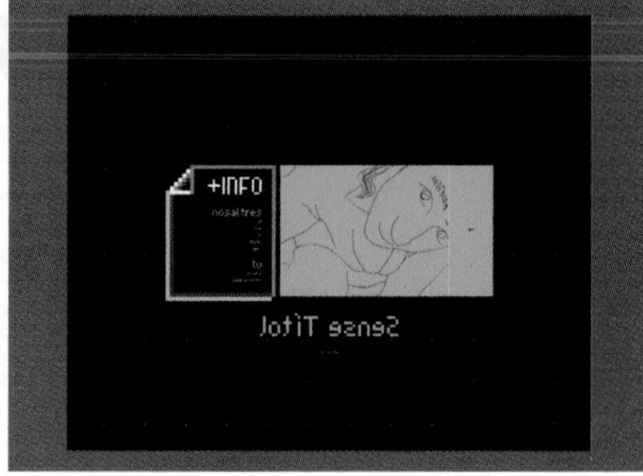

Info

Design: Sense Titol <www.sensetitol.com>. /// **Programming**: Marc Guardiola (Sense Titol). /// **Tools**: Adobe Photoshop, Macromedia Flash, Macromedia Freehand. /// **Contents**: photo, animated GIFFs, uncompressed sounds, own music creation. /// **Awards**: DOPE Awards, e-Creative, Cult Favourites (Site of the Month), Pixelmakers, Design Collector, FWA, Best Flash Animation Site, Moluv, Website Design Awards. /// **Cost**: 600 hours.

SEPTIME CREATION

FRANCE

www.septime-creation.com

2005

Concept

Our website doesn't fit in the traditional websites' layout (header, content, footer), we created a fullscreen application with animated elements and text, transitions, explosions, growing plants... /// Notre site ne correspond pas aux présentations traditionnelles (titre, contenus, pied de page). Nous avons créé une application en plein écran avec des éléments et des textes animés, des transitions, des explosions, des plantes qui poussent... /// Unsere Website entspricht nicht dem traditionellen Layout einer Website (Überschrift, Inhalt, Fuβnote), wir haben eine den gesamten Bildschirm einnehmende Anwendung geschaffen, mit bewegten Elementen und Text, Übergängen, Explosionen, wachsenden Pflanzen...

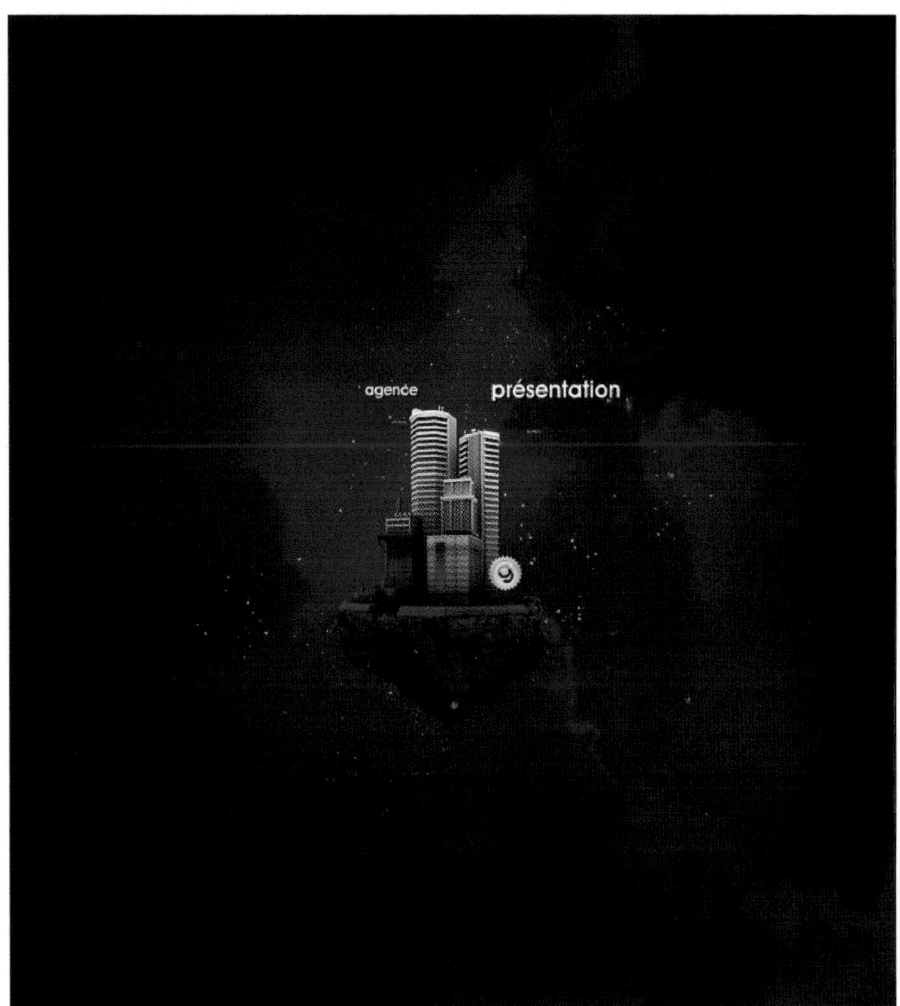

Info

DESIGN: (Septime Creation) Art Direction: Ulysse Lacombe, Marketing Director: Guillaume Bousquet, Graphic Design: Nicolas Combes, David Polonia. /// **PROGRAMMING**: Romain Moussac. /// **TOOLS**: Macromedia Flash, PHP, Adobe Photoshop, Adobe Illustrator, Autodesk 3ds Max. /// **CONTENTS**: animation, music. /// **AWARDS**: FWA, Flash Kit, TINY, e-Creative, Crossmind, Website Design Awards, Design TAXI, Frenchnfresh.com, NewWebPick, DOPE Awards, Praktica.net, Res72.com, Pixelmakers.com.br. /// **COST**: 552 hours.

SIERRAS NORTE

SPAIN

www.sierrasnortedeextremadura.com

2005

Concept

We created a 1:1 map for the user to visually navigate the zone, while the client can manage all the related information by using a customized CMS. /// Nous avons créé une carte à échelle 1:1 pour que l'utilisateur navigue visuellement, pendant que le client gère toutes les informations associées grâce à un CMS sur mesure. /// Wir haben eine 1:1-Karte mit visueller Navigation erstellt. Nach Anklicken der vorgesehenen Punkte wird die nötige Information mit Hilfe des maßgeschneiderten CMS ermittelt.

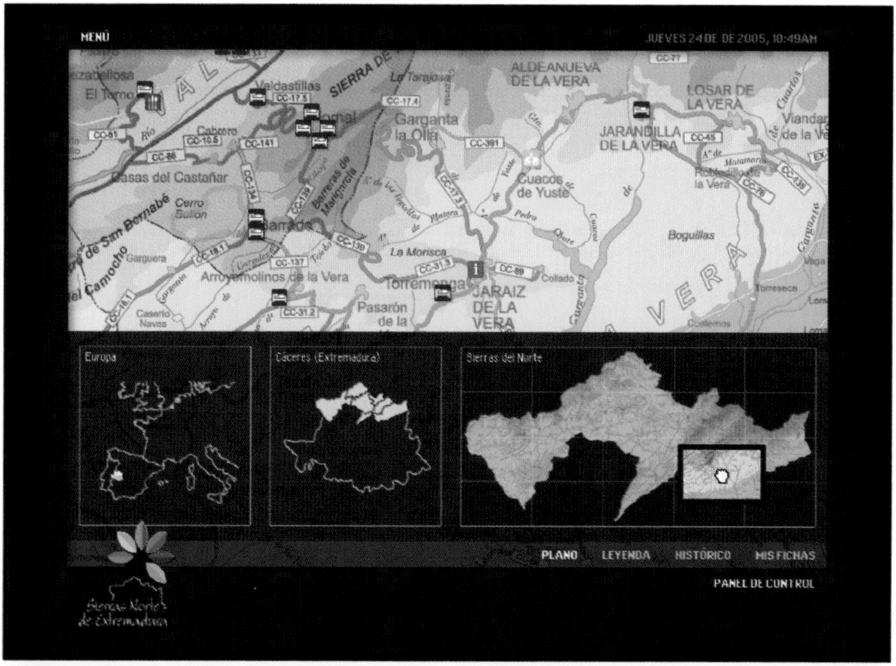

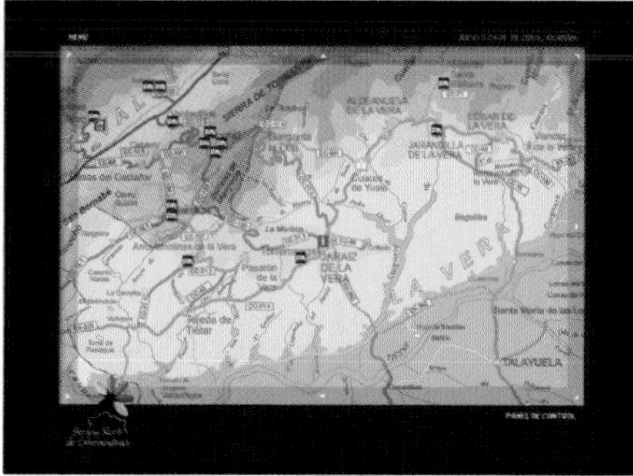

Info

DESIGN: Granatta New Media Design <www.granatta.com>. /// **TOOLS**: PHP, MySQL, Macromedia Flash, Macromedia Freehand, Macromedia Fireworks, XHTML, CMS, CSS. /// **CONTENTS**: text, photo. /// **COST**: 650 hours.

SIMONDS HOMES

AUSTRALIA

www.simonds.com.au

2005

Concept

Functional "Back Button", entirely CMS driven, live sorting of data with "Home Selection Wizard", ability to collect a custom set of favourite houses. /// Un « bouton de retour » fonctionnel, entièrement géré par CMS, un tri des données en temps réel avec « Assistant de sélection de maison », et la possibilité de faire une liste personnalisée de ses maisons préférées. /// Die Besonderheit dieser Website ist ein auf CMS basierender, funktioneller „Back-Button". Hinzu kommt die Möglichkeit der Sortierung in Echtzeit mit Hilfe von „Home Selection Wizard" und eine Ablagefunktion, um ausgewählte Häuser zu speichern.

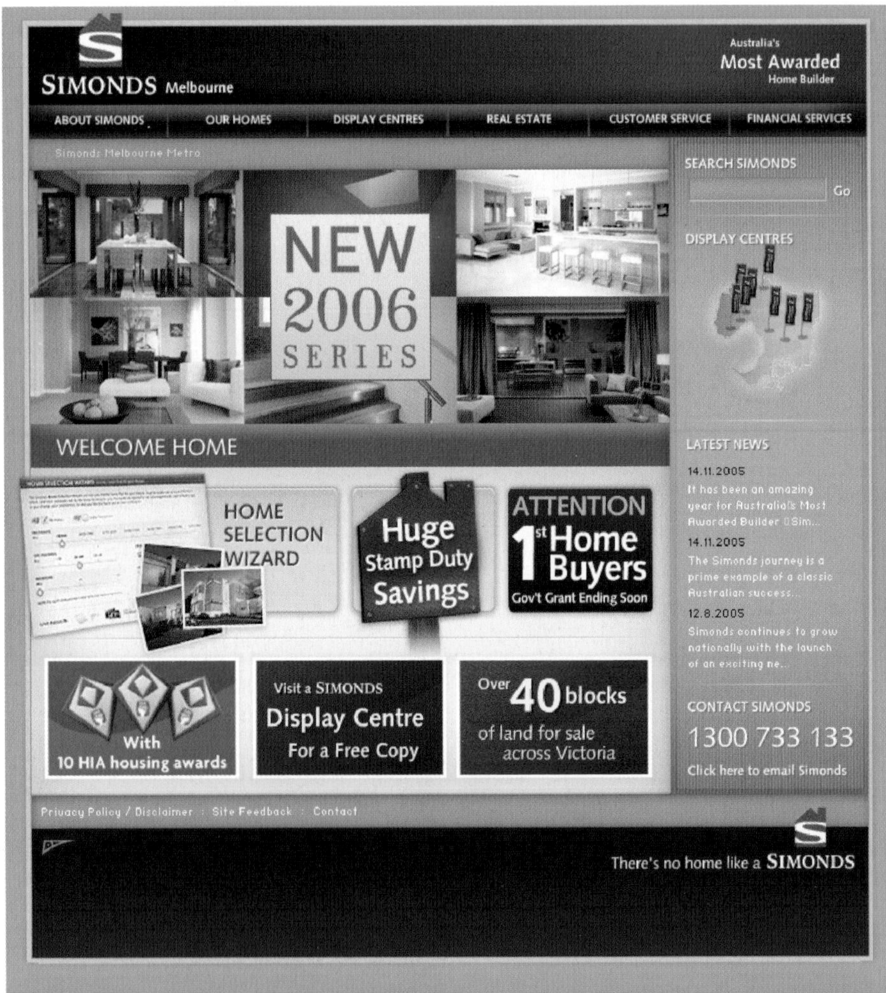

Info

Design: Dave Budge (Visual Jazz) <www.visualjazz.com.au>. /// **Programming**: Stephen Woolcock (Visual Jazz). /// **Tools**: Macromedia Flash, Adobe Photoshop, ASP, Microsoft SQL, Javascript. /// **Contents**: details of Simonds houses, photos, floorplans, house specifications, vr tours, company info. /// **Awards**: FWA (Site of the Day), Macromedia Asia Pacific. /// **Cost**: 800 hours.

SLG ADVERTISING

USA

www.slg-inc.com

2004

This website is a direct reflection of 2 people striving to push the boundaries of story telling on the web. We came together on a small budget -&- a swift delivery schedule and delivered a breath taking experience. /// Ce site est le reflet direct des efforts de deux personnes pour repousser les limites de la narration sur Internet. Nous avons travaillé ensemble avec un budget limité et un délai de livraison assez court, et le résultat est époustouflant. /// Diese Website stellt eine direkte Reflexion von zwei Menschen dar, die danach streben, die Grenzen des Geschichtenerzählens im Internet zu erweitern. Wir haben uns zusammen getan. Das Budget war klein und die Lieferung musste schnell erfolgen. Das Resultat war atemberaubend.

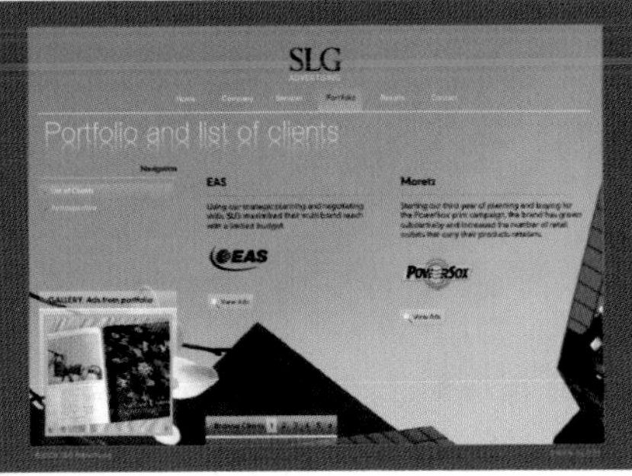

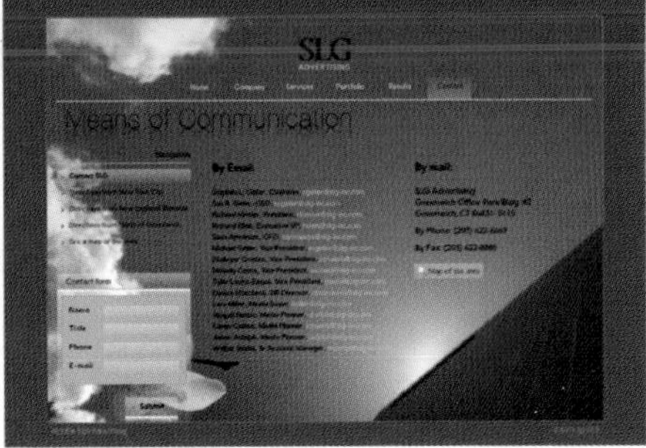

DESIGN: Rasmus Blaze <www.woerk.com>. /// **PROGRAMMING**: Diet Strychnine Corp. <www.dietstrychnine.com>. /// **TOOLS**: Adobe Creative Suite, Macromedia Flash. /// **CONTENTS**: flash. /// **COST**: over 200 hours.

SOFAKE

www.sofake.com

USA

2002

Concept Sofake doesn't take itself too seriously or try too hard to explain every detail of itself. Sofake is less shitty than most flash sites. /// Sofake ne se prend pas trop au sérieux, et n'essaie pas non plus d'expliquer tous les détails de sa démarche. Sofake est moins merdique que la plupart des sites Flash. /// Sofake nimmt sich selbst nicht so Ernst und versucht auch nicht zu stark, jedes Detail über sich selbst zu erklären. Sofake ist nicht ganz so schlecht wie die meisten Flash-Websites.

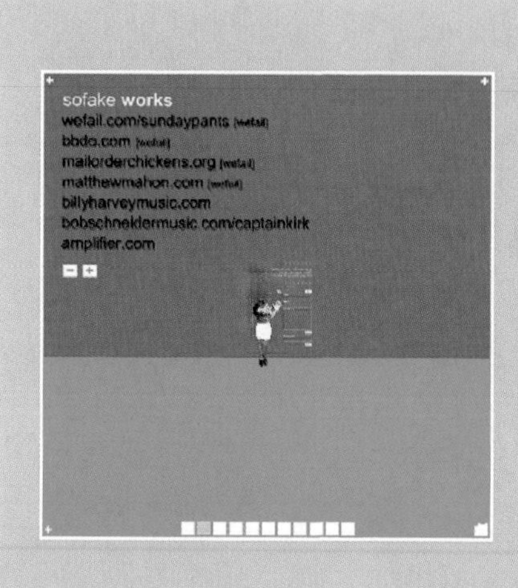

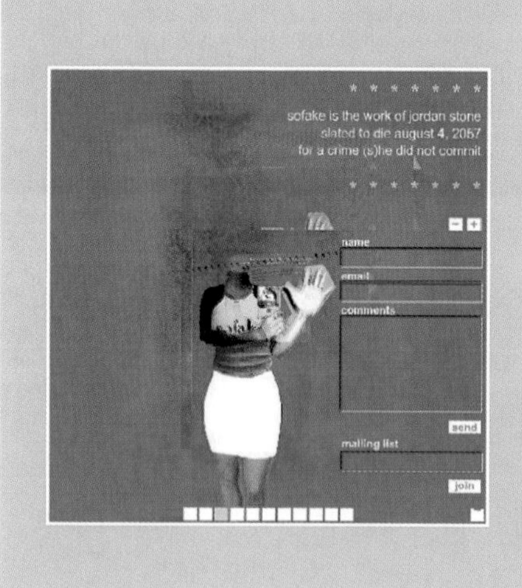

Info **Design and Programming:** Sofake. /// **Tools:** Macromedia Flash, Adobe Photoshop. /// **Contents:** animations, music, games. /// **Awards:** FWA, Bombshock. /// **Cost:** 2 months.

SOLEIL NOIR

FRANCE

www.soleilnoir.net

2005

Concept

The real difference with our website is how we have tried to deal with the graphic and sound design. /// La véritable différence de notre site, c'est la façon dont nous avons essayé de gérer le graphisme et les sons. /// Der Unterschied, der unsere Website ausmacht ist die Art, wie wir versucht haben mit Grafik und Ton-Design umzugehen.

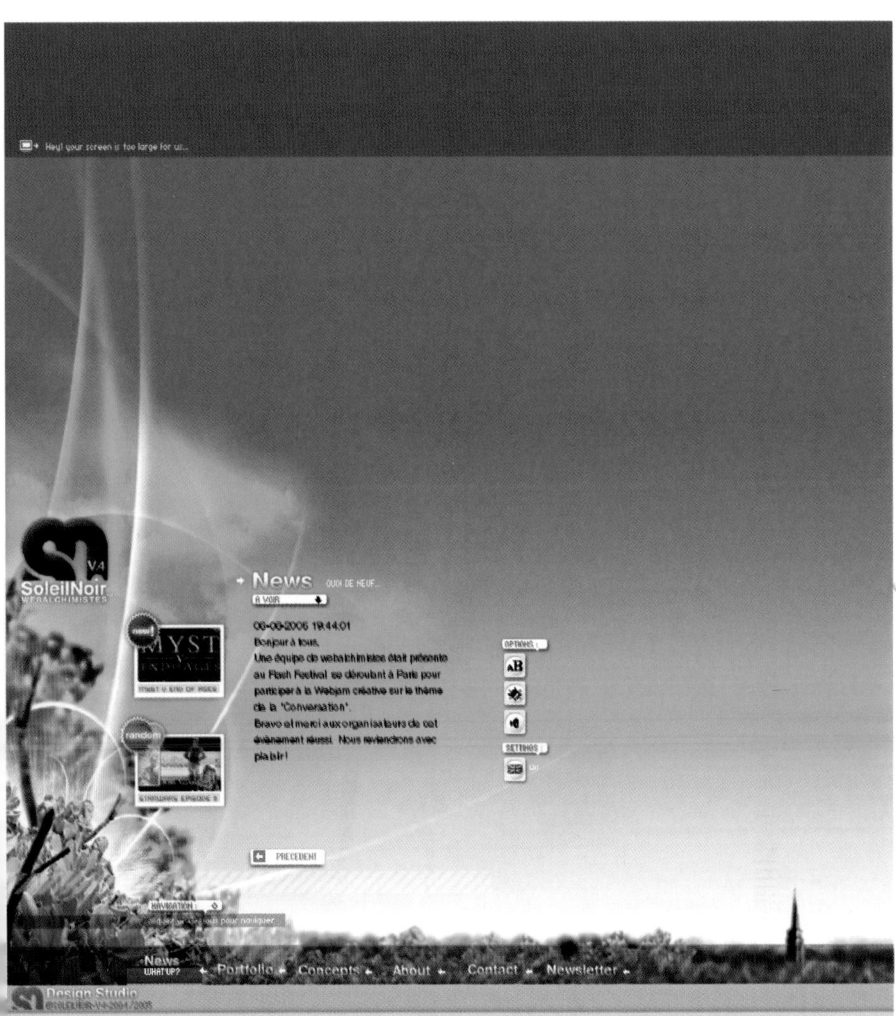

Info

Design: Aster <www.synthesis01.com> (Soleil Noir) <www.soleilnoir.net>. /// **Programming**: Mara <www.marajade.fr> (Soleil Noir). /// **Tools**: Macromedia Flash, PHP content management, MySQL database. /// **Contents**: fully manageable text, audio, pictures and video content. /// **Awards**: FWA, TINY (site of the week), Macromedia. /// **Cost**: 3 weeks from the brief to the online push.

SONIC BOOM

CANADA

www.sonicboom.com

2004

Concept

We wanted to create a seamless experience and did so with a continuous montage of airport imagery that moves to create feeling of speed. The navigation utilizes lateral motion which is not seen very often. /// Nous voulions créer un ensemble homogène et cohérent, alors nous avons fait un montage continu d'images d'aéroport animées qui donnent une impression de vitesse. La navigation utilise le mouvement latéral, ce que l'on ne voit pas très souvent. /// Es ist uns gelungen, nahtlose Übergänge mit Hilfe von Flughafen-Metaphorik und Bewegung zu schaffen, wodurch ein Gefühl von Geschwindigkeit entsteht. Das Besondere an der Navigation ist die horizontale Ausrichtung.

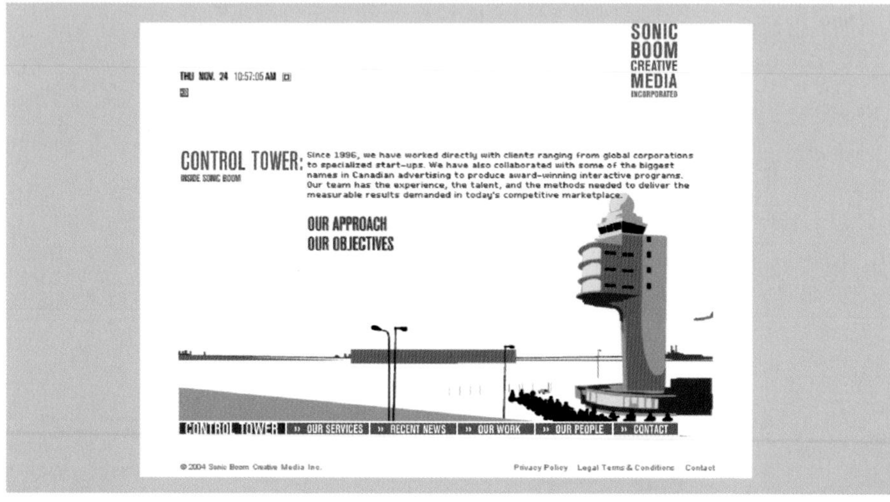

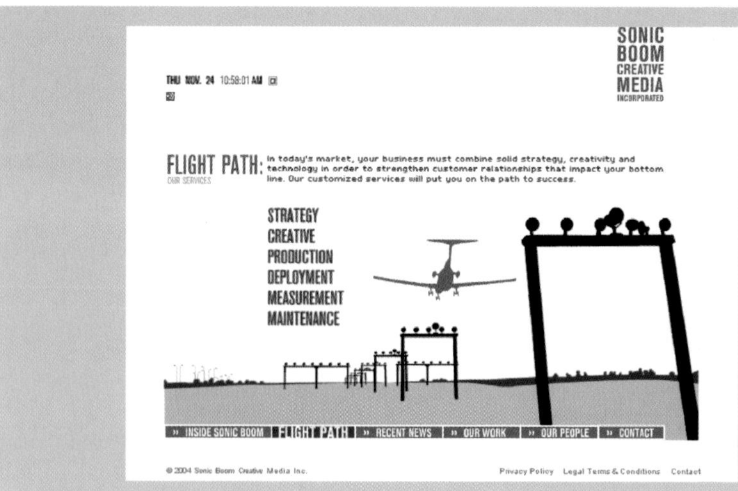

Info

DESIGN: (Sonic Boom Creative Media Inc.) Creative Director: Norman Mayot; Art Director: Chris May. /// **PROGRAMMING**: Flash Developer: Albert Chang; Technical Lead: Craig Denis. /// **TOOLS**: Adobe Illustrator, Macromedia Flash, XML, Microsoft SQL. /// **CONTENTS**: work examples, photos, overviews of work. /// **AWARDS**: Applied Arts 2004, The Advertising & Design Club of Canada (ADCC) 2004. /// **COST**: 250 hours.

SONJA MUELLER

GERMANY

www.sonjamueller.org

2005

Concept

The site offers a horizontally scrolling interface to access Sonja's work, plus a quick-navigation to find specific images, jobs or styles directly. /// Le site présente une interface de défilement horizontal pour accéder au travail de Sonja, et une navigation rapide pour trouver directement des images, des projets ou des styles spécifiques. /// **Die Website verfügt über eine horizontal scrollende Oberfläche zum Einsehen von Sonjas Arbeit sowie eine schnelle Navigation zum direkten Suchen von bestimmten Bildern, Jobs oder Styles.**

Info

DESIGN: Matthias Netzberger, Lars Eberle (Less Rain) <www.lessrain.com>. /// **PROGRAMMING**: Oliver Greschke (Less Rain). /// **TOOLS**: Adobe Photoshop, Macromedia Freehand, Macromedia Flash (AS2), PHP / XML, XHTML, Eclipse. /// **CONTENTS**: portfolio site, photographs by Sonja Mueller. /// **COST**: 2 months.

SPIKEDDB

USA

www.spikeddb.com

2004

Concept

SpikeDDB wanted a modern website that showcased just enough information to intrigue the. So, Firstborn created a website that featured an interface that continually shifted the presentation of content. /// SpikeDDB voulait un site moderne qui présente juste assez d'information pour intriguer le visiteur. Alors Firstborn a créé un site dont l'interface modifie continuellement la présentation des contenus. /// SpikeDDB wünschte eine moderne Website, die gerade genug Information beinhaltet, um Aufmerksamkeit zu erregen. Firstborn erstellte also eine Website, die sich durch eine dynamische Oberfläche auszeichnet.

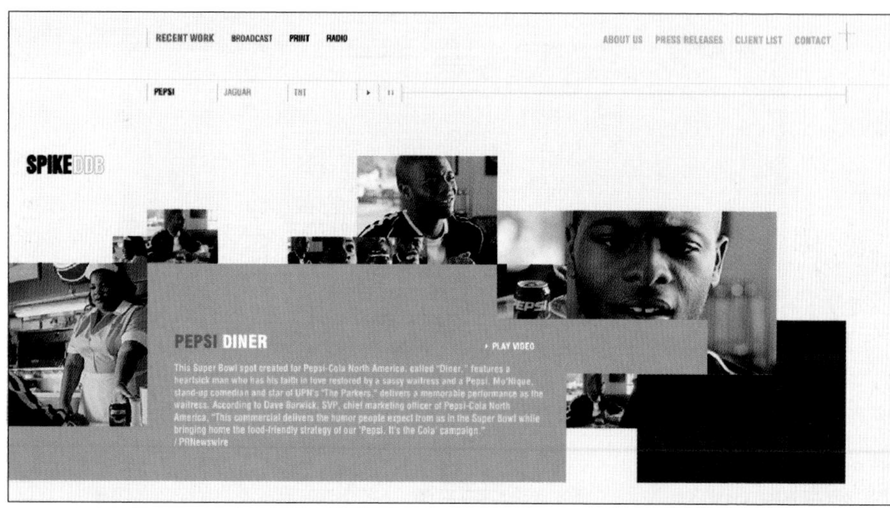

Info

Design and Programming: Joon Yong Park (Firstborn) <www.firstbornmultimedia.com>. /// **Tools**: Adobe Photoshop, Macromedia Flash, Adobe After Effects. /// **Contents**: photos, video, audio. /// **Awards**: FWA. /// **Cost**: 150 hours.

STEPHANE GUILLOT

FRANCE

www.stephaneguillot.com

2005

Concept

Fun and very entertaining concept, the bouncy character of this site lives in a colorful and happy world. In addition to great animation and illustration, the site also features some really catchy music. /// Un concept ludique et divertissant, le personnage sautillant de ce site vit dans un monde coloré et joyeux. Outre les excellentes illustrations et animations, la musique du site est également très entraînante. /// **Das Konzept ist witzig und sehr unterhaltsam. Die federnde Figur dieser Website lebt in einer farbenreichen und glücklichen Welt. Abgesehen von wunderbarer Animation und Illustration lebt die Seite auch von wirklich eingängiger Musik.**

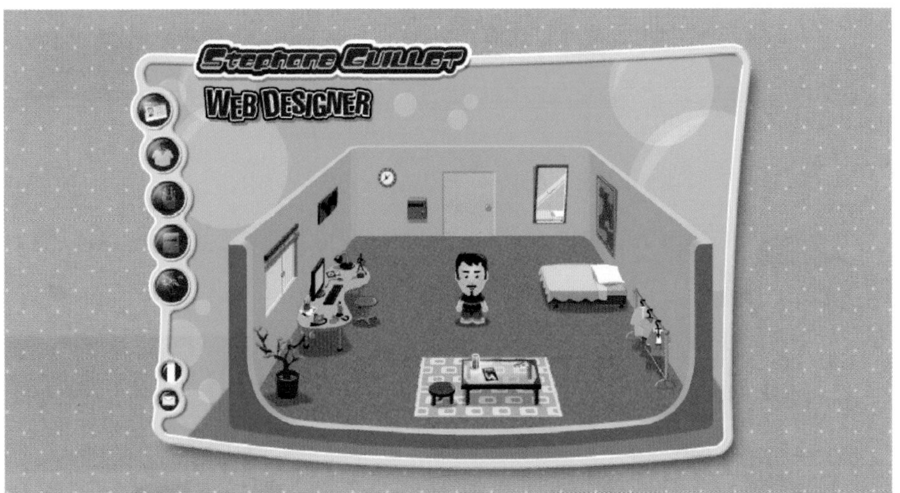

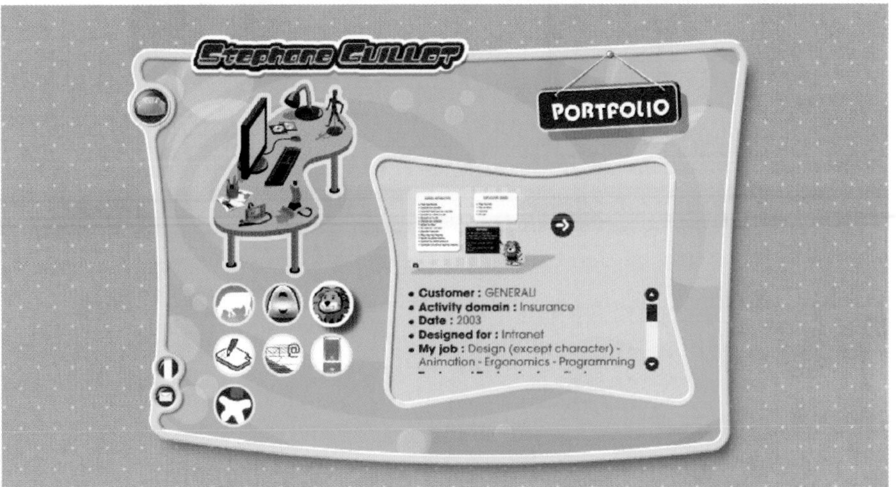

Info

Design and Programming: Stephane Guillot. /// **Tools**: Macromedia Flash, Adobe Illustrator, Adobe Photoshop, SoundForge, Acid, Macromedia Dreamweaver. /// **Contents**: Personal portfolio. /// **Awards**: FWA (Site of the Day), Ultrashock Bomshock, TINY (Site of the Week), Pixelmakers (Site of the Week), ADES Design (Site of the Month), Flash Kit (Site of the Week), Flash LA (Site of the Week), King For A Week (Site of the Week), Design TAXI (Site of the Day), DOPE Awards.

STEREOPLASTIC.COM

GERMANY

www.stereoplastic.com

2004

Concept

Stereoplastic is not only the online portfolio of Mike John Otto. It is a dedication to the combination of retro design with modern graphic design. Each section is a world of its own. /// Stereoplastic n'est pas seulement le portfolio en ligne de Mike John Otto. C'est un hommage à la combinaison du style rétro et de la conception graphique moderne. Chaque section est un monde à part entière. /// **Stereoplastic ist nicht nur das Online-Portfolio von Mike John Otto. Es ist eine Verneigung vor der Verbindung von Retro-Design mit modernem Grafik-Design. Jeder Bereich ist eine Welt für sich. Glatte Übergänge und ein konstantes Look & Feel erlauben dem Benutzer, den Stil von Stereoplastic zu erforschen.**

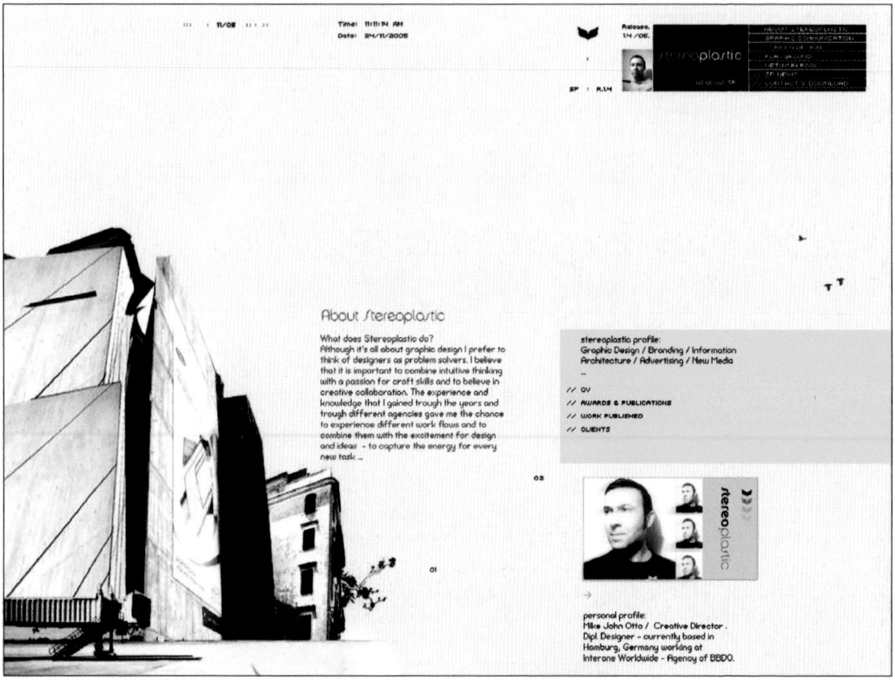

11/05
Time: 11:11:14 AM
Date: 24/11/2005
Release.
14 /05.
stereoplastic
SP : R.14
About Stereoplastic
What does Stereoplastic do?
Although it's all about graphic design I prefer to think of designers as problem solvers. I believe that it is important to combine intuitive thinking with a passion for craft skills and to believe in creative collaboration. The experience and knowledge that I gained trough the years and trough different agencies gave me the chance to experience different work flows and to combine them with the excitement for design and ideas - to capture the energy for every new task ...
stereoplastic profile:
Graphic Design / Branding / Information Architecture / Advertising / New Media
// CV
// AWARDS & PUBLICATIONS
// WORK PUBLISHED
// CLIENTS
02
01
stereoplastic
personal profile:
Mike John Otto / Creative Director .
Dipl. Designer - currently based in Hamburg, Germany working at Interone Worldwide - Agency of BBDO.

Graphic Communication
FREIRäume

Release 14
News 11/05

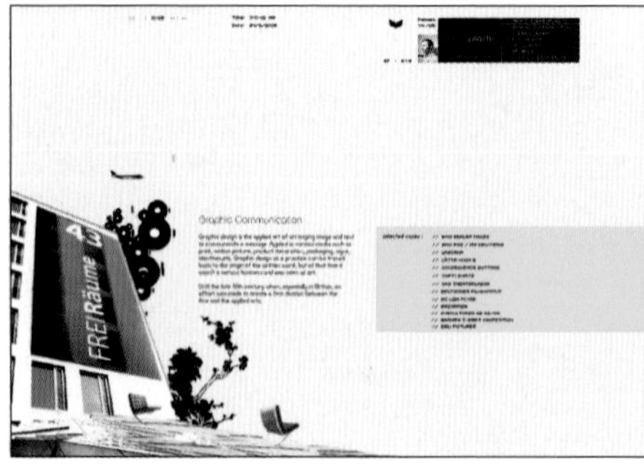

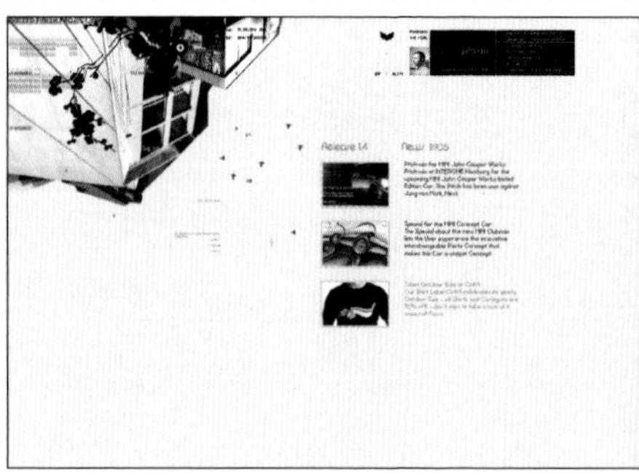

Info

DESIGN: Mike John Otto (Stereoplastic.com). /// **PROGRAMMING:** Mike John Otto, Oliver Hinrichs. /// **TOOLS:** Xhtml, php, Adobe Photoshop, Macromedia Flash, Macromedia Dreamweaver, Macromedia Freehand, Reason. /// **CONTENTS:** photo, music, animations, movies, illustrations. /// **AWARDS:** Linkdup, Styleboost, Design is Kinky, Lookom, Newstoday, Surfstation, Res72, k10k, Highflooter, FWA, American Design, bd4d - published in many design magazines worldwide. /// **COST:** 4 months.

STIFF + TREVILLION

UK

www.stiff-trevillion.com

2005

Concept

The focus of this site is an award-winning architecture portfolio. The navigation is concealed until required, creating a clean canvas for the images to be showcased. /// Le point fort de ce site est un portfolio d'architecture primé. La navigation est invisible jusqu'à ce que l'on en ait besoin, ce qui permet d'avoir un fond dégagé pour mettre les photos en valeur. /// **Der Schwerpunkt dieser Website liegt auf einem preisgekrönten Architektur-portfolio. Die Navigation ist verborgen und erscheint erst, wenn nötig und schafft so eine klare Fläche für die zu präsentierenden Bilder.**

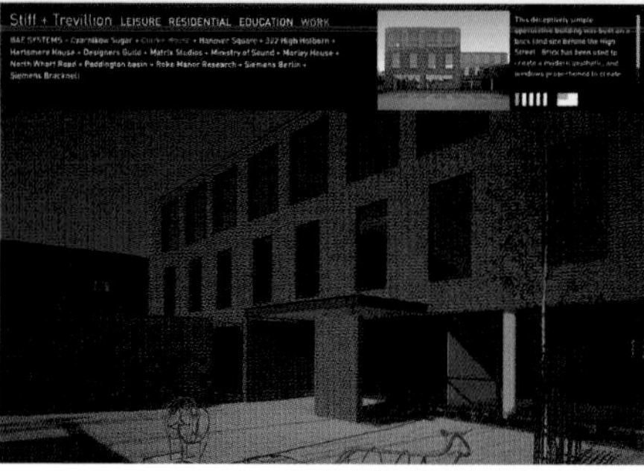

Info

Design and Programming: Ten4 Design <www.ten4design.co.uk>. /// **Tools:** Macromedia Flash, Adobe Photoshop, xml, php. /// **Contents:** photographic architecture portfolio. /// **Cost:** 1 month.

SUBSOCIETY

SWEDEN

www.subsociety.se

2005

Concept

The site profile was to give the user an exciting website with high quality design and creative interactions. /// Le profil du site était censé propose à l'utilisateur un site passionnant avec un graphisme de grande qualité et des interactions créatives. /// **Es sollte dem Benutzer eine aufregende Website angeboten werden, mit einem Design hoher Qualität und kreativen Interaktionen.**

Info

Design and Programming: Kristian Sörefelt (Subsociety). /// **Tools**: Adobe Photoshop, Macromedia Flash, PHP, Autodesk 3ds Max, Autodesk Combustion /// **Contents**: portfolio. /// **Awards**: FWA (site of the day), Website Design Awards (site of the month), Kirupa (site of the week), e-Creative (site of the day), Pixelmakers (site of the day), Moluv (display of excellence), Flash Kit, TINY (site of the Week). /// **Cost**: 200 hours.

SUKILAND

FRANCE

www.sukiland.com

2003

Concept

An original, timeless, ludic and animated design (the central character and the blues spots) with a simple navigation. All of that to do Sukiland a living website and pleasant to visit... /// Un graphisme original, intemporel, ludique et animé (le personnage central et les taches bleues), et une navigation simple. Tout cela pour faire de Sukiland un site vivant, agréable à visiter. /// **Es handelt sich hierbei um ein originelles, zeitloses, spielerisches und animiertes Design (die zentrale Figur und die blauen Flecken) mit einer einfachen Navigation. Das Ganze macht Sukiland zu einer lebendigen Website, die man gern besucht...**

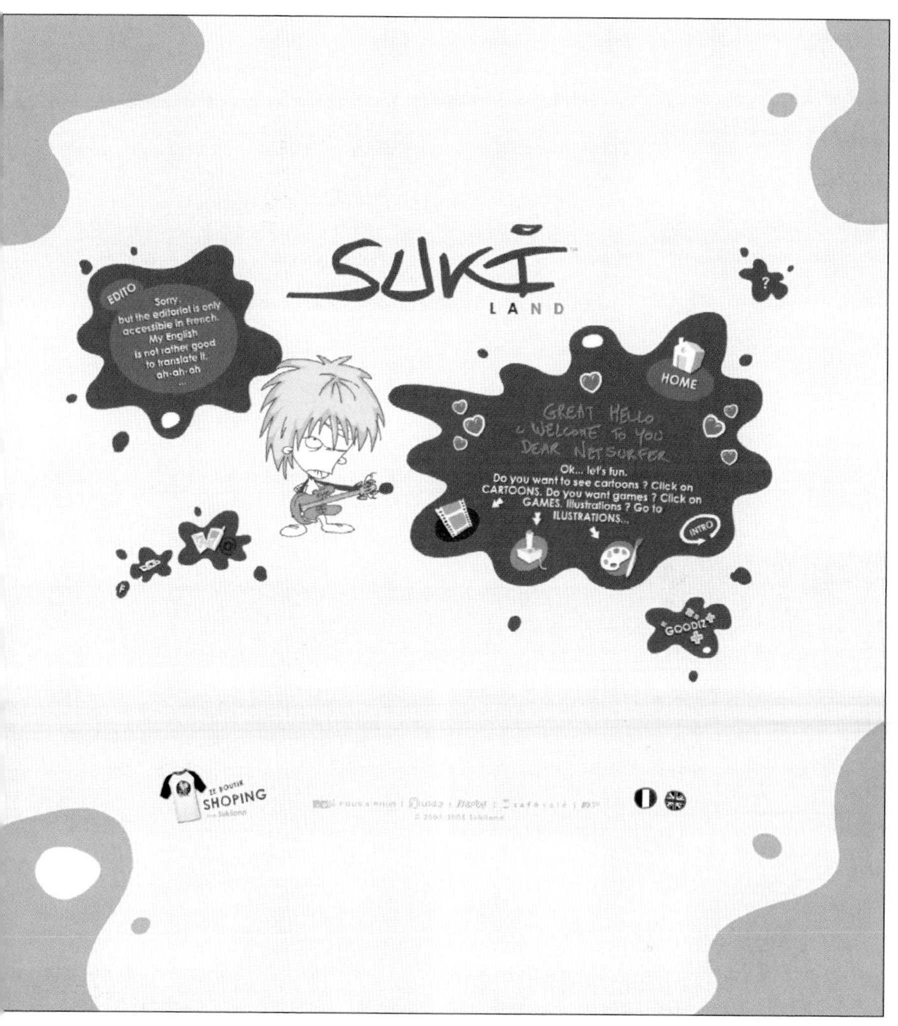

Info

DESIGN AND PROGRAMMING: Sukiland. /// **TOOLS:** Adobe Photoshop, soundforge, php, Macromedia Dreamweaver. /// **CONTENTS:** cartoons, games and illustrations. /// **AWARDS:** FWA, TINY, NewWebPick, e-Creative, Moluv, Golden Web Award, Design Firms, Canadian Web Awards, Click of the Day, Butterfly. /// **COST:** 3 weeks for the first version. Each animation of the character was made into 1 to 2 days, as each update 1 to 2 days too.

SUNGLASS

ITALY
2005

www.sunglass.it

Concept

Sunglass is an institutional web site made for a Curved Glass Company... the on line project speak the architectural's language. /// Sunglass est un site institutionnel réalisé pour une société de verre bombé... Le projet en ligne parle le langage de l'architecture. /// **Sunglass ist eine Firmen-Website für die Curved Glass Company... das Online-Projekt basiert auf der Sprache der Architektur.**

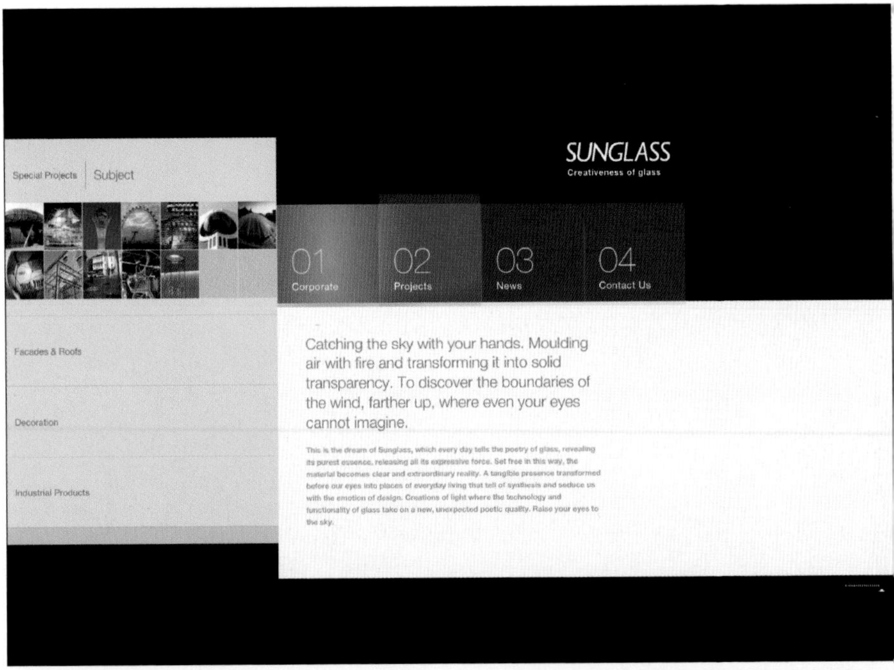

Special Projects
Subject
Facades & Roofs
Decoration
Industrial Products
SUNGLASS
Creativeness of glass
01
Corporate
02
Projects
03
News
04
Contact Us
Catching the sky with your hands. Moulding air with fire and transforming it into solid transparency. To discover the boundaries of the wind, farther up, where even your eyes cannot imagine.
This is the dream of Sunglass, which every day tells the poetry of glass, revealing its purest essence, releasing all its expressive force. Set free in this way, the material becomes clear and extraordinary reality. A tangible presence transformed before our eyes into places of everyday living that tell of synthesis and seduce us with the emotion of design. Creations of light where the technology and functionality of glass take on a new, unexpected poetic quality. Raise your eyes to the sky.

SUNGLASS
01
02
03
04
NARDINI

SUNGLASS
01
02
03
04
NARDINI

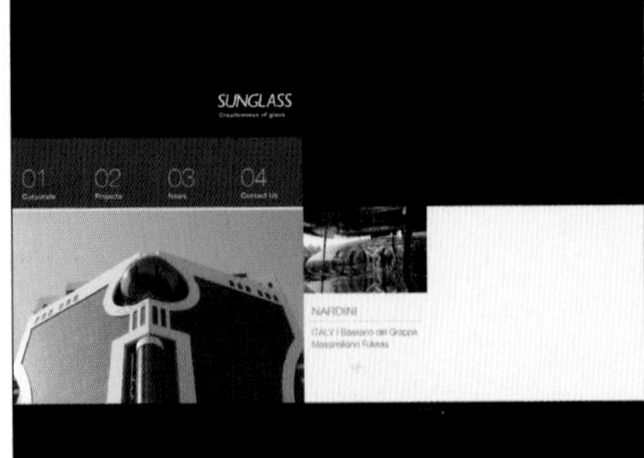

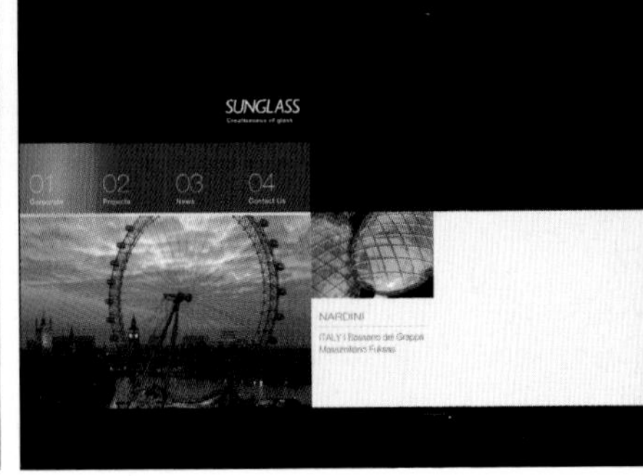

Info

Design: Alessandro Orlandi & Matteo Giuricin. (FISHOUSE) <www.fishouse.net>. /// **Tools:** Macromedia Flash, Adobe Photoshop. ///
Contents: photo, music. /// **Cost:** 500 hours.

HONDA SUZUKA CHALLENGE

CANADA

http://suzuka.sonicboom.com

2004

Concept

We wanted to push the envelope on the feeling the game had with panning and zooming and motion, which was influenced by the method in which racing on television is filmed. /// Nous voulions repousser les limites des sensations de jeu avec des panoramiques, des zooms et de l'animation. Tout cela a été influencé par la façon dont les courses sont filmées en télévision. /// **Wir wollten bis an die Grenzen gehen und das Gefühl eines Wettbewerbs mit Schwenken, Zoomen und Dynamik erzeugen, genauso, wie ein Rennen im Fernsehen erlebt wird.**

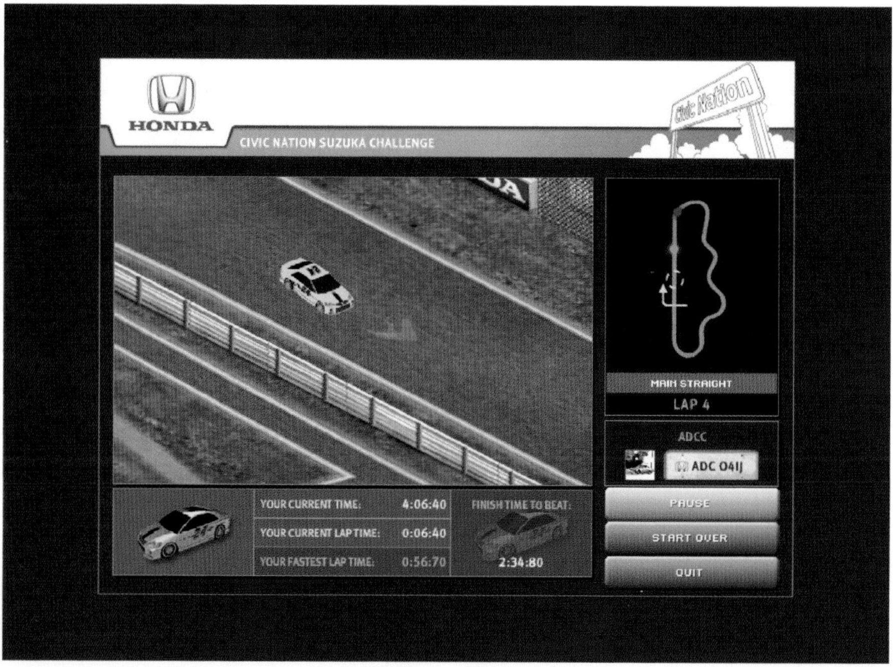

Info

Design: (Sonic Boom Creative Media Inc) Creative Director: Norman Mayot; Art Director: Richard Ho; Designer: Shaun Withers. /// **Programming:** Flash Developer: Craig Swann; Flash Developer: Emmanuel Adams; Technical Lead: Craig Denis. /// **Tools:** Adobe Illustrator, Macromedia Flash, XML, Microsoft SQL. /// **Contents:** the actual Honda Suzuka race track was remodeled for the game, from an isometric viewpoint. /// **Awards:** The Advertising & Design Club of Canada (ADCC) 2005. /// **Cost:** 200 hours.

SYNAPSE

USA

www.synapsedev.com

2005

Concept

This site achieves an immersive and hands-on feel through user controlled multidimensional animations that are seamlessly integrated with the layout's use of full-screen graphics. /// Ce site fait plonger l'utilisateur dans le vif du sujet en lui permettant de contrôler des animations multidimensionnelles parfaitement intégrées à l'utilisation que la présentation fait des graphismes en plein écran. /// Diese Website schafft ein eindringliches und realitätsnahes Gefühl, und zwar durch die vom Benutzer gesteuerten, mehrdimensionalen Animationen, die nahtlos und unter Ausnutzung der vollen Bildschirmgröße in die Layout-Grafiken integriert sind.

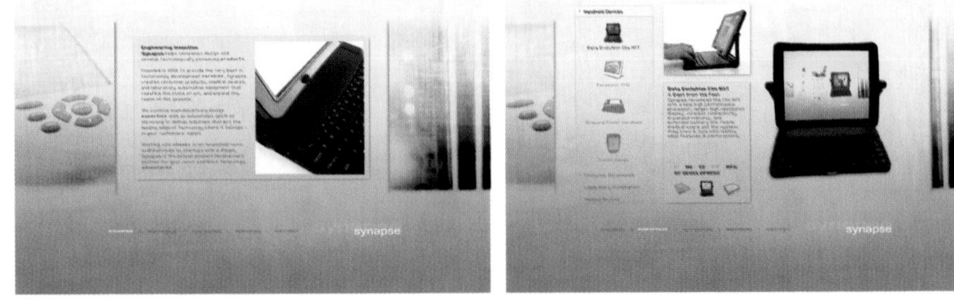

Info

Design and Programming: CrashShop <www.crashshop.com>. /// **Tools:** Adobe Photoshop, Macromedia Flash. /// **Contents:** photos, animation. /// **Cost:** over 300 hours.

TGSNT

USA/BRAZIL

www.tgsnt.com

2004

Concept

TGSNT offers aspiring animators all the information needed online to produce an award winning flash film short. The site also features the Cave Dudez playing the popular TGSNT Miniball game. /// TGSNT donne aux apprentis animateurs toute l'information nécessaire pour produire un court-métrage en Flash digne d'être primé. Ce site présente aussi les Cave Dudez en train de jouer au fameux jeu de Miniball de TGSNT. /// **TGSNT bietet aufstrebenden Animatoren alle Informationen, die benötigt werden, um einen preisverdächtigen Flash-Kurzfilm produzieren zu können. Ein wesentliches Merkmal der Website sind weiterhin auch Cave Dudez und das populäre TGSNT Miniball-Spiel.**

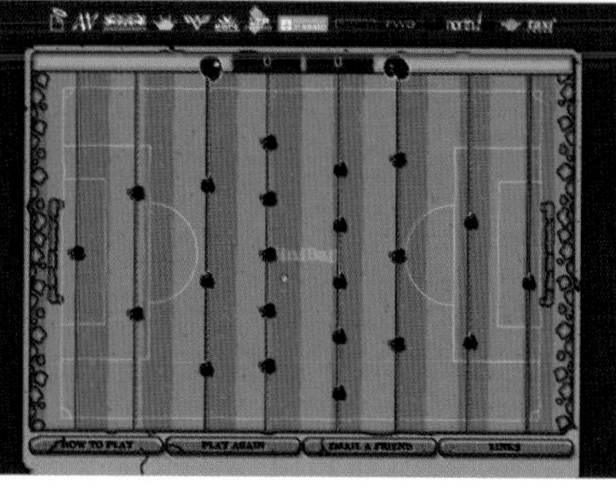

Info

Design: ZOOLOOK <www.zoolook.com>. /// **Programming:** Nicholas Da Silva (ZOOLOOK). /// **Tools:** Adobe Illustrator, Adobe Photoshop, Macromedia Flash, Macromedia Dreamweaver, Macromedia Fireworks, php, Apple Quicktime. /// **Contents:** animation and films; games. /// **Awards:** Cineme 2004 Official Selection; FWA; Page.Thinks; Pixelmakers; Ades Design; King for a Week; NewWebPick; DOPE Awards; TINY; Plasticpilots; Netdiver; Design TAXI; LookNorth.CA; Turkey Awards. /// **Cost:** 490 hours.

THEDOFL

KOREA

www.thedofl.com

2004

Concept

I tried to show a lot of portfolios with easy and intuitive navigation. Above all, I used real motion with interaction for profile section. /// J'ai essayé de montrer de nombreux portfolios avec une navigation facile et intuitive. J'ai surtout utilisé Real motion avec de l'interaction pour la partie profil. /// Ich habe versucht, viele Portfolios mit einfacher und intuitiver Navigation zu zeigen. Für den Profil-Bereich benutzte ich darüber hinaus interaktive „Real Motion".

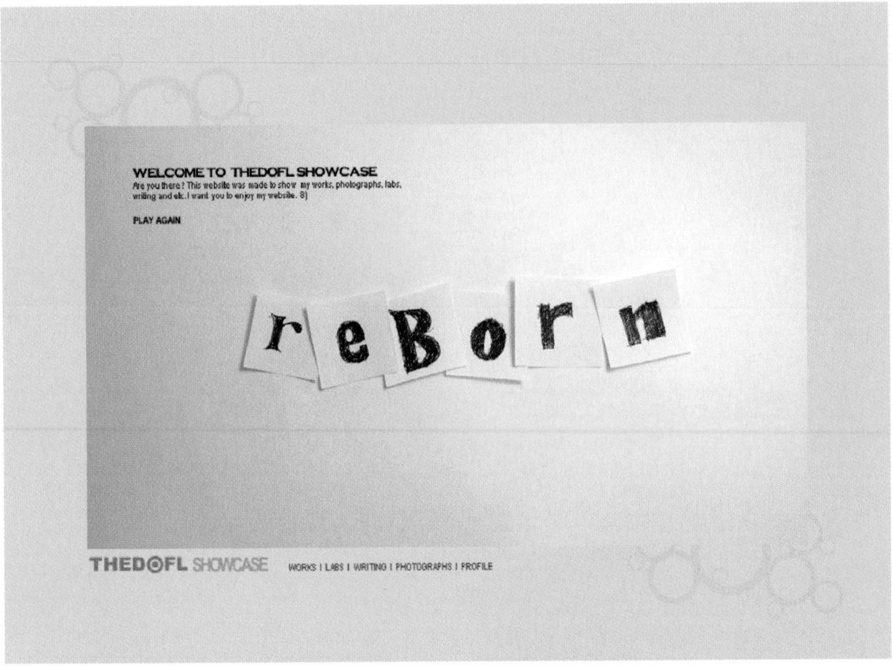

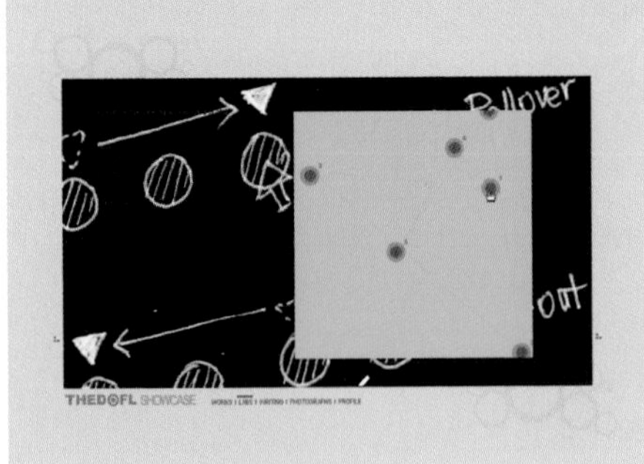

Info

Design and Programming: DOFL Y.H. YUN <www.thedofl.com>. /// **Tools:** Adobe Photoshop, Macromedia Flash, xml, php. /// **Contents:** design, photo, animation. /// **Awards:** ASTRAL Awards (Silver), 2004 blue league self promotion portfolio awards, Netdiver, DOPE Awards. /// **Cost:** 45 days.

THE MAP OF DESIGNERS

KOREA

www.thedofl.com/project/themap

2005

Concept

I tried to make the visual map to show relationship of members who visit community website. People can leave their traces and the other people can see that by real time. /// La carte visuelle montre les relations entre les membres qui visitent le site de la communauté. Les gens peuvent laisser une trace, et les autres visiteurs le voient en temps réel. /// Ich habe versucht, eine „Visual Map" zu erstellen, und die Bezüge von den die Gemeinschaftssite besuchenden Mitgliedern aufzuzeichnen. Surfer können Spuren hinterlassen, andere können diese in Echtzeit betrachten.

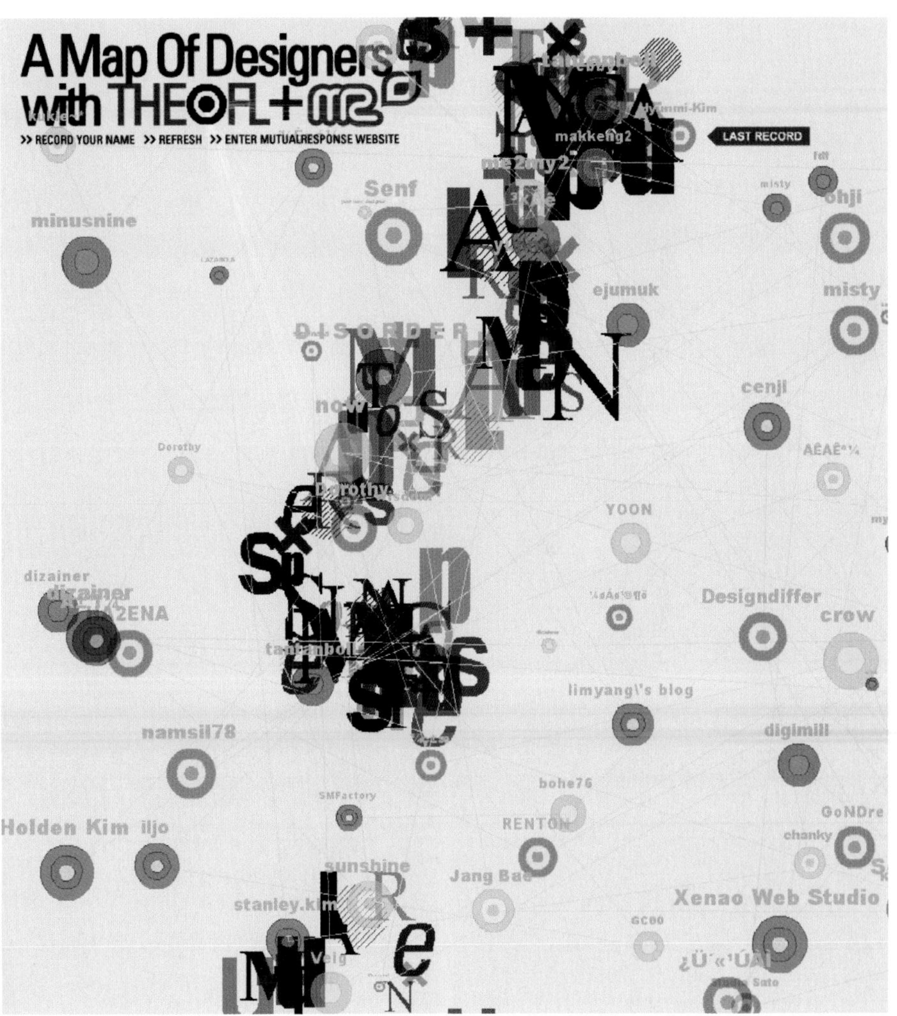

Info

DESIGN AND PROGRAMMING: DOFL Y.H. YUN <www.thedofl.com>. /// TOOLS: Macromedia Flash, xml, php. /// CONTENTS: text infomation. /// COST: 1 week.

TIGER BEER

UK

www.tigerbeer.co.uk

2004

Concept

This is a flash site with more personality than most. Using everything we knew about creative design, 'animation as marketing' and client content management we took Tiger Beer into their new era. /// Ce site Flash a plus de personnalité que la plupart des autres. Nous avons utilisé tout ce que nous savions du graphisme créatif, des « animations marketing » et de la gestion de contenu client, et nous avons fait entrer Tiger Beer dans une nouvelle ère. /// Dies ist eine Flash-Website mit mehr Persönlichkeit als die meisten anderen. Wir versetzten Tiger Beer in eine neue Ära, indem wir alles einsetzten, was wir über kreatives Design, ‚Animation als Marketing' und Client Content Management wussten.

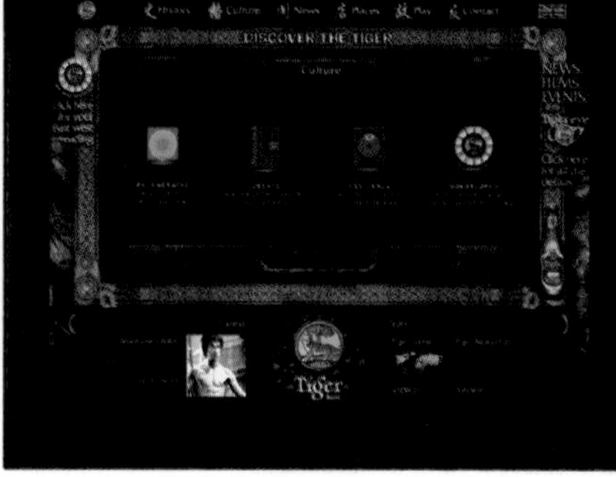

Info

Design: Tim Dillon (Onscreen Creative) <www.onscreencreative.com>. /// **Programming**: Rob Thomson, Zulma Repatlet <www.marotori.com>. /// **Tools**: Macromedia Flash and html mixed site with php CMS. /// **Contents**: creative product information, animation trilogy created to promote site, design direction creating new brand approach, sound design, Flash animation. /// **Awards**: Ireland based innovation awards 2004. /// **Cost**: 7 months.

TIJUANA FLATS

USA

www.tijuanaflats.com

2005

Concept

The important thing to us was the our ability to match the brand's high energy and eccentricity. It's fun and it doesn't take itself too seriously. /// Pour nous, le plus important, c'était que notre travail soit en harmonie avec la grande énergie et l'excentricité de la marque. C'est plein d'humour et ça ne se prend pas trop au sérieux. /// Unsere Fähigkeit, die große Energie und die exzentrische Verhaltensweise der Marke aneinander anzupassen, war uns sehr wichtig. Nicht ganz ernst gemeint, der Spaß steht im Vordergrund.

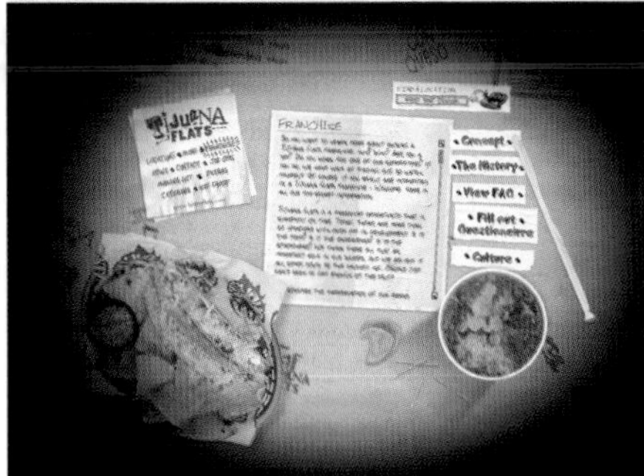

Info

Design: PUSH <www.pushhere.com>: Creative Director: Chris Robb, Senior Art DirectorMark Unger. /// **Programming**: Mindflood <mindflood.com>. /// **Tools**: Adobe Photoshop, Macromedia Flash, Adobe After Effects, Flash Remoting, AmfPHP, MySQL, Custom CMS. /// **Contents**: photo, mp3 spot player, animation, customer and franchise communication points, menu download. /// **Awards**: Communication Arts (site of the week), The One Club Creative Showcase, Best Flash V2 Corporate Site Showcase. /// **Cost**: 320 hours over 4 months.

TISHARA

USA

www.tishara.net

2005

Concept

I designed this page to emulate a white board where I place the user as the designer going through all of the various media that Tishara has to offer. /// Dans cette page, j'ai simulé un tableau blanc où je mets l'utilisateur à la place du designer explorant tous les différents supports que Tishara propose. /// Ich habe diese Seite als eine freie Arbeitsfläche entworfen. Der Benutzer ist der Designer, ihm stehen alle verschiedenen Medien zur Verfügung, die Tishara anbietet.

Info

Design and Programming: Chris Pierantozzi <chrispierantozzi@hotmail.com>for CyTek Studios. /// **Tools**: Adobe Photoshop, Adobe After Effects, Key Light, Macromedia Flash. /// **Contents**: photos, video, and resume of Tishara Lee Cousino. /// **Awards**: FWA, TINY. /// **Cost**: 120 hours.

TRANTOR

ITALY

www.trantor.tv

2005

Concept

Trantor is a full Flash chat site, the task was to build a 3D environment where the user can move his avatar and interact with other users. /// Trantor est un site de chat entièrement en Flash. Il fallait construire un environnement en 3D où l'utilisateur puisse déplacer son avatar et interagir avec les autres utilisateurs. /// Trantor ist eine mit Flash kreierte Chat-Seite. Die Aufgabe bestand darin, eine 3D-Umgebung zu schaffen, in der der Benutzer seinen Avatar bewegen und mit anderen Benutzern agieren kann.

Info

DESIGN: magicsocket. /// **PROGRAMMING**: Mario Ballario, Marco Corti (magicsocket). /// **TOOLS**: MySQL, PHP, AmfPHP, Macromedia Flash, Adobe Photoshop. /// **CONTENTS**: chat, animation, photo. /// **AWARDS**: Res72, Moluv, Pixelmakers. /// **COST**: 2000 hours.

TROPPA

SPAIN
2005

www.troppa.com

Concept

This is a photo-based website, where photographs are the theme and the main graphical resource. Flash items are aligned on top and bottom of the web in order lend space to the photos. /// C'est un site basé sur les photos, qui sont le thème et la principale ressource graphique. Les éléments Flash sont alignés en haut et en bas du site afin de laisser de l'espace aux photos. /// Dies ist eine auf Fotos basierende Website. Die Fotografien sind das Thema und die grafische Hauptquelle zugleich. Flash-Elemente sind angeordnet oben und unten auf der Seite, damit genügend Fläche für die Fotos verbleibt.

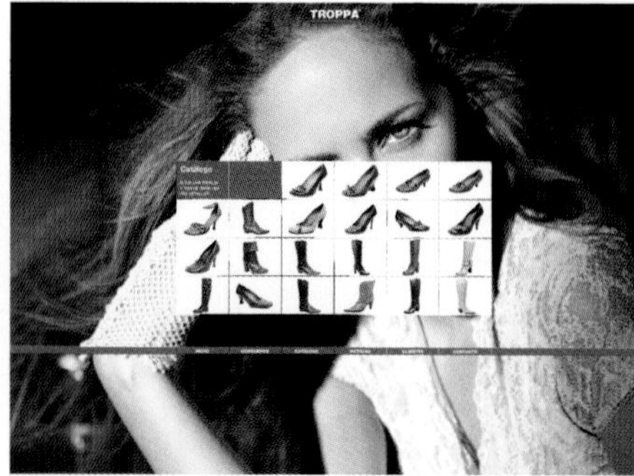

Info

Design: Sense Titol <www.sensetitol.com>. /// **Programming:** Marc Guardiola (Sense Titol). /// **Tools:** Adobe Photoshop, Macromedia Flash, Macromedia Freehand. /// **Contents:** photo, uncompressed sounds, own music creation. /// **Awards:** Pixelmakers. /// **Cost:** 200 hours.

THEODORE TRANKU & ASSOC.

ITALY

www.tta.it

2005

Concept

Balance, intuition and effectiveness in the graphic and motion. Expression and corporate image of the prestigious agency of public connections Theodore Tranku & Associates. /// Équilibre, intuition et efficacité dans le graphisme et le mouvement. Un site d'entreprise qui transmet l'expression et l'image de la prestigieuse agence de relations publiques Theodore Tranku & Associates. /// **Typisch für die Website der Agentur Theodore Tranku & Associates sind das Gleichgewicht, intuitive und effiziente Grafik und Bewegung sowie Ausdruck und Bilder.**

italiano

close

Agency

Founded in 1963 in Milan, TT&A is Italy's oldest independent, full-service public relations agency. We offer our Italian and international clients a complete range of strategic consulting and implementation services.

TT & A
THEODORE
TRANCU
& ASSOCIATES SRL

TT&A - THEODORE TRANCU & ASSOCIATES S.r.l - Public Relations and Stakeholder Dialogue Consultants

Copyright ©2005 TT&A. All rights reserved.

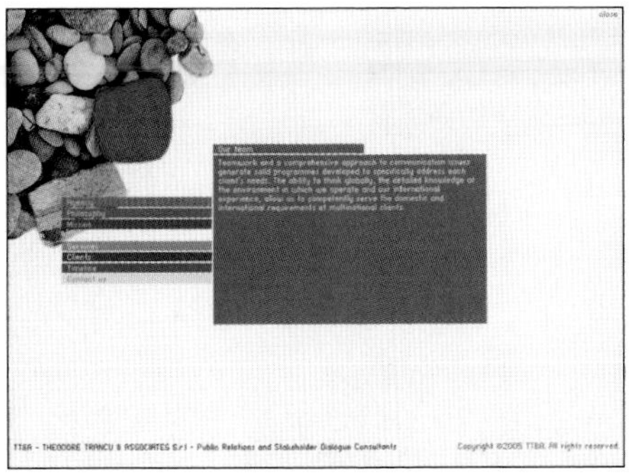

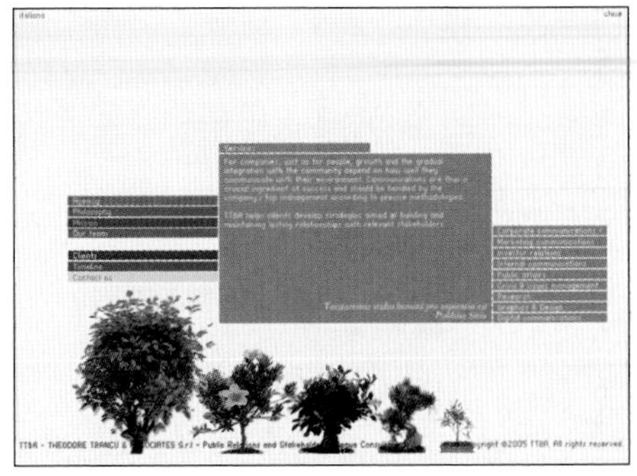

Info

DESIGN AND PROGRAMMING: Libero Cavinato <www.liberonline.com>. /// **TOOLS**: Macromedia Flash, Adobe Photoshop. /// **CONTENTS**: animation, programming, photo. /// **AWARDS**: Flashforward 2005 New York in Navigation section (Finalist). /// **COST**: 100 Hours.

TYPEFLAKE

USA

www.typeflake.com

2003

Concept

This is a little something to play around with that combines all the great aspects of the holidays with good design. Create your own personal greeting by simply typing a message! /// Voici un petit quelque chose pour s'amuser, qui combine le thème des fêtes de fin d'année et un bon design. Créez votre propre carte de vœux simplement en tapant un message ! /// Es handelt sich hier um ein kleines Spielzeug, eine Verbindung von Urlaubsgefühl und gutem Design. Der Benutzer hat die Möglichkeit, auf einfache Weise einen persönlichen Gruß zu verfassen.

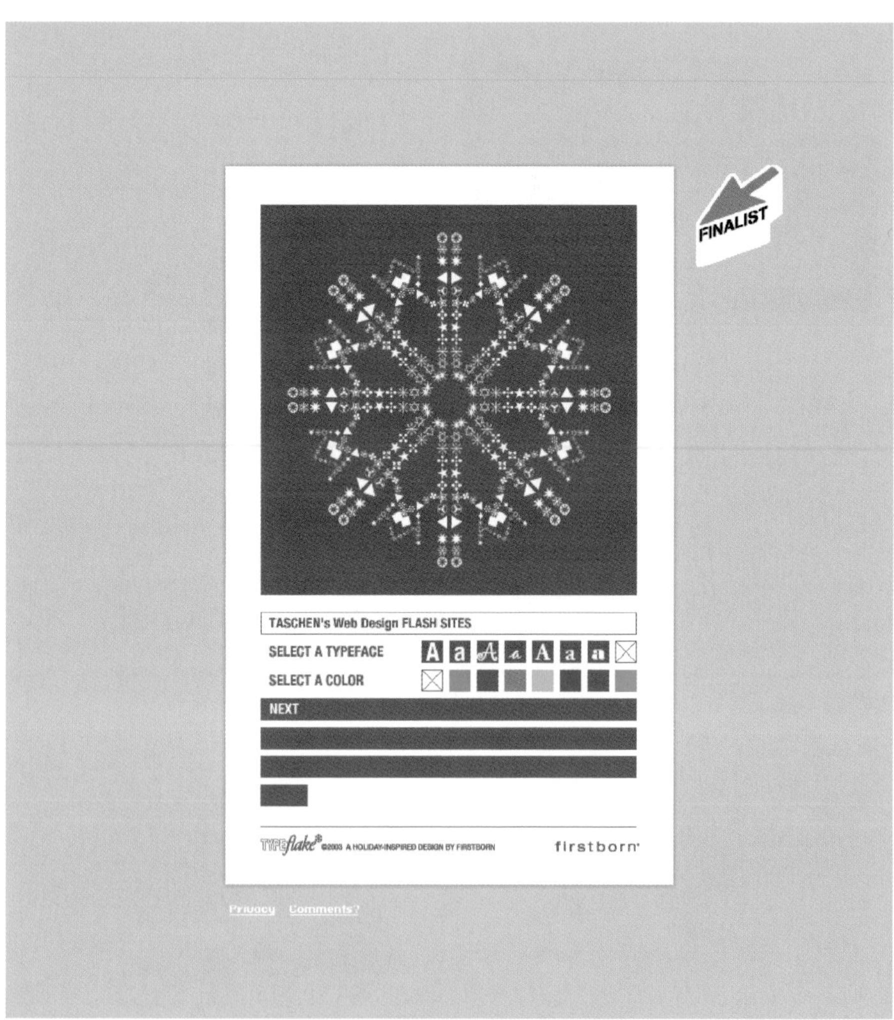

Info

Design: Vas Sloutchevsky (Firstborn) <www.firstbornmultimedia.com>. /// **Programming**: Gicheol Lee, Robert Forras. /// **Tools**: Adobe Photoshop, Macromedia Flash, Macromedia Dreamweaver/ASP, SQL Server 2000. /// **Contents**: Animation. /// **Cost**: 180 hours.

SHREK DVD LAUNCH

AUSTRALIA

www.universalpictures.com.au/shrek

2004

Concept: **As well as standard DVD website content (dvd info, screengrabs, wallpapers), we also created a Music Mixer for Pinocchio, games and a 'send a burp to a friend' utility.** /// Outre les contenus classiques pour un site de DVD (infos sur le DVD, captures d'écran, papiers peints), nous avons également créé un mixeur de musique pour Pinocchio, des jeux et un outil « envoyer un rot à un ami ». /// **Zusätzlich zu einem Standard-Inhalt für eine DVD Website (DVD-Info, Screenshot, Desktop-Hintergrund zum Downloaden), haben wir auch einen Musik-Mixer für Pinocchio, Spiele und ein ‚send-a-burp-to- a-friend'-Werkzeug programmiert.**

Info: **DESIGN:** Robert Dennis, Ronald Kurniawan, David Brown, Brad Eldridge, Leonardo Zamboni (Soap Creative) <www.soapcreative.com.au>. /// **PROGRAMMING:** Ashley Ringrose, Adam Johnson (Soap Creative). /// **TOOLS:** Adobe Photoshop, Adobe Illustrator, Macromedia Flash, xml. /// **CONTENTS:** DVD information, film information, trailers, games. /// **COST:** 300 hours.

WEBSHOCKER

SLOVENIA

www.webshocker.net

2005

Concept

Site is powered by Webshocker Flash CMS application. Unique site navigation makes exploring the site very enjoyable. /// Le site se base sur une application de CMS Flash de Webshocker. La navigation originale rend l'exploration du site très agréable. /// Die Website wird unterstützt durch eine Webshocker-Flash-CMS-Anwendung. Die einzigartige Navigation macht das Erforschen der Website angenehm.

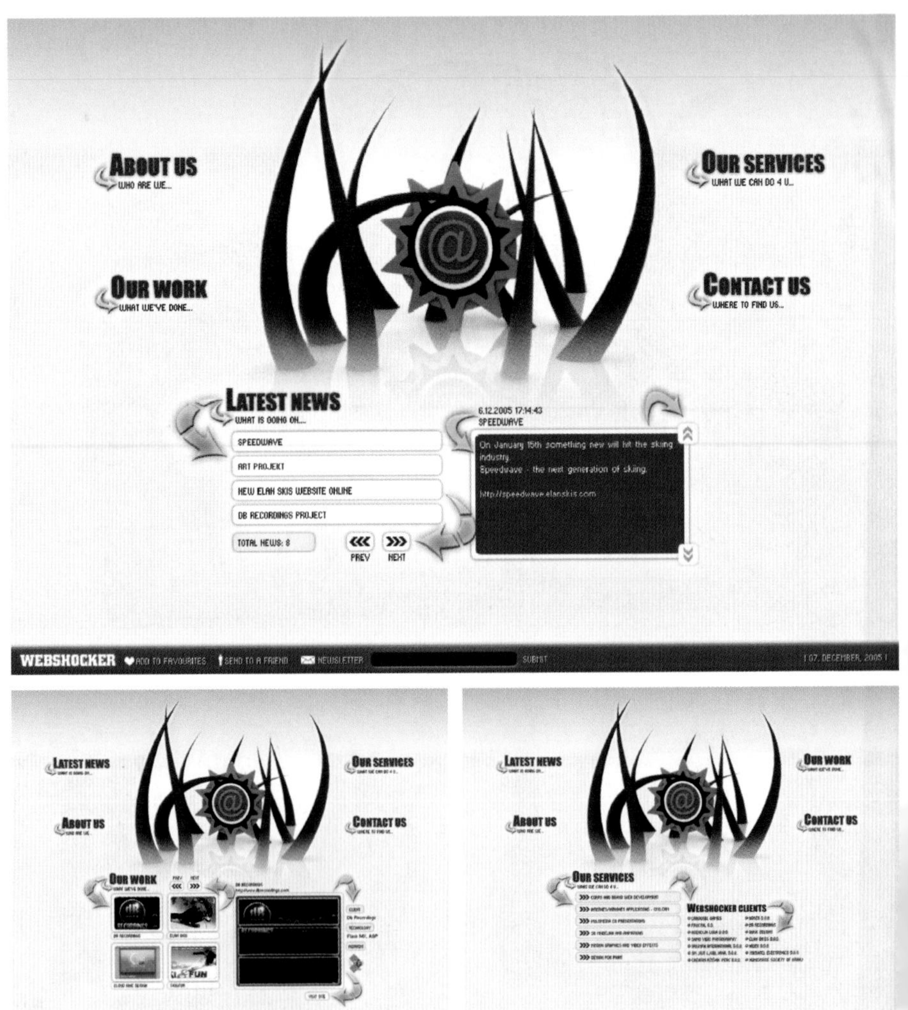

Info

DESIGN AND PROGRAMMING: Webshocker. /// **TOOLS**: Webshocker Flash CMS, Macromedia Flash, Adobe Photoshop, Autodesk 3ds Max, ASP. /// **CONTENTS**: photo, animations, 3D. /// **AWARDS**: FWA, TINY, DOPE Awards, fcukstar.com. /// **COST**: 150hours.

THE WHITNEY BIENNIAL

USA

www.whitney.org/biennial

2004

Concept

The dynamic artist sorting functionality by theme and medium provides users with the ability to explore 108 artists organically and intuitively. /// La fonctionnalité de tri dynamique des artistes par thème et par support permet aux utilisateurs d'explorer les 108 artistes de façon organique et intuitive. /// **Die Website verfügt über ein dynamisches und funktionelles Werkzeug, um Informationen über 108 Künstler intuitiv nach Thema und Art zu sortieren.**

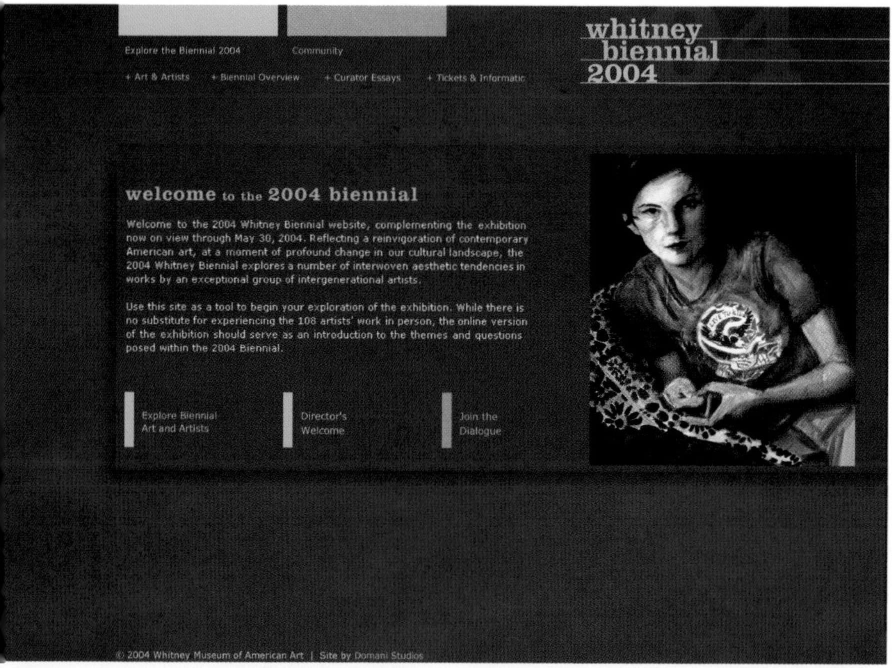

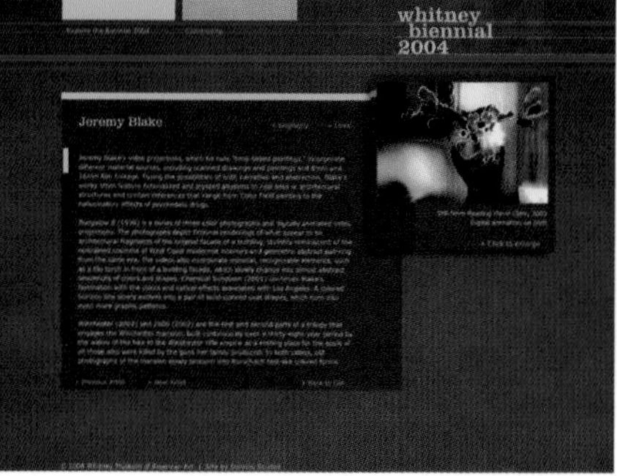

Info

DESIGN AND PROGRAMMING: Domani Studios <www.domanistudios.com>. /// **TOOLS:** Macromedia Flash, Adobe Photoshop, Adobe Illustrator, PHP, MySQL, Unix. /// **CONTENTS:** flash-based website showcasing 108 artists and a real-time proximity-based community dialogue application. /// **AWARDS:** I.D. Magazine 2004 Interactive Media Design Review (Gold), 365: AIGA Annual Design Competition 26, HOW Interactive Annual 2005, Communication Arts' Design Interact. /// **COST:** 2 months (design and development cycle).

WIEDEN+KENNEDY TOKYO LAB

JAPAN
2005

www.wktokyolab.com

Concept

This site can enjoy the sound and the video of "CHANNEL H" of 2nd album of HIFANA. /// Sur ce site, vous pouvez apprécier la musique et la vidéo de « CHANNEL H », du deuxième album de HIFANA. /// Auf dieser Website kann der Benutzer den Sound und das Video von „CHANNEL H" aus dem 2. Album von HIFANA genießen.

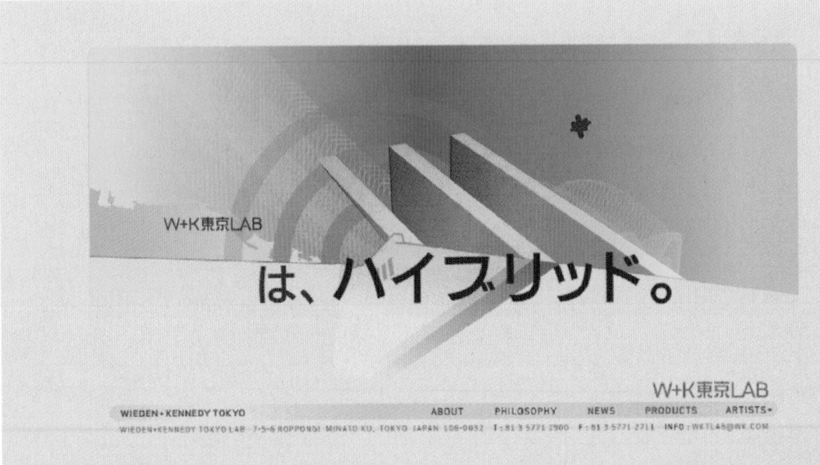

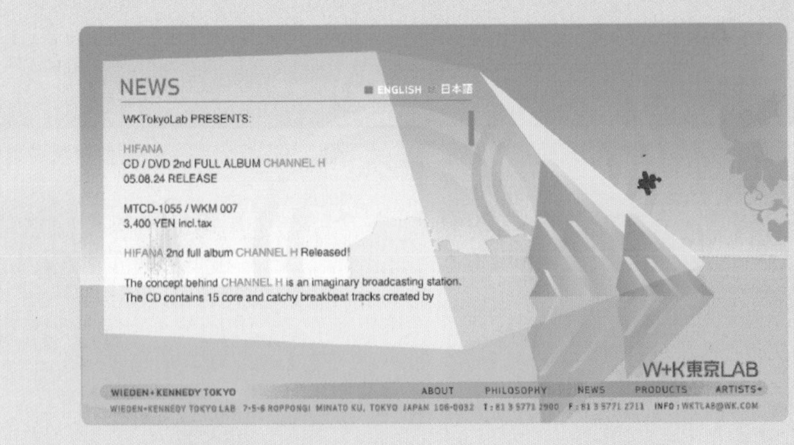

Info

Design and Programming: Haruki Higashi <www.loworks.org>. /// **Tools**: Macromedia Flash, Adobe Illustrator. /// **Contents**: music, film. /// **Cost**: 1 month.

SHIMANO XTR

INTERNATIONAL

http://xtr.shimano.com

2002

Concept

This site employed motion graphics and 3D animation to show and explain how the bike components actually work. /// Ce site emploie des graphismes animés et de l'animation en 3D pour montrer et expliquer comment fonctionnent les éléments d'un vélo. /// **Auf dieser Website wurden bewegte Grafik und 3D-Animation eingesetzt, um die Funktion von Fahrradteilen anschaulich darzustellen.**

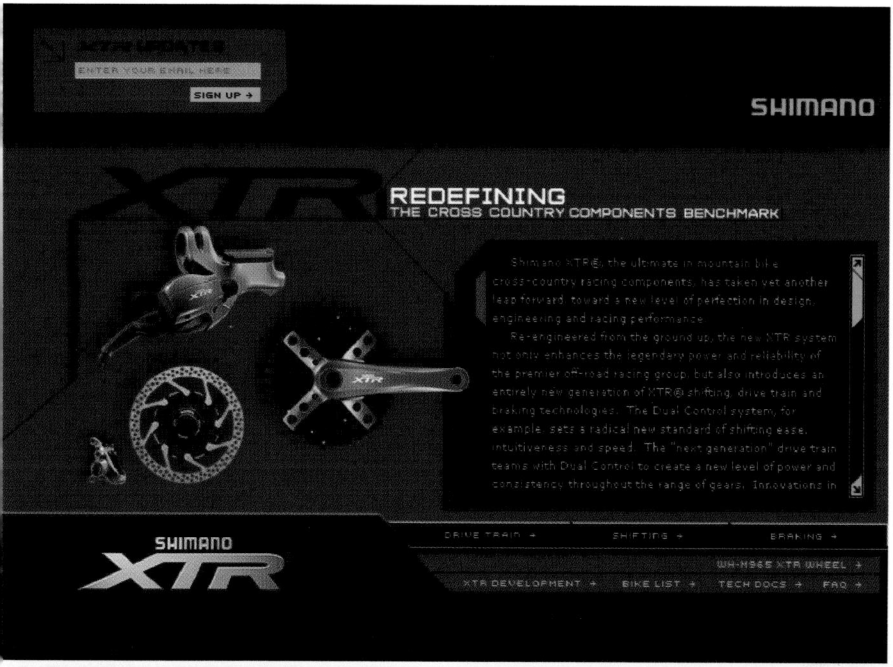

ENTER YOUR EMAIL HERE
SIGN UP →
SHIMANO
REDEFINING
THE CROSS COUNTRY COMPONENTS BENCHMARK
Shimano XTR®, the ultimate in mountain bike cross-country racing components, has taken yet another leap forward, toward a new level of perfection in design, engineering and racing performance.
Re-engineered from the ground up, the new XTR system not only enhances the legendary power and reliability of the premier off-road racing group, but also introduces an entirely new generation of XTR® shifting, drive train and braking technologies. The Dual Control system, for example, sets a radical new standard of shifting ease, intuitiveness and speed. The "next generation" drive train teams with Dual Control to create a new level of power and consistency throughout the range of gears. Innovations in
SHIMANO
XTR
DRIVE TRAIN →
SHIFTING →
BRAKING →
WH-M965 XTR WHEEL →
XTR DEVELOPMENT →
BIKE LIST →
TECH DOCS →
FAQ →

SHIMANO
DRIVE TRAIN
XTR
SHIMANO
XTR

SHIMANO
SHIFTING
SHIMANO
XTR

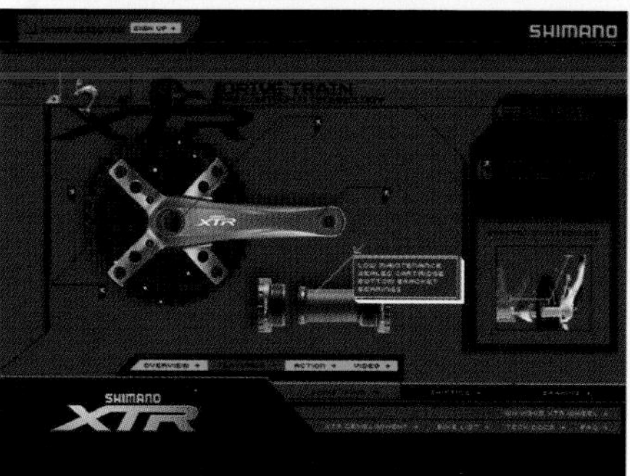

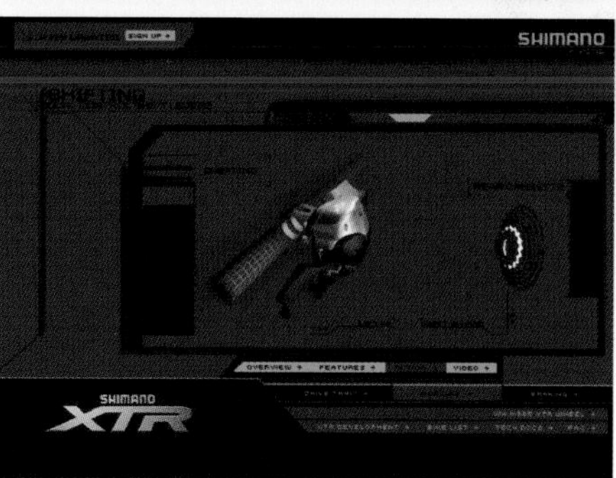

Info

DESIGN AND PROGRAMMING: Juxt Interactive <www.juxtinteractive.com>. /// **TOOLS:** Adobe Photoshop, Macromedia Freehand, Macromedia Flash, Autodesk 3ds Max. /// **CONTENTS:** brand and product information featuring interactive 3D animation and video. /// **AWARDS:** New York Art Directors Club, One Show, Communication Arts. /// **COST:** 3 months.

CREDITS

I would like to thank all studios and professionals participating in the book again, as well all people involved, for their contribution and effort to provide the materials and information that enriched this publication. Also Daniel Siciliano Bretas for his tireless work contacting all the offices we wanted to include in this book and for his work designing and layouting the book. His work has been fundamental to make this a great inspirational series. Moreover, Stefan Klatte for guiding us always in the technical details and helping us making a better job every day.

This volume has taken a step further from the other two volumes. We have a great introduction from Rob Ford, the creator of the Favourite Website Awards and a person with great knowledge about everything related to web design.

We have also introduced here two case stories coming right after the introduction. Kurt Noble from the USA and Pascal Leroy from Belgium demonstrate the way to work with Flash and the path to create cutting edge stuff.

The amazing thing these days is that we are located in different cities and continents, we never met each other personally, and we never had a problem to work together. A brief introduction via e-mail enables us to built solid relationships and share ideas, dreams and gets the work done.

Please do not skip them!

Julius Wiedemann

IMPRINT

Web Design: Flash Sites

To stay informed about upcoming **TASCHEN** titles, please request our magazine at **www.taschen.com/magazine** or write to **TASCHEN**, Hohenzollernring 53, D-50672 Cologne, Germany, contact@taschen.com, Fax: +49-221-254919. We will be happy to send you a free copy of our magazine which is filled with information about all of our books.

Design & Layout: **Daniel Siciliano Brêtas**
Production: **Stefan Klatte**

Editor: **Julius Wiedemann**
Assitant-editor: **Daniel Siciliano Brêtas**
French Translation: **Aurélie Daniel**
German Translation: **Dorota Pawlucka**
Spanish Translation: **Raquel Valle**
Italian Translation: **Marco Barberi**
Portuguese Translation: **Margarida Seiça**

Printed in Italy
ISBN 978–3–8228–4047–4

Web Design: Portfolios
Ed. Julius Wiedemann / Flexi-cover, 192 pp. / € 6.99 / $ 9.99 / £ 5.99 / ¥ 1.500

Web Design: Studios
Ed. Julius Wiedemann / Flexi-cover, 192 pp. / € 6.99 / $ 9.99 / £ 5.99 / ¥ 1.500

Web Design: Music Sites
Ed. Julius Wiedemann / Flexi-cover, 192 pp. / € 6.99 / $ 9.99 / £ 5.99 / ¥ 1.500

"These books are beautiful objects, well-designed and lucid." —*Le Monde*, Paris, on the ICONS series

" Buy them all and add some pleasure to your life."

60s Fashion
Ed. Jim Heimann

70s Fashion
Ed. Jim Heimann

African Style
Ed. Angelika Taschen

Alchemy & Mysticism
Alexander Roob

American Indian
Dr. Sonja Schierle

Angels
Gilles Néret

Architecture Now!
Ed. Philip Jodidio

Art Now
Eds. Burkhard Riemschneider, Uta Grosenick

Atget's Paris
Ed. Hans Christian Adam

Bamboo Style
Ed. Angelika Taschen

Ingrid Bergman
Ed. Paul Duncan, Scott Eyman

Berlin Style
Ed. Angelika Taschen

Humphrey Bogart
Ed. Paul Duncan, James Ursini

Marlon Brando
Ed. Paul Duncan, F.X. Feeney

Brussels Style
Ed. Angelika Taschen

Cars of the 50s
Ed. Jim Heimann, Tony Thacker

Cars of the 60s
Ed. Jim Heimann, Tony Thacker

Cars of the 70s
Ed. Jim Heimann, Tony Thacker

Charlie Chaplin
Ed. Paul Duncan, David Robinson

China Style
Ed. Angelika Taschen

Christmas
Ed. Jim Heimann, Steven Heller

Design Handbook
Charlotte & Peter Fiell

Design for the 21st Century
Eds. Charlotte & Peter Fiell

Design of the 20th Century
Eds. Charlotte & Peter Fiell

Marlene Dietrich
Ed. Paul Duncan, James Ursini

Devils
Gilles Néret

Robert Doisneau
Ed. Jean-Claude Gautrand

East German Design
Ralf Ulrich/Photos: Ernst Hedler

Clint Eastwood
Ed. Paul Duncan, Douglas Keesey

Egypt Style
Ed. Angelika Taschen

Encyclopaedia Anatomica
Ed. Museo La Specola Florence

M.C. Escher

Fashion
Ed. The Kyoto Costume Institute

Fashion Now!
Eds. Terry Jones, Susie Rushton

Fruit
Ed. George Brookshaw, Uta Pellgrü-Gagel

HR Giger
HR Giger

Grand Tour
Harry Seidler

Cary Grant
Ed. Paul Duncan, F.X. Feeney

Graphic Design
Eds. Charlotte & Peter Fiell

Greece Style
Ed. Angelika Taschen

Halloween
Ed. Jim Heimann, Steven Heller

Havana Style
Ed. Angelika Taschen

Audrey Hepburn
Ed. Paul Duncan, F.X. Feeney

Katharine Hepburn
Ed. Paul Duncan, Alain Silver

Homo Art
Gilles Néret

Hot Rods
Ed. Coco Shinomiya, Tony Thacker

Hula
Ed. Jim Heimann

India Bazaar
Samantha Harrison, Bari Kumar

London Style
Ed. Angelika Taschen

Steve McQueen
Ed. Paul Duncan, Alain Silver

Mexico Style
Ed. Angelika Taschen

Miami Style
Ed. Angelika Taschen

Minimal Style
Ed. Angelika Taschen

Marilyn Monroe
Ed. Paul Duncan, F.X. Feeney

Morocco Style
Ed. Angelika Taschen

New York Style
Ed. Angelika Taschen

Paris Style
Ed. Angelika Taschen

Penguin
Frans Lanting

20th Century Photography
Museum Ludwig Cologne

Pierre et Gilles
Eric Troncy

Provence Style
Ed. Angelika Taschen

Robots & Spaceships
Ed. Teruhisa Kitahara

Safari Style
Ed. Angelika Taschen

Seaside Style
Ed. Angelika Taschen

Signs
Ed. Julius Wiedeman

South African Style
Ed. Angelika Taschen

Starck
Philippe Starck

Surfing
Ed. Jim Heimann

Sweden Style
Ed. Angelika Taschen

Tattoos
Ed. Henk Schiffmacher

Tiffany
Jacob Baal-Teshuva

Tokyo Style
Ed. Angelika Taschen

Tuscany Style
Ed. Angelika Taschen

Valentines
Ed. Jim Heimann, Steven Heller

Web Design: Best Studios
Ed. Julius Wiedemann

Web Design: Best Studios 2
Ed. Julius Wiedemann

Web Design: E-Commerce
Ed. Julius Wiedemann

Web Design: Flash Sites
Ed. Julius Wiedemann

Web Design: Music Sites
Ed. Julius Wiedemann

Web Design: Portfolios
Ed. Julius Wiedemann

Orson Welles
Ed. Paul Duncan, F.X. Feeney

Women Artists in the 20th and 21st Century
Ed. Uta Grosenick

ICONS